A MANAGER'S GUIDE TO GLOBALIZATION

Six Keys to Success in a Changing World

A MANAGER'S GUIDE TO GLOBALIZATION

Six Keys to Success in a Changing World

Stephen H. Rhinesmith

ASTD

THE AMERICAN SOCIETY FOR TRAINING AND DEVELOPMENT
Alexandria, Virginia 22313

IRWIN
Professional Publishing
Burr Ridge, Illinois
New York, New York

Sponsoring editor:	Cynthia A. Zigmund
Project editor:	Gladys True
Production manager:	Ann Cassady
Compositor:	The Wheetley Company
Typeface:	10/12 Times Roman
Printer:	Book Press, Inc.

Library of Congress Cataloging-in-Publication Data

Rhinesmith, Stephen H.
  A manager's guide to globalization : six keys to success in a
changing world / Stephen H. Rhinesmith.
     p.   cm.
  Includes bibliographical references and index.
  ISBN 1-55623-904-1
  1. International business enterprises—Management. 2. Executives—
Psychology. I. Title. II. Title: Globalization.
HD62.4.R48   1993
658′.049—dc20   92-19470

Printed in the United States of America
   6 7 8 9 0   BP   9 8 7 6 5

To Kathe

Foreword

by John Naisbitt

Stephen Rhinesmith's superb *Manager's Guide to Globalization* could not have arrived at a better time. It is clear in today's business environment that our human resources hold the competitive edge in the global economy. For hundreds of years a country's natural resources and capital were the measure of its wealth. First Japan, and then South Korea (and the other three economic tigers) proved that you don't have to have natural resources for economic success. Capital is now a globally traded commodity.

That leaves the quality of a country's human resources as the distinguishing characteristic in global competitiveness. How well a country or a company develops its human resources will be the measure of its participation in the global economy of the 1990s.

But as Dr. Rhinesmith points out, the changes in how we manage have as yet been no match for the technological changes and the geopolitical restructuring of the world in which we must now operate. Dr. Rhinesmith helps us reconceptualize the role of management in this new world and redefine the skills needed by managers of global organizations to be responsive and effective in this new arena. He guides us in the transition from, as he puts it, "a limited, fixed world view to an open, free-flowing constantly changing world."

For the first time in this book, relationships between global mindsets and effective management behavior have been systematically spelled out. Dr. Rhinesmith leads us through answers to the questions "What are the global mindsets needed for this new world? What new competencies do managers in global organizations need to have? And how can we develop a human resource system that can better prepare managers for the world they will face in the twenty-first century?" These are critical questions for our organizations today and Dr. Rhinesmith provides intriguing insights based on his years of experience in the international arena.

A Manager's Guide to Globalization is aimed primarily at middle and upper managers of large international, multinational, and globalizing companies who are facing the new complexities and uncertainties of a changing world. The book will be supremely useful in helping these managers understand what it really means to "go global." There is no other publication to date that comes close to providing as much theory and practice on the issue of the human side of globalization.

Dr. Rhinesmith's "six keys to success in a changing world" will help managers understand in a very personal, readable way the highly competitive, complex, multicultural, uncertain, and ever-changing world of global management. These six keys—managing competitiveness, complexity, organizational adaptability, uncertainty, multicultural teams and personal, and organization learning—constitute new management skills that are the gateway to personal and organizational success on a global basis and represent many of the new directions for the manager of the future.

Dr. Rhinesmith's basic message is that we must look toward the bigger, broader picture with a more systems view of the world and that we must learn to deal with the contradictions and ambiguities which a broader world view thrusts upon us. Both of these ideas are difficult for many managers. Having been raised in a world of limited functional specialization with a reasonable degree of certainty built into professional expertise, many managers today have lived with a very different paradigm than that described in this book. The challenge raised by Dr. Rhinesmith is for them to develop broader, more flexible mindsets and to back these up with a personal ability to deal with less structure and more openness to the unfolding of complex events, many of which cannot be planned for in advance.

While the subject matter of this book is broad, it has been organized in a way that is very teachable. It can be used by human resource managers to reexamine their performance appraisal systems for global management skills, as well as to develop new management and executive training programs to help managers address the important issues outlined by Dr. Rhinesmith.

Dr. Rhinesmith does not claim that all his insights are new. In fact, one of the important aspects of the book is its excellent bibliography which is probably the best yet compiled in the field of global human resource management. Drawing from literature in business, comparative management, psychology, sociology, anthropology, philosophy, and intercultural relations, Dr. Rhinesmith has successfully addressed the three levels of globalization—strategy/structure, corporate culture, and people—that he believes are necessary for an integrated approach to future global management.

Dr. Rhinesmith has given us nothing less than a new paradigm for the future management of global corporations. Any leader interested in articulating a global plan, aligning a global corporate culture to this plan, and mobilizing employees to develop the global mindsets and skills necessary for personal and organizational success will find this book a must for their business management strategy.

Introduction

It is now clear that global change will be a way of life in the 1990s and beyond.

The forces of technology, political freedom, territorial dispute, ethnic rivalries, economic competition and entrepreneurial ingenuity are stronger than all the centuries of social, political, and economic fabric that have woven the world into its current form.

At the center of these changes, as always, will be people. Employees, managers, and leaders of organizations struggling to adapt to the new world rushing toward them—and away from them.

MANAGEMENT IN CRISIS

Behind these people are managers who are supposed to have new ideas, new methods, and new ways of helping others cope with massive change.

But it seems that as managers we also are struggling to find new paradigms to understand the changes occurring, let alone creating new development strategies that can help people adjust more rapidly to constant change.

There are many managers whose eyes glaze over as their CEO announces that the new initiative for the coming year is globalization. There are even more managers who have been at a loss for concepts, methods, and plans when confronted with the task of "making our people and culture more global."

If one looks at the transformation that has taken place in science and technology since World War II, it is clear that the theories, methods, and applications of science have dramatically affected the speed, size, and ease of everything we do.

But if we look at the methods of social science and adult education we are using today to help people deal with these accelerating scientific changes, we see that we are still fixed on many of the ideas and methods of the 1950s and 1960s in recruitment, selection, experiential training, compensation and benefits, and career development.

To be sure, there have been changes in our ability to help managers and employees adjust to changing world conditions. But the changes made in personal development theory and technology are small when compared with the changes in science and technology.

Yet our organizations and people are confronted with a new, accelerating world and are asking for assistance in new patterns of thinking and new paradigms for a new age. As managers we still have a long way to go to catch up with their needs—and ours.

SYSTEMS THINKING AND NEW PARADIGMS

One assumption behind this book is that today's manager in a global organization is responsible for more than just business strategies and tactics to achieve organizational objectives. More than ever, global managers need to think systemically and open-endedly about organizations as cultures that must adapt and change to survive. To achieve this, the people inside these organizations must be managed in a way that enables and allows them to work freely with change.

To be a global manager, it is not necessary to be a systems theorist, but it *is* necessary to be able to think in a systemic yet open, playful, creative, intuitive way. Amazingly, Chester Barnard, one of the first management theorists, recognized this need in his *Functions of the Executive* in 1938.

> The executive functions, which . . . are the basis of functional specialization in organizations, have no separate concrete existence. . . . The (more appropriate) pertinent to (executive functioning) are 'feeling,' 'judgement,' 'sense,' 'proportion,' 'balance,' and 'appropriateness.' It is a matter of art rather than science, and is aesthetic rather than logical. For this reason it is recognized rather than described and is known by its effects rather than by analysis. [p. 235]

It is noteworthy that it has taken us over 50 years to realize the fundamental nature of Barnard's observation after two generations have tried to manage *functions* rather than *systems.*

The global manager is ultimately the facilitator of personal and organizational development on a global scale. To achieve this, one must not only be attentive to and a developer of organizational cultures, values, and beliefs that reach well beyond our own cultural, technical and managerial backgrounds, but one must also be a consummate reframer of the boundaries of the world in which one operates.

These **boundaries** include:

* Boundaries of space, time, scope, structure, geography and function.

- Boundaries of functional, professional and technical skills relevant for a past age.
- Boundaries of thinking and classification of rational versus intuitive, national versus foreign, we versus they.
- Boundaries of cultural assumptions, values, and beliefs about the world, our relations with others, and our understanding of ourselves.

This transition from a limited, fixed world view to an open, free-flowing constantly changing world view is not easy to make. Many of us, as individuals and organizations, will need to learn how to learn again, because the ways we have been taught are inadequate for the dynamic, holistic, interdependent flow of the future.

In the end, to be successful global managers we must find new paradigms for living and working in global organizations. And we must develop new technologies for assisting people to learn to play with flexible mindsets, few fixed rules, and the constant readjustment of goals, objectives, and strategies.

Globalization is about changing organizations, but first it is about open people. *It is impossible to develop a free-flowing competitive global organization with structured, inhibited people.*

To achieve this transformation, there is a fourfold challenge for us all.

- First, we need to learn how to play with organizations and our world views in ways that are **open-ended,** rather than closed systems.
- Second, we need to practice **new behavior** that emphasizes openness to change, thinking the unthinkable, and preparing ourselves to take advantages of surprises.
- Third, we will have to develop methods for **helping others** understand and practice these new behaviors in ways that do not duplicate our own learnings, but add to the process of generating new forces to help shape the future.
- Fourth, we will need to structure our organizations, systems, and relationships so that we **concentrate not on winning the current game, but redefining it** so that it can continue to be played from different angles for creative advantage.

Globalization is ultimately the business of mindset and behavior change. The human factor—as Gorbachev, Yeltsin, and other reform leaders have learned—appears to be the key to change and development whether on an organizational, social, economic, or political level.

The human factor, as we shall see, is also the key to organizational resilience, creativity, and survival. The test for managers throughout the world today is to determine what can be done to radically transform people's thinking and behavior *within the context of democratic ethics,* where people have the right and freedom to choose the form and practice of their own development.

This democratic ethical issue lies at the heart of organization change in a free society. We have seen from Mao Tse-tung, Stalin, and others that vast social, economic, and organizational changes can be achieved through the use of totalitarian terror. We have also seen, at least in the case of Russia, that these vast changes can come unraveled in moments, even after 70 years.

The basic dilemma of organization change is that it must be freely adopted by the people that it affects who are many times against its introduction. In some ways, the entire field of organization development can be summed up as enabling people in organizations to identify and become committed to changes that will meet the best long-term interests for themselves, their organization, and society.

Since, as we shall see at many points throughout this book, there are inherent contradictions in personal, organizational, and societal life and there are varying cultural interpretations of what these best interests are and how they can best be met, one can begin to understand some of the complexity involved in global organization development.

BUILDING BLOCKS FOR THIS BOOK

The thought-prints of James Carse run throughout this book. His wonderful little work, *Finite and Infinite Games,* has been an inspiration in keeping me focused on the bigger picture and purpose of globalization.

Finite and Infinite Games is a lesson in paradigm shifting, in reframing, in play, and in what it is to be fully human and open for surprises. There are no more central lessons for the manager in a global organization.

This book, with Carse's help, attempts to define some of the elements of globalization that are important for managers who will learn to play the infinite game of constant change in the global world of tomorrow.

On a more mundane level, I have tried to integrate many of the disparate pieces of global organizational strategy, structure, culture, management, and human resource policies that form the organizational matrix within which the global manager must work to achieve corporate competitiveness in the coming decade.

In Chapter One we start the game of play by examining the globalization phenomenon to determine its relevance for different kinds of companies at different levels of international and global development. Since the ultimate focus of this book is to develop your capacity as a manager in a global organization and redirect your thinking toward holistic, integrated, open systems management, this warm-up chapter hints at some of the themes we will face in the expansion and reconceptualization of the subject in the remainder of the book.

Chapter Two introduces the more integrated conceptual framework within which we will operate, noting the levels of globalization—strategy/ structure, corporate culture, and people—which are the fluid and changing parts of globalization. It also introduces six management competencies, each with its own associated mindsets, characteristics, and actions, around which the rest of the book is organized.

Chapter Three represents a summary of what is relatively well known about global organizations, that is, forming and developing global strategies and structures. Through a review of the strategic and structural issues involved in global business we also provide some basic terminology and definitions for managers approaching international business for the first time.

A major theme of this book, however, is that globalization is *not* just a matter of strategy and structure. Too often senior executives believe they have a global organization if they operate around the world. We shall see that this is far from the whole picture for today's globally competitive organization.

In Chapter Four we examine the nature of organizational complexity, note some of the fundamental contradictions of global organizational life— centralization versus decentralization, global efficiency versus local responsiveness, geographic versus functional priorities—which need to be managed, and discuss ways successful corporations have found to manage these challenges.

In Chapter Five we explore the importance of corporate culture as the means through which organizations maintain their adaptability. There is a great deal of discussion today about the ability of corporations to respond rapidly to constant change in their environments. It is clear that this cannot be achieve through continuous reorganizations. It is our thesis that global organizations maintain their adaptability through their global corporate cultures and global managers who are constantly monitoring and altering information systems, task forces, and international decision architectures to enable their organizations to be resilient to global changes while operating in a reasonably fixed structure.

In Chapter Six we probe the power and possibility of multicultural teamwork. Since teams are a fundamental element of organizational life today, and a global corporate culture depends very much on managing and leading multicultural teams, we will look at multicultural teams as organisms that use their diversity for creative answers to manage organizational complexity and adaptability.

In Chapter Seven we will explore the implications of redefining chaos as an infinite game to be played through continual change and renewal. With world change increasing in its speed and complexity, many global players feel they are being overtaken by chaos. If one concentrates only on the rules of the current game, then increasing chaos threatens the current organization. If, however, chaos is seen as an opportunity to redefine the boundaries of the systems and the rules of the game, then change can be used for competitive advantage. To do this, however, we must learn to flow with as well as control our organization's response to an uncertain environment.

The dynamics noted thus far obviously have enormous implications for the development of managers in global enterprises. In Chapter Eight we explore what can be done to help managers develop the mindsets, qualities, competencies, and behaviors for successful management in a global organization. We also examine a strategically-linked, and integrated approach to human resource development, review some developmental literature on individual, group, and organizational life cycles, and reflect on HRD challenges for the 21st century.

Finally, we turn to Chapter Nine. Here we use Carse's quotations to review themes that run throughout the book. Focusing on Carse's idea that "a finite game is played for the purpose of winning, an infinite game is played for the purpose of continuing the play," we examine how to focus on continuing the play for a successful and productive life.

THE SECOND STORYLINE

There is a second storyline that runs throughout this book, which I want to alert you to in advance—it is the movement from functional expertise to the broader, bigger picture; from stability to change; from structure to process; from individual responsibility to teamwork and play. **The second storyline is movement to a global mindset.**

I have come to the fundamental conclusion that successful global management is, first and foremost, a state of mind. This state of mind has been referred to as a global perspective, global mindset, and matrixed mind by various authors in recent years.

My own developing awareness of this shift from rational, procedural, structural answers to an infinite, open-ended, flexible, playful game has made me realize that ultimately this requires a change not only of mindset, but of philosophy and perhaps, in the end, personal style, if not personality.

In the end, I believe **we are facing a radical shift in the definition of effective management. Rather than being rewarded for creating order out of chaos, we may be entering an era in which creating chaos out of order is the key to personal and organizational survival.** If this is the case, then I, by management experience and training, am the wrong person for the new world and you may be also.

But if this transition seems reasonable to you as it does to me, we have two choices. One, we can curl up in a corner and hope that stability is regained and predictability will allow us to anticipate the joys of the daily known—like eating, sleeping, and reading the newspaper filled with descriptions of all the chaos the world is in. Or we can become an active player in this infinite game and decide that we will try to understand what this new world is demanding, even if it is not our natural bent.

Hopefully, after reading this book you will choose the latter course. To help reflect on the journey you are about to undertake, I have created an outside observer and guide to this book called "the global mind." Remembering my days as a comparative European literature and philosophy major at Wesleyan University, I decided to take a chapter from some of the original thinkers about life and its challenges—the Greek chorus.

The Greek chorus was a companion to the audience in the great Greek plays of the 4th century BC. In these, the chorus reflected on what was happening on stage, noting issues of importance and suggesting to the audience lessons that might be learned. It provided a counterpoint line of reasoning about what they were seeing, feeling, and thinking.

In this book, the Greek chorus has become the global mind. Prior to each chapter, there will be "Forethoughts from a Global Mind" that will introduce the subject and provide a context within which to approach the next portion of the book. The global mind has both a left and right brain, just like humans, with the left controlling rational, linear, analytical thinking and the right controlling open, associative, intuitive patterns. Ultimately, the global mind tilts toward its right side as the dominant side for global management.

At the end of most chapters, their will be two applications sections. The first, "Key Practices and Tasks" will suggest actions that you can take to carry out the competency discussed in the chapter. In the second, "Afterthoughts for Global Mindsets" the Greek chorus performs its other role of summing up the lessons from the play.

At times this journey may be difficult. At times, I hope it will be enlightening. In the end, becoming a manager in a global organization will probably involve some fundamental challenges to the way you think of yourself and the world today. To this extent, becoming a global manager may encourage you to experiment with new perceptions of yourself, your potential, and your relationship to your work and the world around you.

Stephen H. Rhinesmith

Acknowledgments

This book, while quickly written over the last year, has been over 30 years in its development. As a result, many people have made contributions to me and my understanding of the issues I address. While not exhaustive by any means, I would like to acknowledge my debt to the following people and institutions who have contributed to my global education.

• To AFS (American Field Service) Intercultural Programs which gave me my first glimpse of the rest of the world at age 17 as an AFS student to Germany, and which later twice entrusted me with the responsibilities and personal fulfillment of its presidency.

• To Pat Galagan and Nancy Olson of the American Society for Training and Development and the late John Williamson at Wilson Learning Corporation who first encouraged me to think systematically about globalization.

• To John Naisbitt who was there when I needed encouragement and who role-modeled the joys of writing about things you care about.

• To my clients, Pedro Mata, Wim van Bergen, and Chris Dennis at Grace Cocoa, Pat Walker and June Maul at AT&T, Walt Winkler at ARCO International, Claudia Stoeffler of Siemens Corporation, Jim Radzwick and Alice Wright of Bristol-Myers Squibb, Sharon Richards of INTEL, Pierre Casse and Donal O'Hare of the World Bank—all of whom gave me the chance to test and develop my ideas.

• To the participants in the 1991 Summer Institute for Intercultural Communication who helped me think through an integrated approach to globalization.

• To my colleagues at the Forum Corporation, Allan Ackerman, Joan Bragar, and Diane Nerby, who pushed me through the last phases of the conceptualization, and reconceptualization, of this book.

• To my colleagues at Training Management Corporation, Danielle Walker, Jane Silverman, and especially Kim Sullivan, who has creatively translated my ideas into training materials.

• To authors I have never met, but greatly admire and who have influenced me enormously—James Carse, Christopher Bartlett, Sumantra Ghoshal, Ives Doz, C. K. Prahalad, Kenichi Ohmae, Paul Evans, Fritjof Capra, and Peter Vaill.

- To authors and friends I have known for many years, Robert Moran, Phil Harris, George Renwick, Nancy Adler, Gerard Egan, Cliff Clarke, Charles MacCormack, Michael Tucker, Bob Stableski, and Reed Whittle who have helped me expand my original cross-cultural expertise to broader areas.
- To Ed Stewart whose seminal work in identifying and conceptualizing patterns of American culture has deeply influenced me for the past 25 years in all my cross-cultural thinking and behavior.
- To the Peace Corps, where I had my original opportunities for multi-cultural team building.
- To friends and colleagues, Warner Burke, Jan Clee, Bill Paul, Lars Cederholm, Daryl Conner, and Rick Boyatzis, who took the time to read and comment on various stages of the manuscript.
- To my undergraduate and graduate advisers, Herb Arnold and Marshall Singer, who instilled in me a curiosity to reach out beyond myself intellectually and a belief that I could have an original idea.
- To my wife, Kathe, my sons, Christopher and Colin, and my parents who have given up so much family time in order for me to write this book.

S.H.R.

Contents

*Chapter One**

Going Global

No one can play the game alone.

Carse, p. 45

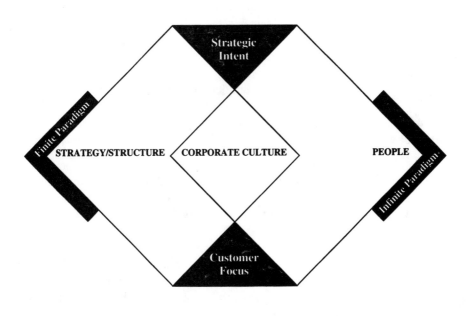

FORETHOUGHTS FROM A GLOBAL MIND

No one plays the global game alone, so as a global mind, I will be your guide and companion through this journey. I have a definite point of view. I believe in constant change and growth rather than stability, and I have a

*Parts of this chapter have appeared in the *Training and Development Journal* in "Developing Leaders for a Global Enterprise" (1989) and "An Agenda for Globalization" (1991).

definite objective—to help you develop a global mindset and to feel comfortable with a world in transformation.

As we begin, there are three important things you should keep in mind.

- Things today are not what they were—and will be different again tomorrow.

- This will require some revision of old thinking, as Mikhail Gorbachev used to say.

- If you want to be a successful global manager you will have to learn not only new information, but new ways of thinking, feeling, and behaving.

If you will keep these first three ideas in mind, you will have begun the journey toward developing a global mindset.

This chapter starts out in a logical, rational form. I have constructed this chapter to make you feel comfortable—while raising some questions about the feasibility of maintaining that feeling if you want to be a manager in a global organization.

As we proceed through the remainder of this journey, you will feel a distinct shift from the logical and simple to the intuitive and complex. This is one of the shifts in the nature of the world that I referred to above. But let's not get ahead of ourselves. Let's begin.

Globalization has arrived in the world, but not in most of the world's organizations. Yet there is little doubt that to be viable during the next century *all* organizations, whether domestic or international, will need to become more global in their outlook, if not in their operations.

It is somewhat ironic that conventional wisdom about the inability of U.S. firms to compete effectively in the global marketplace usually focuses on inadequate spending in technology, plants, and equipment. There is growing evidence that the real vulnerability may lie in the lack of global mindsets in key managers.

In this book, we will describe six keys to success that global managers need to master if they are to meet the challenge of managing global organizations in the years ahead. These keys include the development of global mindsets, as well as competencies, practices, and tasks that enable you as a global manager to *act* on these mindsets. We will also describe a set of characteristics that global managers develop after they have behaved in a global way over a period of time.

CHANGES IN MANAGEMENT THINKING AND MBA EDUCATION

The human factor may ultimately come to represent the new competitive edge for global corporations. One presumed strength of U.S. firms is the level and quality of their management and leadership training. The reality, however, as it relates to global thinking, appears from recent research and experience to be just the opposite.

Recent changes in the curricula of some of our most prestigious business schools have begun to try to correct this. Carnegie-Mellon University polled a business school alumni group who said that competing effectively on a global basis would be the most difficult challenge for the next decade. As a result, Carnegie-Mellon and other business schools, are emphasizing international and global business perspectives and are giving greater attention to the human factor in aligning organizations to strategic objectives.

The Wharton School of Business, for example, which made its reputation in the 1970s and 1980s for producing graduates with broad financial training, has set its sights on turning out business leaders, rather than just financial experts. The new $2 million overhaul of their curriculum will have the following characteristics.

1. Place greater emphasis on people skills.
2. Add more global perspective.
3. Foster creativity and innovation.
4. Promote real-world problem solving.
5. Examine business issues from the viewpoint of several disciplines.

This "MBA for the 21st Century" as *Business Week* calls it, is one manifestation of new thinking that will be necessary for global organizations in the next decade (*Business Week,* May 13, 1991). Business in the United States is increasingly recognizing the need for a global perspective in everything from the sourcing of finances, technology, new materials, and people, to scanning the globe for new markets and competitors.

Most American companies, however, are short on people with the training and experience needed to play the global game at the same skill level as the Japanese, Dutch, Germans, or Swedes. These countries have been forced by the nature of their geography, home market, and competitive advantage to compete internationally—and even globally—over the last 40 years.

The United States, on the other hand, has remained more insular from an economic, if not political and military, perspective. Our greatest strength of the past—a domestic market unsurpassed anywhere in the world—has now oddly enough put us at a disadvantage in the new business game that demands global thinking, global marketing, and global adaptability.

To change these thinking patterns in a fundamental way may take years, if not a generation. During that time, our corporations, not our school system, will need to take the lead in identifying the new skills and thinking patterns necessary to prepare our managers to become more globally effective.

CULTURAL PREREQUISITES FOR EFFECTIVE GLOBAL COMPETITION

What will it take to enable the United States to effectively compete on a global basis?

First, we will need to realize that the new game will not be played or driven by the U.S. business model. Clinging to traditional American views of competitiveness and marketplace success will increasingly threaten our corporations' ability to compete globally in the years ahead. There is some evidence that these attitudes are already changing. A recent United Research Company/Harris survey of 150 CEOs in Forbes 500 companies found that the greatest opportunity and challenge for the future was the global market with its attendant challenges to operate differently.

Second, we will need to modify certain barriers, misconceptions, and beliefs if our enterprises are going to work with multinational teams and strategies in a way that is managerially competitive. Some of the barriers we will need to recognize and work with appear in research by Andre Laurent, a professor at INSEAD business school in France, who makes the following key observations based on his study of multinational corporations (Laurent, 1986).

1. *Multinational companies do not and cannot submerge the individuality of different cultures.* As strong as a corporate culture may be, people never give up their own national backgrounds and preferences. People can adapt, but in periods of crisis or uncertainty, they will retreat to their own sets of beliefs and cultural values. Since crisis and uncertainty are prime characteristics of global organizations, national culture often plays an important role in people's day-to-day behavior.

2. *Contact with other nationality groups can even promote determination to be different.* It is paradoxical that many people withdraw when confronted with cultural differences, and reinforce their determination not to adjust and not to give up their own values. Unless intercultural contact is supported and guided to be a positive experience, it can often lead to the reinforcement of negative stereotypes. And others will resist integration or

homogenization, as they may see it, by emphasizing their own cultural heritage, history, and beliefs.

3. *It is useless to present new kinds of management theory and practice to individuals who are culturally unable or unwilling to accept it.* For example, performance reviews are difficult in most multinational corporations because of differences in personal style. Americans see themselves as open, direct, and blunt; Asians tend to be much more indirect, oblique, and subtle in giving feedback. Thus, something as apparently basic and common as a performance appraisal system probably cannot be implemented uniformly on a global basis.

Several other key cultural paradigms that affect our ability to rethink the new global game are worth noting.

1. The "we are all alike" syndrome is one that many of us have experienced when we have visited a foreign land and come back with the initial perception that all people are very much alike—we are just one, big human race.

2. A second stage of understanding, however, comes when we begin to uncover subtle, more specific differences. We then realize that although people have some significant similarities in their needs and feelings, they can also have strong differences in the way they *meet* these needs and *express* these feelings.

3. Finally, a third stage is reached after continued contact with the realization that people are both different and similar. As a result, an organization, leadership, or management model must address both common and uncommon threads. *Ultimately, we must acknowledge and address the diverse behaviors and beliefs which other people hold.*

The prevailing attitude of senior executives in many American companies seems to be, "If we can get our corporate culture and values right, then no matter where we operate around the globe, issues of strategy and local behavior will be predictable and consistent."

What some are saying is that the template for values, beliefs, and behaviors of the enterprise must come from the values, beliefs, behaviors, and attitudes of the parent corporation. It is becoming clear that this is the wrong starting point. **Diversity—both domestic and international—will be the engine that drives the creative energy of the corporation of the 21st century. Successful global managers will be those who are able to manage this diversity for the innovative and competitive edge of their corporations.**

The difficult task for senior management today is to turn around the traditional thinking that suggests that values, beliefs, and behaviors need to be highly standardized from a central, corporate perspective. This shift in thinking will be particularly difficult for those American enterprises that have done little in the last 30 or 40 years to educate and train their managers to organize and manage the firm's resources from a multicultural or international perspective.

Most of the current writing and thinking about global organizations focuses on marketing, resource allocation, technology transfer, and organizational structure as they relate to information flow, strategy, and control requirements. Little attention has been given to the management and human development needs that arise in the evolution from a domestic business to one that operates from a true global perspective. This book is an attempt to help you focus on some of these issues which are so important in transforming America's local corporations into global organizations.

TEAM PLAY

The global game cannot not be played alone, as the introductory quotation from James Carse notes. Rosabeth Moss Kanter, in *When Giants Learn to Dance* (1989), claims that the global economy is looking more and more like a corporate Olympics—a "series of games played all over the world with international as well as domestic competitors" (p. 18).

She notes that these global games are increasingly *team* sports, requiring collaboration across national, cultural, social, ethnic, and economic differences. While there are many different games played in wide-ranging ways, and according to many different rules, the teams that win most are characterized by "the strength, skill and discipline of the athlete, focused on individual excellence, coupled with the ability to work well within a well-organized team" (Kanter, 1989, p. 19).

We will see that teamwork and good interpersonal and group cooperation are increasingly forming the bedrock of organizational life in the 1990s and beyond. Teamwork and team *play* are both important to global organizations. Global managers must redefine work and play as part of their ability to manage in different societies. After all, what is play in North America, may be work in Asia, Latin America, or the Middle East and vice versa. Strict separation of work and play, as has been the tradition in countries like Germany, is more permeable in the Middle East and may need to become even more permeable to be successful on a global basis.

CONTINUOUS PLAY

Global games may be team efforts, both domestically and internationally, but the rules of the games are changing. In some cases, the objective is no longer to win, but to continue the play, because the game is filled with constant change, making the rules, the boundaries, and even the end unclear.

As Kanter describes it, the "game" may be changing from baseball to croquet as described in *Alice in Wonderland*. In this game nothing remains stable.

> The mallet Alice uses is a flamingo, which tends to lift its head and face in another direction just as Alice tries to hit the ball. The ball, in turn, is a hedgehog, another creature with a mind of its own. Instead of lying there waiting for Alice to hit it, the hedgehog unrolls, gets up, moves to another part of the court and sits down again. The wickets are card soldiers ordered around by the Queen of Hearts, who changes the structure of the game seemingly at whim by barking out an order to the wickets to reposition themselves around the court. [Kanter, 1989, p. 19]

If technology is the flamingo, employees and customers the hedgehogs, government regulators and corporate raiders the Queen of Hearts, then the reality of a new world begins to emerge. Managers of global corporations deal with constant change in a constantly changing game that cannot be won—but must be continually played in new ways.

SEA CHANGES

Robert Reich, in his book, *The Work of Nations* (1991), notes "we are living through a transformation that will rearrange the politics and economics of the coming century. There will be no *national* products or technologies, no *national* corporations, no *national* industries. There will no longer be national economies . . . all that will remain rooted within national borders are the people who comprise a nation. 'American' corporations and 'American' industries are ceasing to exist in any form that can meaningfully be distinguished from the rest of the global economy" (Reich, 1991, p. 3 and 77).

Reich notes that many corporations are becoming "global webs" in which products are international composites. "What is traded between nations is less finished products than specialized problem-solving (research, product design, fabrication), problem-identifying (marketing, advertising, customer consulting) and brokerage (financing, searching, contracting) services, as well as certain routine components and services, all of which are combined to create value" (Reich, 1991, p.113).

Reich proceeds to argue that a nation's commitment to the development of its *people* is the prime way to ensure global competitiveness. If this is true on a national basis, it is certainly true on an organizational level. For this reason, we have chosen to examine the needs and methods of helping people like you become self-confident, competent global managers.

Peter Drucker, one of the most thoughtful management philosophers of the 20th century, has also noted that we are in the middle of a sea change in political and economic history. He writes in his far-sighted book, *The New Realities* (1989), that:

> Sometime between 1965 and 1973 we passed over the divide and entered 'the next century.' . . . No one except a mere handful of Stalinists believes anymore in salvation by society. . . . The last such 'divide' was crossed exactly a century earlier, in 1873, when the crash of the Vienna stock market marked the end of the Liberal era, the end of one hundred years in which laissez-faire was the dominant political creed. [p. 7]

Salvation by society, as Drucker calls it, has given way to the "triumph of the individual" as heralded by John Naisbitt and Patricia Aburdene in *Megatrends 2000* (1990). Drucker notes that the era dominated by the Liberal Democratic doctrines and policies first formulated in the 1870s is now becoming as ineffectual as laissez-faire policies and ideas were during the last quarter of the 19th century.

Jack Welch, the transformational leader of General Electric, has a prescription for productivity, growth, and competitive advantage in this new global age. He, like Reich, believes this will be gained through "people power" in companies where the corporate cultures are guided by "speed, simplicity and self confidence." Frank P. Doyle, Senior Vice-President for Corporate Relations staff at GE noted during a recent meeting that "people are becoming the winning edge determining the competitiveness of companies and countries" (*Paradigm 2000 Newsletter,* Vol I, Number 2 June/July 1990, p. 6).

On the home front, AT&T has introduced a new Language Line which provides 24-hour instantaneous interpretation services by phone in 143 languages and dialects. Someone must be going global, because there is obviously a business need for interpreters! Call 1–800–752–6096.

One new concept of going global explained by Dr. Frank de Chambeau of Coopers & Lybrand is a 150-hour workweek spread out over 14 time zones—constantly on-line.

Other views on the new world view facing the global manager of the future include:

> Globalization means attaining and maintaining a 360-degree focus. [Natasha Wolainsky, President, Strategic Business Alliances]
>
> If a guy wants to be a chief executive 25 or 50 years from now he will have to be well-rounded. His education and experience will make him a total entrepreneur in a world that has changed into one huge market. . . . He'd better speak Japanese or German and understand history . . . and he'd better know those economics cold. [Lee Iacocca]

For the first time in its history mankind as a whole and not only the individual representatives, has begun to feel that it is one entity, to see global relationships between man, society and nature, and to assess the consequences of material activities. We must have a new outlook and overcome mentality, stereotypes and dogmas inherited from the past—gone and never to return. . . . It is a system that organically blends all main spheres of security . . . military, political, economic and humanitarian. [Mikhail Gorbachev's address to the International Forum for a Nuclear Free World, 1987]

The world is going to be so significantly different it will require a completely different kind of CEO (with) multi-environment, multi-country, multi-functional, maybe even multi-company and multi-industry experience. [Ed Dunn, Corporate Vice-President, Whirlpool Corporation] (All quotes from *Paradigm 2000*, Vol. 1, Number 1. April/May, 1990, pp. 9–10).

In 1989, the chairman of the then NCR Corporation, Gilbert Williamson, was asked about American competitiveness and how much it drives his corporate strategy. He replied "I don't think about it at all. We at NCR think of ourselves as a globally competitive company that happens to be headquartered in the United States" (Reich, 1991, p. 119).

To date, globalization has had the greatest impact on the telecommunications, electronics/computer, finance, pharmaceutical, chemical, transportation, and automotive industries. If you are in one of these industries, you know it. If you aren't, get ready—because it's just a matter of time before you will be going global.

HRD IMPLICATIONS OF GLOBALIZATION

All this talk of a new global world moves the human resource function into a new orbit. HRD can no longer focus only on *compliance* (compensation, benefits, and labor relations), but must now include *facilitation* (of global attitudes, knowledge, skills, and corporate culture).

A 1985 review of international human resource literature entitled "International HRM: Fact or Fiction?" concluded that little had been written in the international arena beyond articles on issues of expatriate selection, orientation, training, relocation, compensation, and re-entry (Patrick V. Morgan, 1986). No attention was paid to the role of HRD as a strategic partner for business units in achieving their global business objectives.

A more recent review in 1989 with a more forward-looking title, "Shaping the Global Workplace," reported that little progress had been made in the ensuing four years (Stephanie Overman, 1989).

Yet, all the statistics and recent writings underscore the growing importance of being more globally oriented. Tom Peters, in his recent book, *Thriv-*

ing on Chaos, notes that "every firm over two million dollars in revenues should take steps to examine their international market opportunities in the next 12 months. And every firm over \$25 million should be alarmed if it is not doing 25% of its business globally, including some with Japan" (Peters, 1988, p.150).

While this may be a bit of an overstatement, it places the emphasis on the right "syl-la-ble," as they say. Survival and competitiveness in the future will depend on an organization's global capacities; this, in turn, will depend foremost on its people.

The challenge for all of us involved in management, as well as in the development of management, is to begin to change the context in which we think about our human development responsibilities. We clearly need to discard traditional models and views and begin to think from a global rather than a domestic paradigm. In the process, we must challenge and change many of our views about hiring, training, controlling, motivating, and measuring our managers.

This change will require a long-term commitment, probably three to five years for most large enterprises simply to get moving. In all likelihood, it will take a full generation to implement the approach. By that time, we will have a whole new game to worry about.

CONTEXTS AND LEVELS OF GLOBALIZATION

Ask Andy Grove, the scion of Silicon Valley and founder of INTEL, whether INTEL is a global corporation. He will answer emphatically "yes." Ask Dov Frohman, director of INTEL's Research Center in Israel, the same question and he will just as emphatically answer "no." Ask Sharon Richards, cross-cultural coordinator for INTEL and she will answer "yes" in strategy, but "no" in the skills and attitudes of the people and the corporate culture of the company.

Who's right? All three are. And that's the first problem with globalization. Nobody—even in the same company—seems to have the total picture of how to make globalization work.

INTEL, in fact, is working conscientiously to integrate and align its global strategy, structure, culture, and people. But most U.S. firms are confused about how to globalize and particularly about how to drive a global perspective down through the human side of an organization.

There is a great deal of interest today in selecting, training, and preparing managers to work in global organizations. CEOs are defining *globalization* as a major corporate objective of the 1990s, much like *quality* and *customer focus* were driving corporate objectives of the 1980s.

FIGURE 1-1
Contexts and Levels of Globalization

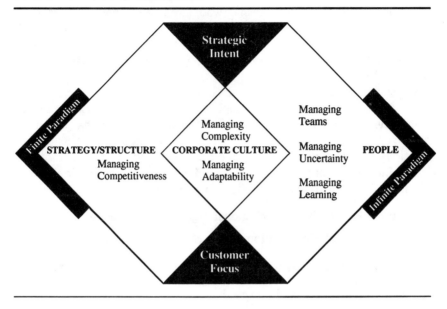

Unlike the 1980s, however, we do not have a W. Edwards Demming, Crosby, or Juran to help us define exactly what global management entails. How do we make sense of all this? How do we organize the themes and trends of the world into something which global managers can deal with on a day-to-day basis?

We have chosen to divide organizational life into three levels of activity: strategy/structure, corporate culture, and people (see Figure 1-1). An integrated approach to managing global organizations addresses all three levels. The problem facing executives, managers, and employees of globalizing corporations is that few people within an organization comprehend all three areas. As in the INTEL example, senior managers usually concentrate on global strategy and structure. Middle managers complain that various aspects of the corporate culture prohibit them from acting globally. And human resource people focus on building better interpersonal and cross-cultural skills.

To make matters worse, the situation is no better on the outside. External consultants are biased in one direction or another, or know only one level of the issue. Business school academics are versed in global strategy and structure, but not in cross-cultural relations. Cross-cultural experts focus on psychology, with little understanding of strategic business issues.

Authors like Bartlett and Ghoshal, who have written about globalization, have spoken of the importance of "administrative heritage" (corporate culture) for globalization, but have emphasized that strategy and structure determine the competitive success of a global company (Bartlett and Ghoshal, 1990).

Other writers, like Copeland and Griggs, who have written eloquently about cultural factors affecting people engaged in global business operations, have not applied these same cultural issues to a global corporate culture and the problems of managing flexibility and adaptiveness of corporations as well as individuals (Copeland and Griggs, 1985).

The framework for this globalization guide is built on four basic elements of which the first two are shown in Figure 1-1. These are:

• Four *contexts* within which global organizations operate.

• Three *levels* of globalization within each organization.

The other two elements will be described in the next chapter. These are:

• Six *mindsets* for global perspectives.

• Six *competencies* for global effectiveness.

Contexts

All organizations operate within four contexts that determine their mission, values, and corporate culture. These four **contexts** include:

1. The *finite, or fixed paradigm* of the world against which the initial strategy and structure of a globalizing organization are set.

While some fixed structure and strategy is necessary for operating a worldwide organization, this finite or fixed part of a global organization must be seen as a base and not the operational answer to future market opportunities. **Any part of a global organization that is fixed must be secondary to that which changes.**

2. The *customer focus* through which all organizational objectives, strategies, and tactics must be viewed.

It has by now become an article of faith that management and organizational success in the 1990s must be customer driven and focused. This is as true of a global organization as a domestic one, but mindsets become more complex as a variety of social, cultural, and personal values and beliefs must be responded to in a sensitive manner.

3. The *strategic intent* of the organization which defines the purpose, mission, and vision of what it is trying to achieve in the global arena.

Just as customer focus has become a major external filter for the operation of all organizations, a clear strategic intent has become the internal locus of operation. In other words, managers and organizations operate within a constant sensitivity to the needs of the customer *and* the needs of the stakeholders.

4. The *infinite, or constantly changing paradigm* of the world against which people and organizational processes must operate to ensure continued organizational survival and success.

The first three contexts represent *grounding* for global management. The fourth, constant change, represents the need for global managers and organizations to not just manage, but constantly *seek change* if they are to survive and prosper in a global environment.

This constant *balance,* between those aspects of organizational life which must remain constant and those which must be flowing and responsive to change, constitutes one of the most challenging and difficult aspects of global management. While all managers in the world face a similar dilemma, when considered on a global basis, the complexity and uncertainty of management increases considerably.

These four contexts establish the dynamic within which a global organization and its managers must operate.

Levels

For globalization to be successful, an organization must align its global strategy at three **levels**—strategy/structure, corporate culture, and people. Failure to do this has been the single reason that many organizations have foundered in their attempts to go global.

Level I: Strategy/Structure. *Strategy/structure* defines the relatively fixed mix of centralization-decentralization and geographical-functional-business-product structure to be used for the best competitive advantage.

A global organization relocates some functions on a global scale to places other than headquarters. A multicentered organization that can serve all parts of the firm anywhere in the world emerges.

Philips, for example, is establishing "centers of competence" in regions of the world where national cultural values and behavior best match the competence. Its long-range technology development center was moved from the United States to the Far East to take advantage of longer-term thinking and reward patterns. IBM and Digital Equipment Corporation have moved their R&D facilities to Italy where intuitive, innovative behavior has been highly successful.

Thus, in a global organization, the human resource challenge becomes recruitment, selection, training, and succession planning on a global scale from global sources. Global and cross-cultural training and career path planning become necessary for managers, regardless of their domestic or international assignments.

Level II: Corporate Culture. *Corporate culture* contains the values, norms of behavior, systems, policies, and procedures through which the organization adapts to the complexity of the global arena.

The foremost concern of any global corporation is the speed and agility with which it can respond to new developments anywhere in the world. To achieve this, the corporation must master a structure that allows quick decision making, must develop a common vision and value system that provides guidance for decentralized management, and must be constantly scanning the environment for new trends and directions.

Developing a global corporate culture involves not only understanding, skill, and the reallocation of resources, but also the ability to deal with issues of identity, power, and psychology that are always difficult to overcome in any organizational change. The quandary has most often been described as the choice between global integration and local responsiveness.

The pressures for global integration include the importance of international customers, the presence of multinational competitors, and the investment intensity of new technologies. It is easy to see how each of these areas can take on a global, rather than national identity and function. The hard part is getting there.

Dow Chemical is a good example of a company that utilizes high-speed information tools to operate integrated global production scheduling. Using a computerized linear programming model, the company weighs everything from currency and tax rates to transportation and local production costs to identify the cheapest maker of each product. In some instances, Dow's computer network chooses among factories on three continents to supply customers throughout the world (Kupfer, 1988, p. 48).

Electrolux, the Swedish company which made 100 acquisitions in the 1980s on both sides of the Atlantic, is an example of a corporation that needed to develop conflict resolution tools for management of their highly diverse multinational conglomerate.

With a history of extreme decentralization, Electrolux had to move from a company of "hundreds of independent villages" to a set of flexible "networks"—with product development, manufacturing, and supply all spanning international borders. Electrolux experienced tension on at least four different levels: between product divisions and marketing companies; between these two types of entities and country managers; between country managers and international product area managers; and between country managers and the international marketing coordinators.

To cope with these ongoing issues, they allocated international responsibility for decisions in a clear and decisive manner to the country manager level for sales activities and to central departments for other activities. They also co-opted the country managers into a new forum, called "The 1992 Group," to oversee the development of all aspects of product line strategy.

Finally, they emphasized quick decision making and stated (in an understated manner) in their internal literature that, "It is not quite 'proper' to fail to reach an agreement in areas of conflicting interests" (Evans, Doz, and Laurent, 1989, p. 121).

Robert Reich describes a new role which he considers necessary in global corporations—that of the strategic broker. He claims that one of the tasks of these people is "to create settings in which problem-solvers and problem-identifiers can work together without undue interference" (Reich, 1991, p. 88).

The strategic broker is a facilitator and coach, finding people who can work creatively together, giving them the resources necessary and providing the freedom to solve basic problems and resolve ongoing tensions within the organization. This is a combination of Peters and Waterman's "skunk works" and Tichy and Devanna's "transformational leader" (Peters and Waterman, 1982 and Tichy and Devanna, 1986).

Recent research in Europe has identified five distinct elements critical to building a global corporate culture (Evans, Doz, and Laurent, 1990, p. 118).

1. *A clear and simple mission statement* (e.g., IBM's four goals—profit, quality, efficiency, and growth; and its three values: attract, motivate, and retain).

2. *The vision of the chief executive officer* (e.g., GE's Jack Welch wants the company to be number one or two in all GE's businesses).

3. *Company-controlled management education* (e.g., Ericsson and Olivetti both have global management development centers in Britain, not Sweden or Italy, their home countries).

4. *Project-oriented management training programs* (e.g., ICL, the British computer company, put its top 2,000 managers through a one-week seminar in order to change its corporate culture).

5. *Emphasis on the processes of global corporate culture* (e.g., ICI, BP, and Philips have board-level involvement in all appointments of the top 100 managers).

Developing a global corporate culture with appropriate management practices depends heavily on changing the individual attitudes and skills of executives, managers, and employees in the organization. Without a change in people's mindsets, the best vision or global strategy will never get off the ground.

Level III: People. The *people* level of our model involves the development of human resources to manage teams, uncertainty, and personal and organizational learning in a way that enables the organization to continuously improve in spite of constant global, market, and competitive change.

In the end, a global organization's people, and especially its global managers, constitute *the most critical factor* in the organization's ability to survive and grow. People represent an organization's purpose, mission, values, and mindsets that are the generative juices, which *enable* it to respond in creative ways to unanticipated surprises.

At the center of any globalization effort are, therefore, a handful of *global managers* who understand the world and are prepared to manage the complexity, adaptability, teams, uncertainty, and learning that global organizations face in competing on a worldwide basis and meeting the needs of a wide range of customers in many countries.

But many American firms, such as AT&T, who are striving to become more global have found that their greatest problem is the lack of management with global mindsets—from top to bottom.

These mindsets, and the new behavior that they stimulate, extend all the way from global scanning for markets, products, and competitors to individual cross-cultural skills in adapting to new cultures, working in multicultural teams, and serving divergent local client needs.

Many companies over the years have developed excellent international relocation and compensation policies. Associations such as the Employee Relocation Council, as well as the international practice areas of many professional personnel and human resource associations, have spent years sharing information about the best practices in international relocation, compensation, and benefits packages.

Predeparture and in-country training has been uneven in cross-cultural issues, language, and adjustment support. Recent surveys indicate that while up to 70 percent of expatriates transferred overseas receive some form of language training, fewer than 50 percent receive any predeparture cross-cultural training. But some form of in-country orientation is usually provided by the local expatriate community.

Few companies train headquarters staff in how to work with foreign trainees; expertise in resolving interpersonal and cross-cultural conflicts is rare. Very few companies train American employees to sell, negotiate, or manage relationships internationally or to do business in foreign cultures.

At Level II: Corporate Culture, the driving force is the interest, perceptions, and values of leadership. It is fairly clear by now that leaders set the priorities, perceptions, values, and interests of corporations and establish the recognition and reward systems which encourage behavior the leaders feel is critical for the corporation to achieve its strategic objectives. The resulting corporate culture allows the organization to be resilient and adaptable to changes in the environment.

Global leaders are responsible for *articulation* of the global business strategy and structure, *alignment* of the corporate culture to support this strategy and structure and *mobilization* of the people to execute these strategies. Managers in global organization support these activities and ensure that the organization operates in such a manner that these activities are efficiently and effectively carried out. The mindsets and competencies that global managers need to carry out these responsibilities is the subject of this book.

At Level III: People, the driving force *should* be human resource professionals, who in partnership with line management provide a human resource system that stimulates individual and organizational learning. Too often in the past, HRD professionals have lagged behind in their capacities to develop people with the appropriate mindsets and competencies for the future. In successful global organizations, however, you will find the HRD function is increasingly sophisticated and a major partner with line management in achieving all levels of global success.

GLOBALIZATION LEVELS AND CORPORATE OBJECTIVES

Finally, it is important to note how these various levels of globalization fit with your company's objectives. Figure 1-2 provides an overview of this relationship. Each level of globalization has its own drivers that set corporate objectives.

At Level I: Strategy/Structure, the drivers are the nature of the business and the environment in which your company is operating. The business objective, profitability, is achieved through a strategy and structure which enable your business to respond effectively on a global basis.

FIGURE 1-2

Globalization Levels and Corporate Objectives

Globalization Level	Corporate Objective	Driver of Objective
I. Strategy/Structure	Profitability	Nature of the business and business environment —technology —competitors —customers —suppliers
II. Culture	Responsiveness	Leadership interests, perceptions and values expressed through —articulation of strategy —alignment of culture —mobilization of people
III. People	Learning	Human resource system in partnership with line management to develop global mindsets and competencies.

It is important to note that the drivers of a global company's strategy and structure are not just technology, competition, and customers, but also suppliers. Many companies are finding that they need to be more global not only to serve global customers, but also to more effectively utilize the advantages offered by global suppliers.

What should corporations do to develop people with the mindsets and skills to execute global strategies? How can they take an integrated approach to globalization that allows global strategy and structure to be supported by a global corporate culture and a globally minded workforce? Much needs to be done, both by the professional and academic consulting community, as well as by corporate leaders and human resource practitioners. We shall turn to one answer to this question in the next chapter.

AFTERTHOUGHTS FOR GLOBAL MINDSETS

The themes in this chapter suggest a number of directions you might consider in developing the global mindset that everyone says is a prerequisite to becoming a global manager.

1. As Carse notes, "No one can play the game alone"—meaning that *teamwork* and interpersonal relations are going to be key to your success as a global manager. If these are areas you need to develop, you'd better run, not walk, to your local training department or nearby continuing education program and explore opportunities to help you understand the interpersonal and group dynamics of effective teamwork.

2. *Cultural factors* are going to play a strong role in every aspect of global business. It is clear that the world is headed toward ethnic heterogeneity and you would be well-advised to start thinking more about cultural differences and understanding how and why people from different cultural backgrounds think and behave the way they do. There are a number of good books cited in the bibliography. I would start with Stewart and Bennett, *American Cultural Patterns: A Cross-cultural Perspective* (1991), which is by far the best book on the subject.

3. It is clear that *something is going on that is bigger than all of us.* Whether you want to call it a sea change or not is your own choice. The fact is that the world is in constant change and it seems that the managers who are successful have somehow adjusted to a life that appears to be somewhat out of control. If you've been thinking that it's just a matter of time before things settle down again, you may have a long wait. It might be better to see uncertainty as opportunity and begin now to determine how you can learn to take advantage of it.

4. You might *try some new reading.* The Economist is a good weekly publication with a European perspective. *The World Monitor* is a good view of the world from the American side. *World Press Review* will give you a summary of world events from different viewpoints of publications around the world. The *Financial Times* provides an excellent daily overview of world events from a European perspective, and the *Japan Times* fills in the Asian viewpoint. This assumes, of course, that you're reading a national newspaper like the *New York Times* or *Wall Street Journal* each day.

5. Finally, think about the question raised by Robert Reich. "Who is them and who is us?" Reich writes:

> Corporation A is headquartered north of New York City. Most of its top managers are citizens of the United States. All of its directors are American citizens, and a majority of its shares are held by American investors. But most of Corporation A's employees are non-Americans. Indeed, the company undertakes much of its R&D and product design, and most of its complex manufacturing outside the borders of the United States in Asia, Latin America and Europe. Within the American market, an increasing amount of the company's product comes from its laboratories and factories abroad.
>
> Corporation B is headquartered abroad, in another industrialized nation. Most of its top managers and directors are citizens of that nation, and a majority

of its shares are held by citizens of that nation. But most of Corporation B's employees are Americans. Indeed, Corporation B undertakes most of its R&D and new product design in the United States. And it does most of its manufacturing in the U.S. The company exports an increasing proportion of its American-based production, some of it even back to the nation where Corporation B is headquartered.

Now, who is "us"? [Reich, 1990, p.53]

Chapter Two

Global Mindsets and Competencies

Finite games can be played within an infinite game, but infinite games cannot be played within a finite game.

Carse, p. 8

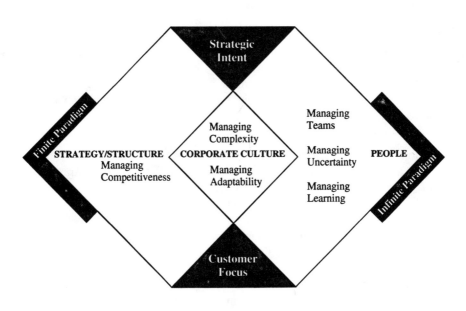

FORETHOUGHTS FROM A GLOBAL MIND

Now that you have an overview of some of the elements of going global, we'll move on to the fundamental challenge of globalization: developing and implementing an integrated approach that includes not only corporate strategy and structure, but also a global corporate culture and people with global mindsets and competencies.

Since you are a manager in a globalizing organization, you know how much your company's ability to achieve its globalization goals depends on you and people like you. You also know how hard it is to understand what globalization is all about and what people really mean by global mindsets. In this chapter, you will be introduced to some additional pieces of this puzzle called globalization. This piece has to do with you, your mindsets, and your skills.

These are areas which have not been well-developed and, when they have been explored, the explorers have many times been looking for other things and have therefore not fully mapped out the territory they were passing through. They may note that *process* is important, but they seldom see it as dominant. Only the total quality management (TQM) movement and those interested in Japanese management practices have come to understand the *power of process as the focal point for global competitiveness.*

This chapter provides a framework for the rest of the book. Here we'll define the terms of global management and outline how the various elements are related. You may find this a little theoretical, but if you can stay with it, you will understand the many elements involved in managing successfully in a global organization.

So walk around this chapter and make it friendly for yourself. It's the integrating centerpiece that makes the fundamental case that in the end will enable you to become a productive manager in a successful global organization.

Most of the professional and academic research that has been conducted in the area of global attitudes, behavior, and skills has concentrated on cross-cultural adjustment skills and international attitudes that extend beyond ethnocentric images to a more multicultural perspective.

Professionals concerned with this area come mainly from the behavioral sciences—primarily psychology, social psychology, sociology, anthropology, and communications. Few people in such specialties understand global business strategy or know of exemplary global business practices. As a result, integration of these factors into corporate strategy and culture—and the extension of such interests to persons who are not expatriates—has been limited.

The problems that can occur in international business as a result of cultural ignorance are well documented. David Ricks in *Big Business Blunders* (1983) outlines more than 100 examples of cross-cultural mistakes in multinational marketing. Ian Mitroff, in *Business Not As Usual* (1987), also argues that international business executives cannot approach the future based on the past.

Yet a recent study conducted by Korn/Ferry International and Columbia School of Business, *21st Century Report: Reinventing the CEO* (1989), notes that U.S. executives are far behind their European, Japanese, and Latin American counterparts in valuing experience outside the headquarter country and in speaking foreign languages.

Various authors offer recommendations as to the types of skills and attitudes necessary for global success. Henry Ferguson, in *Tomorrow's Global Executive* (1988), outlines specific talents that are needed in planning, motivating, operating, communicating, researching, networking, and negotiating on a global basis.

Lennie Copeland and Lewis Griggs, in *Going International: How to Make Friends and Deal Effectively in the Global Marketplace* (1985), cite marketing, negotiating, communicating, managing people, training and transferring skills, knowing business and social etiquette, getting things done, dealing with headquarters, dealing with the field, and managing personal and family life.

In the July/August 1990 *Harvard Business Review*, Bartlett and Ghoshal describe the most encouraging recent attempt to bridge the gap between strategy/structure, culture, and human resource policy. Their article, "Matrix Management: Not a Structure, a Frame of Mind," argues that "top-level managers in many of today's leading corporations are losing control of their companies . . . because their companies are incapable of carrying out the sophisticated strategies they have developed over the past 20 years." Bartlett and Ghoshal argue for more attention to the "effective management of human resource tools to broaden individual perspectives."

Most current training in this area has concentrated on personal cross-cultural adjustment of staff and families transferred overseas. There have also been courses on international negotiation, marketing, strategy, and finance for people traveling internationally on business.

Occasional public seminars can be found on such topics as multicultural team building, and cross-cultural conflict management, counseling and coaching, but little systematic work has been done in this area.

The Walt Disney Company recently undertook a series of cross-cultural orientation sessions for its Orlando-based managers. The program was designed to help the U.S. managers deal with French trainees coming to Orlando in preparation for the 1992 opening of Euro Disneyland. Such a program is the exception rather than the rule for most corporations involved in international staff exchanges.

GLOBAL MINDSETS

Beyond these infrequent seminars, how can managers develop the mindsets and competencies to meet the changing, emerging, and increasingly complex conditions we have been describing?

There is a great deal of discussion these days about global mindsets. Thus far, however, there has been little systematic attempt to define exactly what a global mindset is or what it would look like. There is a general feeling that it is something that a global manager must have, that it represents a certain curiosity about the world and a willingness to deal with broad global and foreign issues, but there has been little attempt to define what a manager with a global mindset might look like.

Glen Fisher, in his recent work on mindsets, has described them as "differing ways that the subject at hand is perceived, understood and reasoned about" (Fisher, 1988). This is similar to what Joel Barker has called a "paradigm." He defines this as a "set of rules and regulations that does two things: (1) it establishes or defines boundaries; and (2) it tells you how to behave inside the boundaries in order to be successful" (Barker, 1992, p. 17).

For our purposes, we will define a mindset as a predisposition to see the world in a particular way that sets boundaries and provides explanations for why things are the way they are, while at the same time establishing guidance for ways in which we should behave. In other words, a mindset is a filter through which we look at the world.

A mindset is a way of being rather than a set of skills. It is an orientation to the world that allows you to see certain things that others do not see. A global mindset means that we scan the world from a broad perspective, always looking for unexpected trends and opportunities that may constitute a threat or an opportunity to achieve our personal, professional, or organizational objectives.

Warren Bennis, in his differentiation between managers and leaders has captured many of the mindsets to be effective globally. He offers this list.

- The manager administers; the leader innovates.
- The manager is a copy; the leader is an original.
- The manager maintains; the leader develops.
- The manager focuses on systems and structure; the leader focuses on people.
- The manager relies on control; the leader inspires trust.
- The manager has a short-range view; the leader has a long-range perspective.
- The manager asks how and when; the leader asks what and why.
- The manager has his eye on the bottom line; the leader has his eye on the horizon.
- The manager accepts the status quo; the leader is his own person.
- The manager does things right; the leader does the right things. [Bennis, 1990, p. 44]

From 25 years of management and research in this area, I have found that people with global mindsets tend to approach the world in six specific ways.

1. People with global mindsets drive for the *bigger, broader picture.*

People with a global mindset are constantly looking for *context.* They are concerned about the backdrop against which current events are happening. This backdrop may be historical, but it is more likely to be concerned with current and future trends on a broad, global basis. A global mind is never content with one explanation of an event, never satisfied with one task when it can manage a project, never happy with a project when it can manage an organization. Likewise, people with global mindsets are constantly scanning the geographical horizon to learn more about potential markets and competitors, new technology, and new suppliers.

It should be noted that there is also a great need today for managers with global mindsets in domestic organizations. Many people will argue that there is no longer any such thing as a domestic organization of any consequence, because if you are successful domestically, there is an increasing possibility that a foreign competitor will enter your market to challenge your position. As we will see in the next chapter, many organizations that market to domestic customers are also finding a need to be more globally oriented and to globally source materials, technology, capital, and even people who can help them provide the best product at the highest quality and lowest cost.

Global scanning, therefore, is an important skill for *any* manager of *any* organization, whether domestic, international, or global.

2. People with global mindsets accept *life as a balance of contradictory forces* that are to be appreciated, pondered, and managed.

While most adults will agree that the world is complex, global managers *know* it's complex. Demands of many constituencies in functional, geographical, and various business units are often in conflict. A global manager must learn to live with conflict *management,* rather than *resolution* and must learn to look for opportunity from adversity and creativity from diversity. A global mind does not coerce resolution from opposite forces in life. The concept of *balance* is central for a global mindset, because it entails the simultaneous appreciation of contradictory ideas in a way that does not paralyze, but energizes. This is easier said than done, but is definitely a mindset and philosophy that must be developed to thrive in a global organization. We shall discuss this further in Chapter Four.

3. People with global mindsets trust *process rather than structure* to deal with the unexpected.

Global minds trust process. It's that simple—and that difficult. It is hard to trust process, because we have been taught to analyze, plan, structure, and control as the normal activities of management.

A global mindset, however, recognizes and acknowledges that process is more powerful than structure and that process, not structure, is the key to organizational adaptability. In this definition, we refer to process as a series of activities that form the physiology for the anatomy of an organization. In other words, process is the systems, policies, procedures, and norms of behavior that enable people and organizations to respond rapidly to changes in their environment.

4. People with global mindsets value *diversity* and *multicultural teamwork and play* as the basic forum within which they accomplish their personal, professional, and organizational objectives.

Teamwork *and* team play are fundamental filters for a global mind. Global minds cannot conceive of operating successfully in a global world by themselves. Teamwork and interdependence on others is a basic tenet of global management. In the process, people with global mindsets find tremendous diversity in the world. Multicultural teams have a wide range of expectations concerning how they work together and how they play together. The mindset necessary to manage a multicultural team requires *sensitivity* and flexibility in meeting the needs of diverse people while attaining project and organizational objectives.

5. People with global mindsets flow with *change as opportunity* and are comfortable with surprises and ambiguity.

Global minds are comfortable with surprises, ambiguity, and change. Global managers have experienced enough of the world to know that it is unpredictable for many reasons. Sometimes it is unpredictable because it is too complex; sometimes because it is simple, but different; sometimes because it is unknowable. Feeling comfortable with ambiguity, accepting surprises, and seeing change as opportunity are all part of the global mindset necessary for success in a world in rapid evolution.

6. People with global mindsets continuously seek to be *open* to themselves and others by rethinking boundaries, finding new meanings, and changing their direction and behavior.

These people are constantly searching for improvement in their own lives and the lives of others. They are seeking to develop themselves not *against* surprises, but *for* surprises. James Carse contends that this is the difference between being trained and educated. To be trained, is to be prepared *against* surprises, to be educated, is to be prepared *for* surprises. In this sense, global managers *must* be educated, rather than trained, because global management is *full* of surprises.

Global mindsets are not *exclusive,* but *inclusive.* When global mindsets become exclusive, they risk alienating many people in the world on whom they are dependent. When global mindsets think too small, they exclude

FIGURE 2-1

Comparison of Domestic and Global Mindsets

Domestic Mindset	Global Mindset
Functional expertise	Bigger, broader picture
Prioritization	Balance of contradictions
Structure	Process
Individual responsibility	Teamwork and diversity
No surprises	Change as opportunity
Trained against surprises	Openness to surprises

purposes and goals that are important to others and undermine their ability to be effective global leaders.

These six global mindsets form the foundation for global management competencies. One can tell as much by the verbs used to describe these mindsets as by the nouns. The verbs indicate that these people:

- drive
  - accept
    - trust
      - value
        - flow
          - seek

Global managers are doers, yet they are willing to occasionally step back and go with the flow. They trust process and accept paradoxes, but they also work to understand complexity in a way that has purpose and direction. They value teams and teamwork and continuously seek to improve the quality of life for themselves and others. These are people who live life on many levels—physical, intellectual, emotional, and spiritual—and for whom the world is their playground and their school.

Their global mindsets can be compared with more parochial, domestic mindsets, which are perfectly legitimate for domestic organizations, but often fall short in organizations that operate globally. The contrast might look something like what is shown in Figure 2-1.

Moving managers from a domestic to a global profile is often dependent upon the degree to which an organization educates and rewards behavior in the second column versus the first. This is the human resource challenge that is the subject of this book.

FIGURE 2-2
Global Mindsets and Personal Characteristics

Global Mindset	Personal Characteristic
Broad	Knowledge
Balance	Conceptualization
Process	Flexibility
Diversity	Sensitivity
Change	Judgment
Open	Reflection

GLOBAL MINDSETS AND
PERSONAL CHARACTERISTICS

There is a definite connection between global mindsets and personal qualities or characteristics. It is possible that a characteristic may precede a mindset, or a mindset may lead to certain behavior which, in turn, creates a related characteristic.

Human resource managers have spent years trying to develop screening and selection procedures for identifying global managers. Most have used personal characteristics as the basis for testing, since it has been difficult to test mindsets and there has never been a well-developed theory or method of testing the relationship between personal characteristics, mindsets, competencies, and the capacity to manage globally.

While the framework we are developing here is not empirically derived, it provides a context, based on personal experience, global management training programs, and relevant literature, within which to grapple with the issue of global management and how global managers can be selected and developed.

The list in Figure 2-2 outlines the relationship between mindsets and the personal characteristics that I have found are most often associated with these mindsets.

Knowledge

Constantly driving for the bigger, broader picture will expand one's *knowledge*. A global manager's technical, business, and industry knowledge is the most fundamental quality that allows him or her to successfully manage the competitive process, both domestic and foreign. This knowledge must be broad, as well as deep, and *must* have a well-developed international dimension that includes constant scanning of information and competitive and market conditions on a global basis.

Conceptualization

Second, global managers must have highly developed *conceptual capacity* to deal with the complexity of global organizations. This conceptual ability needs to be present in two forms.

Global managers must be specialized and at the same time holistic in their thinking. As Peter Senge has eloquently noted in his work, *The Fifth Discipline,* managers of learning organizations need to have a "systems view" of the world as well as "personal mastery" of their function. A systems view requires an *intuitive, right-brain* ability to understand different levels of business vision, mission, and strategy and to grasp their implications for global structure, culture, and people.

Global managers must also, however, have *analytical, left-brain* skills to be able to balance contradictory forces and go to the heart of complex issues that are part and parcel of a global organization. It is important not only to be able to live with a balance of irreconcilable demands, but also necessary to use analytical skills to break complicated issues into parts that can be managed and made actionable by others.

Flexibility

Third, global managers are constantly challenged to trust process rather than structure. This is not easy for someone who has become used to one way of life, one world view, and one comfortable skill set. The management of a global corporate culture that is adaptable and capable of dealing with rapid changes in the environment requires managers who are extremely *flexible.* Flexibility allows managers to meet the needs of the organization and to constantly adjust to global and local demands through coordination and allocation of the organization's resources.

I have found that dependence on a structured process of decision making, or even preset understandings of the relationship between different functions, will often lead to failure. Instead, as a result, a global manager has to be able to work with decision-making and problem-solving *processes,* rather than policies and procedures, to achieve results.

Sensitivity

Fourth, since global organizations conduct the majority of their creative and operational work in multicultural teams, global managers must have a *sensitivity* to cultural diversity, which few people possess naturally.

Learning to be cross-culturally sensitive is not easy. It requires not only a sensitivity to others, which is so often stressed, but also a fairly well-developed ego and self-concept (which is often not stressed).

In my experience, I have found that people who adapt best cross-culturally are those who feel relatively secure with themselves. There is always some form of challenge in cross-cultural interactions, and often this challenge is directed at questions about who you are and what you believe in. When faced with such issues, the most successful people are those who have a reasonably well-developed philosophy and approach to life, which is inclusive, rather than exclusive of others.

The ability to operate cross-culturally comes more naturally to some, but in any case, it is a lifelong learning experience. With the wide range of cultures and people in the world, there will always be some that are more difficult for us to deal with than others. Those of us who work internationally, therefore, must be constantly attentive to increase the range of our skills and abilities to work constructively with the broadest range of people and cultures. This requires people who are not only relatively well-integrated and stable emotionally, but also people who have a predisposition to others' views and a willingness to question their own assumptions, values, and beliefs about the world and the way it operates.

Judgment

Fifth, it is clear that the speed and constancy of change in global organizations, as well as their complexity, leads many global managers who have gained their reputations for technical expertise to feel overwhelmed by a lack of certainty. This is not uncommon and may be one of your own motivations for reading this book.

Uncertainty requires new levels of *judgment* which enable you to see change as an opportunity, rather than a threat. Global managers need to be able to intuit decisions with inadequate information and be willing to make decisions based on their experience, rather than refined empirical data. For this reason, most effective global managers have rather broad experience and have demonstrated the ability to operate under many different managerial, organizational, and international circumstances.

Effective global managers also often display a good mix of self-confidence and humility. They are experienced enough to be confident in their judgments, but they are also experienced enough to know that there is infrequently one right answer to any issue of importance and that every major decision requires a certain amount of circumspection, questioning, and listening for new viewpoints.

Imagine how difficult it is for an engineer, who may have been trained that there are correct answers for many technical problems, when he or she has to face the challenge of becoming a global manager in which decisions must be made with a lack of information, with doubts about expertise to make proper judgments about management operations, and with time pressure that will not allow adequate analysis. The interpretation of ethical dilemmas from a cross-cultural perspective, for example, is one of many challenges of judgment that these global managers face.

Reflection

Finally, all successful global organizations are seeking continuous improvement. Continuous improvement, in turn, does not happen without managers who are seeking constant improvement in their own and their organization's performance. And this improvement cannot be achieved without a capacity for *reflection*.

Reflection provides the perspective necessary for dealing with the next round of challenges. It also enables one to weave some sense of development and progress into the fabric of one's life and the life of the organization and people with whom one works. Lifelong learning and education drive most successful global managers, because they recognize that they can never know enough to deal with the world around them. But if they search correctly and long enough, their efforts may lead to vision and even leadership.

These are the six personal characteristics behind the six global mindsets. I want to emphasize again that a characteristic may precede a mindset or a mindset, turned into behavior, may create a characteristic. It really doesn't matter.

With these introductory observations, we are now ready to examine the relationship of mindsets and personal characteristics to global managerial competencies.

COMPETENCIES AND CHARACTERISTICS

If mindsets and personal characteristics are the being side of global management, competencies are the doing side. This definition is somewhat at variance with Boyatzis' definition of a competency as "the knowledge, motive, trait, self-image, social role, or skill essential to performing a job"

FIGURE 2–3
Global Management Competencies and Characteristics

Characteristic	Competence
Knowledge	Managing competition
Conceptualization	Managing complexity
Flexibility	Managing adaptability
Sensitivity	Managing teams
Judgment	Managing uncertainty
Reflection	Managing learning

(Boyatzis, 1982, p. 23). We have chosen to equate competency with "skill" and to denote the other factors "knowledge, motive, trait, self-image, and social role" as personal characteristics.

Following from our previous discussion, we can see in Figure 2–3 how the characteristics we just reviewed provide the backdrop for the six competencies, which form the core of our present study.

These six global management competencies are:

1. *Managing competitiveness* in which managers constantly scan their environment for changes in market, competitive, and supplier conditions, as well as socioeconomic and political trends that may affect the organization and its strategic intent.

2. *Managing complexity* involving the skills to manage trade-offs of many competing interests, as well as the inherent contradictions and conflicts that exist in all global organizations.

3. *Managing adaptability* which entails developing a global corporate culture with the values, beliefs, systems, and norms of behavior that allow it to be responsive to constant change and able to deal with ambiguity.

4. *Managing teams* within a multicultural environment, which requires cultural sensitivity and managerial skills to lead, understand, manage, and supervise people from a wide range of cultures in a broad range of situations.

5. *Managing uncertainty* as a fundamental skill to deal with the increasing chaos of one's environment in a way that provides for continuous improvement, while providing structure and taking advantage of opportunities that arise from the lack of structure.

6. *Managing learning* which requires managers to not only learn about themselves on a continuing basis, but also to train and develop others and

FIGURE 2–4
A Global Manager's Guide to Action

I.	Manage **competitiveness** through *knowledge* by driving for the broader picture.
II.	Manage **complexity** through *conceptualization* by accepting the balance of contradictions.
III.	Manage **adaptability** through *flexibility* by *trusting process* over structure.
IV.	Manage **teams** through *sensitivity* by *valuing diversity.*
V.	Manage **uncertainty** through *judgment* by *flowing* with *change.*
VI.	Manage **learning** through *reflection* by *seeking* to be *open.*

facilitate constant organizational learning so that it can be responsive and adaptive to global change and challenge.

Let's pull all of this together into a framework that outlines the relationship between competencies, characteristics, actions, and mindsets.

A MANAGER'S GUIDE TO ACTION

The best way to understand the relationship between each of the variables in the global competency model is with a formula.

$$C + Ch = f(A \times M)$$

Competency + Characteristic is a function of Action × Mindset.

In Figure 2–4, we have verbally related the six competencies to each of their associated variables. This list is a forthright statement of the conceptual framework for this book and can be your guiding list as we move forward.

By concentrating on the *actions* you can see how to get to the competencies, characteristics, and mindsets we have been reviewing. During the rest of this book, we will explore what further actions you can take to bring all this together.

Another representation of these competencies, characteristics, mindsets, and actions is included in Figure 2–5.

In this fan diagram, each area away from the core represents another competency. At the same time, the diagram provides a list of each of the competencies, characteristics, actions, and mindsets that will be the focus of this study.

FIGURE 2–5
Global Competencies, Characteristics, Actions, and Mindsets

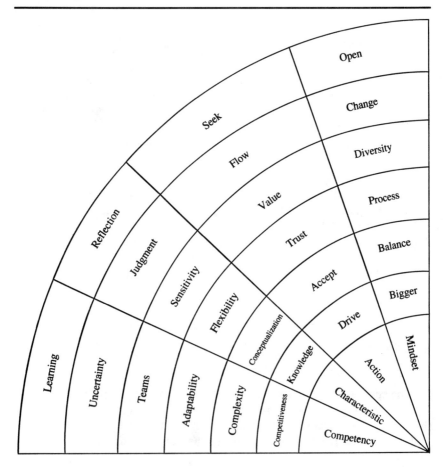

INTEGRATION OF GLOBAL COMPETENCIES
WITH THE LEVELS OF GLOBALIZATION

At this point it might be useful to describe the relationship between the global competencies we have identified and the levels of globalization we discussed in the last chapter.

FIGURE 2-6

Framework for an Integrated Approach to Globalization

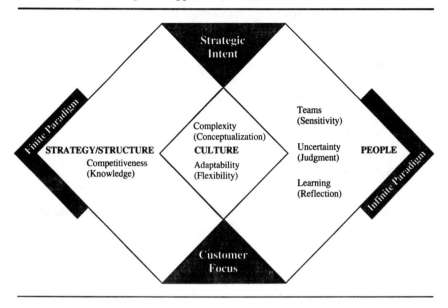

Figure 2-6 demonstrates how the six competencies and personal characteristics are applied to each of the three levels strategy/structure, corporate culture, and people.

To effectively deal with organizational *strategy and structure* (Level I), global managers must learn to manage the **competitive process.** This is dependent upon developing the technical, economic, political, and cultural *knowledge* to operate in a global environment.

Managing a global *corporate culture* (Level II), on the other hand, requires the simultaneous ability to manage organizational **complexity** and **adaptability.** Global managers who successfully manage complexity are able to *conceptually* understand and *focus* the organization on the priorities necessary to achieve the strategic intent of the organization. When this strategy has been formulated, a manager must then be *flexible* to put into place the values, norms, systems, and procedures that translate strategic intent into corporate culture and organizational operations.

To ensure that global strategy is *fully* implemented, however, requires alignment not only of the corporate culture, but also the *people* (Level III) in the organization. Aligning people requires *sensitivity, judgment,* and *re-*

flection. It is carried out through managing multicultural **teams, uncertainty,** and personal and organizational **learning.**

This integrated approach to globalization combines well-known theories of organizational change concerning alignment with the specific competencies that global managers must master. Managers at all levels of a globalizing organization need to master these six competencies for their own unit, department, or division in order to ensure that their organization's global strategy is successfully carried out.

GLOBAL COMPETENCIES, PRACTICES, AND TASKS

One of the most important pieces of our framework involves the translation of a *competency* to specific practices and tasks that enable a global manager to impact his or her environment. This is the *operational* level on which the rest of the book will be built.

For definition purposes, a *competency* is a specific capacity to execute action at a skill level that is sufficient to achieve the desired effect. Each competency requires *practices* that are distinctive and contribute to the competency. These practices, in turn, must translate into a series of *tasks* that global managers execute to be effective.

For example, a global manager who is successful at managing the competitive process (*competency*) will need to constantly scan the global environment for potential competitors (*practice*). To accomplish this, he or she will need to read different publications and perhaps take out a subscription to the *Asian Wall Street Journal* or *The Economist* magazine to supplement current reading of the local or even national newspaper (*task*).

In another instance, to manage complexity successfully (*competency*), a global manager may have to manage relationships that are simultaneously cooperative and competitive, such as strategic alliances with foreign competitors (*practice*). To do this well will require analytical skills (*characteristic*) to determine which aspects of the relationship will be cooperative, and which competitive, and to compartmentalize information, decision making, and operations accordingly (*task*).

In the chapters that follow, I have further defined the six global competencies to outline the practices and tasks that I have found are most often associated with these skills.

FIGURE 2-7
Global Competency Learning Cycle

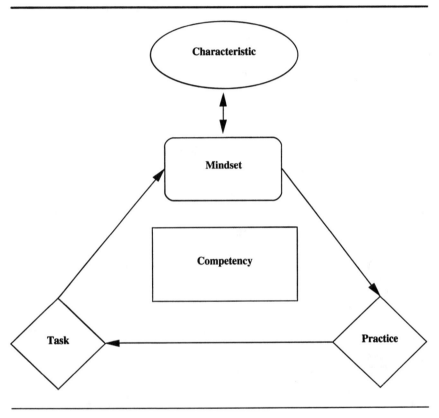

GLOBAL COMPETENCY LEARNING CYCLE (CLC)

The last link in our framework involves an explanation of how all these variables relate to one another. I will try to do this in a way that enables you as a global manager to understand and develop these mindsets, character-istics, and competencies to perform the practices and tasks necessary for effective global management. Figure 2-7 diagrams the relationship among these features in what I have called the global competency learning cycle, abbreviated CLC for competency learning cycle.

In this process, a competency is developed by the constant flow of mind-set to practice to task to mindset. In the application of mindset to behavior, a global manager develops a competence. It is important to remember that a mindset is not a competence. One can only have a competence when mindsets are turned into applied behavior.

Likewise, a characteristic is *not* a competence. A person can be flexible, but *not* apply that flexibility to working with organizational change. Flexibility becomes a global managerial competency when a manager uses his or her natural flexibility to adjust to changes in the organization and to adjust the organization to changes in the environment.

A characteristic, however, is not a part of the formal CLC. It exits either as a *contributing* factor to the original mindset, or as a *result* of the CLC process. It is therefore diagrammed *outside* the CLC.

These six development clusters represent the essence and focus of the leadership development and training necessary to support the global enterprise. In this chapter we have tried to develop an integrated framework for globalization which encompasses both *organizational* analysis of strategy/ structure, corporate culture, and people and *managerial* mindsets, characteristics, and competencies. In the rest of the book, we will explore the context within which these competencies operate and examine specific practices and tasks which you as a global manager can undertake to improve your ability to make a meaningful and significant contribution to your organization's globalization process.

AFTERTHOUGHTS FOR GLOBAL MINDSETS

I hope the message is clear. Global management is a complex business, but one which can be exciting, challenging, and rewarding. You can see the kinds of new behaviors needed in global companies for which few people have adequate preparation. One really has to wonder what some executives think when they set a new global strategy and structure, but do not believe they need an *internal strategic plan* in which they outline the implications of their new strategy and structure for the corporate culture and people in their organization.

If you are going to be a global manager, you need to take responsibility for developing and implementing this internal strategic plan for global success. Without this internal alignment to strategic objectives and structure, your company will never be successful on an ongoing basis.

Some companies get lucky and set a strategy and structure that is good for the short-term, even without a lot of adjustments in the culture and training of their people. But if you and your company are going to play an infinite game, then you have to have the skills to constantly readjust your

strategy, structure, and process based on the new directions that are emerging daily in an increasingly uncertain world. We will explore the relationship
of rapid change to this integrated approach later in our journey.

Chapter Three

Managing Competitiveness

The rules of a finite game are the contractual terms by which the players can agree who has won.

Carse, p. 9

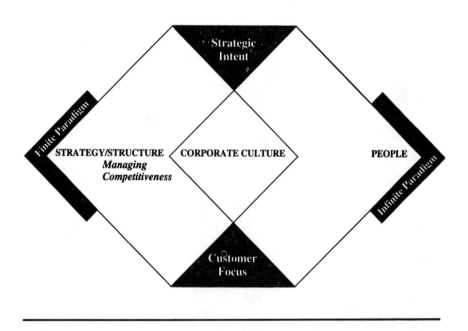

FORETHOUGHTS FROM A GLOBAL MIND

Let's begin our examination of the six keys to success in a changing world with the fundamental responsibility of any global manager—ensuring business competitiveness on a global basis. To achieve this requires attention to your organization's strategy and structure.

You may not be in a position to affect the overall strategy or structure of your corporation. It is important, however, to understand the reasons so many corporations these days are going global and exactly what this means for the strategy and structure of your organization. Without this, you will not have a context for carrying through with the remaining five competencies that constitute the *real* globalization work of the corporation for most middle managers.

Many books have been written on global strategy and structure, most of them very left-brain, written in a belief that you can structure your way to success globally. You can have the best global strategy and structure in the world and still fail if you have not aligned your corporate culture and people to operate within a global mindset.

Strategy and structure are important but insufficient conditions for global success. It is people like *you* who ensure the *implementation* of a global strategy and structure in a way that means the difference between success and failure in global operations. At the same time, all functional activities of a successful global corporation must be strategically linked. For this to happen, there must be a clear strategy—related to a clear customer need, mission, and set of corporate values—which is understood by all managers. **It is useless to build a global corporate culture, infrastructure, and globally oriented work force in a corporation unclear about its destiny.**

FORCES DRIVING CORPORATIONS TO BECOME GLOBAL

The global enterprise is a consequence of several new and sophisticated forces that have come to shape the world economy over the last decade. These include:

1. Aggressive and massive financial accumulation and relatively *free-flowing resource transfer*;
2. Well-defined and *highly efficient communications channels* and information transfer and control systems;
3. *Technology development* and application that seek both leading-edge and low-cost positions in product creation and production; and
4. Clear recognition of the potential for *mass markets, mass customization, and global brands*.

It is also becoming increasingly fuzzy exactly "Who is them?" and "Who is us?" as Robert Reich has noted (Reich, *Harvard Business Review,* 1991 and 1990). Reich describes the global manager's task as coordination of global manufacturing and marketing operations. For example Mazda's newest sportscar was designed in California, financed in Tokyo and New York, its prototype was created in Worthing, England, and it was assembled in Michigan and Mexico using advanced electronic components invented in New Jersey and fabricated in Japan (Reich, 1991, p. 79).

Tom Peters captures the reason chief executives today are thinking globally more than they have in the past—it can best be summed up in three words: **competition, markets,** and **technology.** Here is how he describes the environment to be faced in considering next year's strategy for a maturing product.

- a new Korean competitor
- an old Japanese competitor continuing to reduce costs and improve quality
- a dozen domestic start-ups, each headed by talented people claiming a new technology breakthrough
- one old-line domestic competitor who has slashed overhead costs by 60% and is de-integrating via global sourcing as fast as it can
- another old-line domestic competitor that has just fended off a hostile takeover; in doing so, it may have sold off the division that competes with you to another strong competitor with a greater distribution system
- a competitor that has just introduced an electronics-based distribution system that wires it into each of its 2,200 principal distributors, slashing the time required to fill order by 75 percent
- yet another competitor that is tailor-making its products to suit the requirements or tastes of tiny groups of customers, thanks to a new flexible Computer Integrated Manufacturing (CIM) system
- consumers demanding consistently high quality in every component of the product, from the inner workings to fits and finishes
- a wildly gyrating currency market that confounds your own global sourcing decisions
- the probable interruption of supply from two offshore manufacturing plants where governments have defaulted on loan interest and principal payments. [Peters, 1988, pp. 13–14]

Such a complex environment is very familiar to many global managers today. Let's examine three basic elements contained in this picture—competition, markets, and technology.

Competition

It is clear from this scenario that the first force driving global concerns is **competition.** Many corporations are being forced not only to seek new markets abroad, but also to develop new methods for competitive intelligence gathering that enable them to identify potential entrants into their home markets from anywhere on the globe. As a result, even managers of small, purely domestic corporations have to develop a global perspective to protect themselves from foreign competition.

There are many small to medium-size companies in the United States that in the last 10 years have awakened one morning to find that their purely domestic market was entered by an aggressive, well-financed, and sophisticated foreign competitor. The result is not a pretty sight.

In many instances, however, these American companies could not only have had a fighting chance, but could have won, if they had been scanning *globally* for *potential* competition, rather than being content to view their competition as other American firms operating in their markets.

It is also important to be aware of the role of cross-border acquisitions, mergers, and strategic alliances or domestic downsizings in creating surprise competition, even for the largest corporate giants. Note the examples that Peters has given of the creation of local competition through the downsizing of spin-offs from giant corporations. Likewise, it is possible for a global giant like GE Aerospace to find its primary strategy to operate as number one or two in all its markets wrecked by the strategic alliance of two European companies.

Markets

A second factor driving globalization, as always, is **markets.** New demands for quality, constantly changing tastes, global fads, and short product life cycles are all pushing enterprises to seek global partnerships and alliances to gain access to new markets, or to defend markets that are currently held.

If you ask most major American corporations who have ambitious global expansion plans what is driving their interest, they will respond that their U.S. market is mature and that the newly emerging markets of Eastern Europe, Western European integration, and the rapidly developing markets of the Far East and Latin America are providing new profit opportunities that have to be developed.

These emerging new markets, combined with the maturing of the American market, are attracting American companies from aerospace to telecommunications and consumer products. Coca-Cola estimates that by the end of the 1990s, the United States may account for no more than *10 percent* of its profits. It already makes 80 percent of its profits from operations outside the United States. As Roberto Goizuetta, the Cuban-born chief executive of Coke noted in a recent interview, "Willie Sutton used to say he robbed banks because that is where the money is. Well, we are increasingly global because 95 percent of the world's customers are outside the country. It's that simple" (*New York Times,* November 21, 1991, p. D1).

Even more graphically, Coke's President Robert Keough observes, "When I think of Indonesia—a country on the Equator with 180 million people, a median age of 18, and a Moslem ban on alcohol—I feel I know what heaven looks like!" (*New York Times,* November 21, 1991, p. D1).

Technology

The third force for globalization, **technology,** is changing the face of business everywhere. You do not have to be a manager in a hi-tech business or even a technology-dependent business to use the technology of distribution systems for competitive advantage. You can change the way you carry products or services to customers. Domino's Pizza does not necessarily make better pizza than its competitors, but it has changed the competitive game by redefining *time.* They deliver your pizza in thirty minutes or you get it at a reduced price.

Time, space, and matter, as Stanley Davis wrote in *Future Perfect* (1985) have redefined competition. Much of this in turn has been facilitated by new technological advances. Davis notes that technologically driven changes are enabling companies to also use "matter" as a competitive weapon. Fuji's new disposable camera, miniaturization in electronics, laptop computers, and other advancements from abroad have used technology as the driving competitive force. They are also driving globalization as companies search the world for the latest technology for competitive advantage.

Corporate strategy and structure, as well as every other aspect of organizational life, are dramatically affected by these developments. As a manager trying to understand the implications of globalization for your job, your first realization should be that all of these forces will become increasingly important to your life, and your day-to-day existence will become more complex and less certain. Our purpose in this book is to lay out the dimensions of this trend and provide some guidelines that you can follow to manage your way through this new global environment.

EVOLUTION OF THE GLOBAL ENTERPRISE

There is a great deal of confusion today about exactly what globalization means. For many people, it means doing business abroad either through export, licensing, and distribution agreements; or foreign sourcing of technology, capital, facilities, labor, and material.

While many companies use the term *globalization* for doing business abroad, we will use a more technical definition of globalization as a *stage of development* in international organizational strategy, structure, and culture. As such, it is quite distinct from just doing business internationally, because it is a *way* of organizing corporate life that attempts to respond to the complexity of factors noted in Tom Peters' earlier description.

There are five distinct forms of corporations operating in today's global environment. For some, their current form is a stage in their development toward more complex forms. For others, their current form is the most appropriate for their industry or the nature of their business.

Domestic Enterprise

A domestic business operates solely within its own country—using domestic suppliers and producing and marketing its services and products to customers at home.

But as we have already indicated, a domestic enterprise should not consider itself immune to globalizing forces. International hostile takeovers, cross-border mergers and acquisitions, and new market access by roving global competitors, can all affect the market niche and profitability of the most secure domestic enterprise. Managers of domestic companies, therefore, also need to understand the basic messages in this book.

There is a new form of domestic corporation that has not existed in the past, but it has recently become part of the new global economy. These are domestic companies, like K-Mart, Bloomingdale's, and other retail stores in the United States, who *source* globally for domestic production and sales, rather than manufacturing in the United States for a global *market*.

Traditional wisdom has held that corporations go offshore for markets or cheap raw materials or manufacturing labor. These enterprises, however, see themselves, and are seen by others, as purely domestic corporations, utilizing domestic manufacturing sites to produce products for domestic markets. But they have gone to Tokyo for financing, India for computer scientists, or Germany for technology.

These global domestic enterprises, as they might be called, are created to a large extent by executives and managers who have developed a global mindset, but who enjoy a good profit margin in their home market and have no incentive to market abroad. Traditional wisdom for domestic companies is so strong that most CEOs of small- and medium-size companies never think about going abroad for capital. Yet there are increasing advertisements, even on television, for banks from the Middle East and Far East eager to provide financing for U.S. domestic corporate needs.

When we think of globalization, therefore, we must increasingly think of opportunities for companies that want to remain purely domestic in their manufacturing and sales, but are willing to go global for their sourcing of capital, raw materials, technology, and human resources.

Exporter

The exporter, which includes thousands of small- to medium-size businesses in the United States, is a successful national business that sells or markets its products and services in foreign countries, but operates primarily from its sense of domestic competitiveness and advantage.

This firm has little information about marketplace conditions outside its national boundaries and will most often operate through independent agents or distributors. The exporter tends to be opportunistic and transitional in form, changing from country to country as trends and events that it does not anticipate or understand affect its success.

Managers in export organizations need some sophistication about assessing global market opportunities. They obviously cannot export to countries where there is no demand for their products. Their strategic *business* intent, therefore, must be well developed on a global basis, but their *organizational* structure and skills need not be globally oriented. They can merely find the right in-country representative to handle their buying or selling needs.

International Enterprise

The international organization many times supplements its international sales and distribution capability with localized manufacturing. At headquarters, international operations are often run by an international division, which allows those not involved in international operations to conduct their domestic business fairly independent of any international perspective.

The parent company operates with a centralized view of strategy, technology, and resource allocation, with technology transfer as a key dynamic in headquarters field relations. Decision making regarding customer service shifts to the local or national level for marketing, selling, manufacturing, and competitive tactics, but the core domestic operations remain fairly isolated.

The international corporation is international in its operations and its business strategy, but only its international division is international in its structure and operations. The core corporate culture of the organization is usually unaffected by the international component and there may be little interaction between the international and domestic sides of the business.

The worldwide operations of giants like NEC, Fujitsu, Mitsubishi, and Siemens are evidence that international corporate organization can exist successfully. In these companies foreign operations are still considered to be foreign subsidiaries and are treated as appendages of the home country headquarters.

Multinational Enterprise

The multinational corporation is the next stage in international development. Multinational corporations have become committed to their international businesses to such an extent that they establish mini-replicas of their domestic business in many different countries and markets. In the process, such organizations often pride themselves in turning the management of their foreign operations over to local employees.

One of the objectives of a multinational corporation is to look like a multidomestic organization. In this form they hope that local regulatory authorities will treat the local entity as a national unit. In this way, it can gain domestic competitive advantage by supplementing its operations with globally sourced resources, skills, and technology.

Global Enterprise

Global organizations are an extension of an international or multinational corporation. Instead of *isolating* the international dimension of business as happens in an international corporation, or *replicating* it in many countries as a multinational corporation, the global organization *shares* resources on a global basis to access the best market with the highest quality product at the lowest cost.

Global organizations like IBM, GE, McDonald's, Ford, Shell, Philips, Sony, NCR, and Unilever have shed their national identity, are highly adaptive to changes in the environment, and are extremely sensitive to all global trends that may affect the future. This is a very different and very sophisticated form of organization, as well as business strategy. It requires a completely different mindset and very adaptable managers and corporate cultures.

Global organizations are constantly scanning, organizing, and reorganizing their resources and capabilities so that national or regional boundaries are not barriers to potential products, markets, or new technologies.

In some cases, global enterprises have headquarters outside of their country of origin and may even have *multiple headquarters* for different functions, different product lines, or different businesses (see Figure 3-1). Differentiation and integration are used in these complex organizational structures, with heavy emphasis on the simultaneous management of global

FIGURE 3-1

A Comparison of Multinational versus Global Company Organization

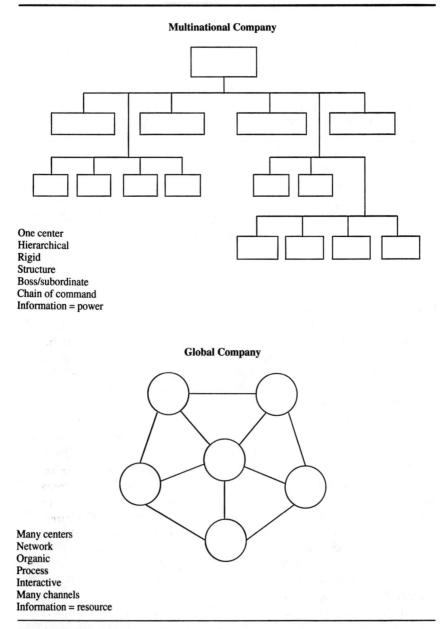

Multinational Company

One center
Hierarchical
Rigid
Structure
Boss/subordinate
Chain of command
Information = power

Global Company

Many centers
Network
Organic
Process
Interactive
Many channels
Information = resource

Source: 1992 Training Management Corporation

FIGURE 3-2
The Components of a Global Strategy

Highest quality product/service
to
Most profitable worldwide market
at
Lowest cost
under
Changing market and competitive conditions
through
Global sourcing of
- Raw materials
- Technology
- Capital
- Facilities
- Human resources

---

efficiency, local responsiveness, and global coordination of policy, people, and resources for the greatest competitive advantage and profitability.

A global corporation is always looking for potential products for businesses. As can be seen in Figure 3-2, a global corporation concentrates on delivering the highest quality product to the most profitable markets from the lowest cost positions with the most appropriate management resources, largely without regard to where dollars, people, resources, and technology reside.

The objective of the global enterprise is to reach and penetrate marketplaces before local or international competitors are equipped to exploit the opportunities. As a result, speed and flexibility, as well as corporate resiliency, become key factors in their successful management. When an organization moves from an international to a global perspective, an essential shift takes place—a shift from the tight control of a bureaucracy to an entrepreneurial, flexible, rapid response capability that is totally comfortable with cross-cultural influences and conditions. We shall explore these in greater detail later in Chapter Five.

Bartlett and Ghoshal (1989) have suggested that there is an additional form in the evolution of the global corporation—the *transnational* corporation. They believe that the transnational corporation combines the *efficiency* of the global structure, the *local responsiveness* of the multinational corporation, and the *technology transfer* capabilities of the international enterprise. These three strategic capabilities are blended together into the transnational corporation through its corporate culture and unique integrating and coordinating mechanisms, which allow it to simultaneously manage all the advantages of the three previous developmental stages.

For our purposes, the characteristics and complexities of transnational corporations will be blended with our discussion of globalization and global organizations. We will incorporate the concerns of the transnational, as described by Bartlett and Ghoshal within global organizations.

FUNDAMENTALS OF INTERNATIONAL STRATEGY

With increasing frequency, the issue of global strategy confronts the global manager with a series of differentiation and integration decisions. On one hand, companies have a clear need for a global strategic intent and broad-based resource, technology, and marketing schemes. At the same time, they need a sense of focus and competitiveness that deals with regional or local conditions, as well as local culture, behavior, and values.

For many international organizations, one of the central executive suite issues of the late 1980s and 1990s is how to organize, integrate, and manage their activities to become global players. This is particularly important for large U.S. firms that are just now beginning to understand that an export mentality—or having offshore divisions or businesses in an international structure—does not mean they are equipped to compete effectively on a global basis.

While our primary focus in this book is on the challenges of managing inside a global enterprise, there are some basic aspects of international market entry and development with which all global managers should be familiar. This is particularly true of human resource managers who are often inadequately acquainted with the business strategy and operations of their organizations.

In order to have internal business partnerships between line and staff departments, cross-functional education will be increasingly necessary. For this reason, we will briefly review some of the basic elements of international business strategy and structure. A fuller review of these ideas, however, can be obtained from a number of books in the bibliography (see Bartlett and Ghoshal (1989), Contractor and Lorange (1986), Doz (1986), Garland and Farmer (1986), Kolde (1985), Lamont (1991), Phatek (1989), Porter (1986), Prahalad and Doz (1989), Young, Hamill, Wheeler, and Davies (1989)).

International Market Entry and Development

International market entry and development is the basic business of most international managers, especially exporters or managers in international and multinational corporations. International market strategies, in turn, must be related to the overall strategic direction of the firm.

Broad distinctions can be made for four different strategies that corporations may undertake—*stability* (remaining in the same business with a similar level of effort), *expansion, retrenchment,* or some *combination* of the above (Young, Hamill, Wheeler, and Davies, 1989, p. 7).

Assuming some desire for growth and development, corporations develop strategies that will allow them:

1. To find new markets, products/services, functions, or technology, or
2. To integrate these activities horizontally, forward, or backward into their current business activity;
3. For economies of scale, cost reduction or competitive advantages;
4. Through reduction in time, inventory, or cost.

Alternative methods of achieving these objectives can involve internal development, external development through acquisitions and mergers, or external development through joint development approaches, strategic alliances, or direct investment abroad.

In the end, internationalization flows through products/services, markets, functions (finance, etc.), and technology. To understand the degree of globalization in your own organization you might want to review the degree to which your products/services, markets, functions, and technology are global in operations (see Figure 3-3).

Another major consideration in international business strategy is the underlying motivations that firms have for doing business internationally. A full description of these motivations is beyond this study, but it is important to have an orientation to some of the basic reasons for international business operations.

Competitive-oriented foreign market entry is probably the most important force driving American companies to more international operations. These moves to defend or improve international market share against competitors, or to respond to strategic partners or suppliers are all important steps in defending the long-term interests and viability of one's company. Failure to recognize that global participation is absolutely necessary for long-term success in today's world can be a fatal flaw in corporate strategy.

Strategic-oriented international development is often directed toward acquisition of scarce technology, or toward diversification and control of cer-

FIGURE 3-3
Ten Globalization Questions for Your Company

Below are a series of questions that will give you a rough estimate of the global nature of your organization. Answer these to see you where you stand.

1. Does your organization's mission statement have a global dimension?
2. Do you source any of your capital, technology, finance, raw materials, or human resources from abroad?
3. What percentage of your corporate profits are derived from overseas?
4. Do you have an international division that worries about international marketing and sales or manufacturing and production, or is everyone in your firm concerned about the international aspect of your corporation's operations?
5. Are the people in your company who take overseas assignments "sent to Siberia," never to be seen again, or are they carefully monitored and reintegrated into better jobs when they return?
6. What is the highest salary level (position) that a foreigner has attained in your company?
7. Do you work on any multicultural teams?
8. Is your R&D spread around the world or done in your home country?
9. Do your managers provide information on the company's international activity, profile, and standing?
10. Does the human resources department place an emphasis on global activities, from recruitment and selection, to overseas assignments in your career path and training and development opportunities that involve staff exchanges, as well as courses on doing business in other countries?

tain industry developments that will allow a long-term advantage. Russia and Eastern Europe are today targets of strategic development, because while their short-term return is small, their long-term potential is great.

Market-oriented foreign development is the third major driving force of many American companies today. This often results either from saturation or reduction of the U.S. market—as in the recent reduction in military spending. Strategies may range from low-profile to aggressive, depending on the political sensitivity of local markets to foreign competition.

Profit-oriented moves abroad are most often made to gain a fast recovery of cash or to save costs. This is especially true of politically unstable or less developed areas of the world. Investments for longer term return generally are geared to world areas with more political stability or where the longer term return, such as in oil, has a very high up-side profit. (Young, Hamill, Wheeler and Davies, 1989, p. 268).

You might want to take a minute and check the motivations underlying your own organization's global operations. It is likely, if you are part of a large organization, that different business or product lines may have different motivations for their foreign operations. Understanding the diversity of basic business motivation is a first step in understanding the need for diversity in a global business organization.

It is important to note that *not all companies should be global in their operations.* The relative importance of overseas production, for example, varies greatly by industry. Aerospace, has traditionally been a very domestically oriented business, often part of the military industrial complex. Oil, tobacco, drugs, rubber, and chemicals, on the other hand, have been more international in their overseas production and operation.

One of the first steps in international market entry and development is to determine a preference for either direct investment or nondirect investment. The latter involves export of goods, services, or expertise through licensing, franchising, contract manufacturing, or turnkey operations (Young, Hamill, Wheeler and Davies, 1989, p. 21).

If the choice is to make direct investment, then assembly and manufacturing facilities are often a likely target, although R&D, financial sourcing, suppliers, and facilities may all be objectives for international operations.

Different industries also exhibit different preferences for internationalization. Contract manufacturing works best with electronics, clothing, and automobiles; whereas equity joint ventures and wholly owned subsidiaries are best in R&D-intensive and advertising-intensive sectors.

Licensing is best in chemical, pharmaceutical, and other processing industries such as processing plastics and electronics. Franchising works most advantageously in soft drinks, fast foods, car rentals, hotels, and personal and business services.

Turnkey operations are best in heavy industry and will increasingly be used in Eastern Europe and Russia, because these areas need completely integrated technological systems to ensure that new technology will operate. This is due as much to the lack of suppliers, as well as to the lack of spare parts, maintenance, and other factors normally available in the infrastructure of more industrialized countries.

This brief overview is just a peek at the many factors that need to be considered in developing international business strategies. This discussion has not attempted to be comprehensive, but only representative of the kinds of business issues with which you as a global manager need to be familiar if you are going to understand the constraints and opportunities available in a global organization.

FUNDAMENTALS OF INTERNATIONAL STRUCTURE

Whatever international strategy a business chooses, it must be supported by an appropriate structure, culture, and the human resources able to implement the strategy. While most of this book will deal with the culture and people issues, it is also important to see the role of structure in global operations, since many executives mistakenly believe that structure is not just *one* piece of globalization, but *the* critical element. While we will try to disprove this assumption, the basics of international structure need to be understood, because the correct structure is a necessary, if insufficient, aspect of corporate globalization.

Prahalad and Doz, *The Multinational Mission* (1989), have conducted a thorough analysis of what they call diversified multinational corporations (DMNCs), or multinational corporations that are in many different businesses. They note that different industries profit from different combinations of global integration and local responsiveness.

Arguing that the management of DMNCs requires the simultaneous management of many different businesses, they have found that different businesses operate differently along two dimensions of global integration and local responsiveness. The electronic components and medical businesses respond well to pressures for global integration, while corningware or lab ware are subject to pressures for local responsiveness (Prahalad and Doz, 1989, p. 24).

Prahalad and Doz (1989), as well as Stopford and Wells (1972), point out that the position of various industries will vary over time. International economic, social, consumer, competitive, and technological forces will push one industry or another into more global integration or local responsiveness. For this reason, constant global scanning of the best international position and structure for various industries becomes an important strategy/structure consideration for all global managers.

Bartlett and Ghoshal have studied nine different corporations and discovered that different industries perform better with different structures. They found that branded packaged product producers (Unilever, Kao, and Procter & Gamble) require a strategy and structure that allows for maximum

FIGURE 3-4

Integration and Differentiation Needs at Unilever

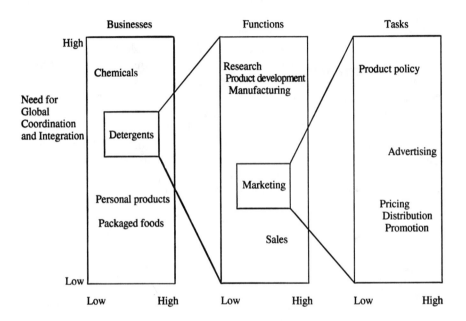

Need for National Differentiation and Responsiveness

Source: Bartlett and Ghoshal, *Managing Across Borders: The Translation Solution.* Boston, Harvard Business School Press 1989, p. 97.

responsiveness to local consumer needs; while consumer electronics (Philips, Matsushita, and General Electric) require the efficiency of global integration for low cost production; and telecommunications switching (ITT, NEC, and Ericsson) operate best through the transfer of technology and knowledge (Bartlett and Ghoshal, 1989, p. 21).

Bartlett and Ghoshal also note that the global efficiency/local respon-siveness mix is set not only by industry, but may also be differentiated by function and task within any given business or corporation as is shown for Unilever in Figure 3-4.

In a diversified global corporation like Unilever we can see what **Prahalad** and Doz noted earlier. Different businesses are different in their need for global integration/coordination, with chemicals at one end, while packaged foods at the other end have a high need for national differentiation and responsiveness.

What is more intriguing, however, is that Bartlett and Ghoshal point out that the classic debate about centralization and decentralization for an entire business is a bogus debate. Instead, different functions, such as R&D may be more naturally coordinated and integrated, while sales are more differentiated and responsive. This is one way of overcoming classic interfunctional rivalries within global organizations.

Finally, Bartlett and Ghoshal note that within functions, it is also possible to spread out different tasks. Product policy is more globally centralized and coordinated, while pricing, distribution, and promotion decisions are more decentralized for national differentiation and local responsiveness.

Strategy and structure are thus intertwined with:

1. The *motivation* of the business.
2. The *nature* of the business.
3. The *function* under consideration.
4. The *task* to be undertaken.

Is it any wonder that many managers are puzzled when confronted with an executive decision to globalize?

NEW DIRECTIONS IN STRATEGY AND STRUCTURE

Emergence of the Enterprise Web

One of the most radical concepts of new organizational form has been outlined by Robert Reich in *The Wealth of Nations* (1991). He describes what he calls the *enterprise web* in which global corporations, to be totally flexible and responsive to the fast-changing demands in their environment, minimize structure, overhead, and payroll through a series of temporal relationships with a range of organizations.

These enterprise webs come in several shapes and sizes, but the most common are:

1. Independent profit centers.
2. Spin-off partnerships.
3. Spin-in partnerships (good ideas, internally produced are sponsored by a corporation in partnership with the creator).
4. Licensing.
5. Pure brokering between problem identification and problem solving.

These forms have been used increasingly in high technology and the auto industries. For example, the Apple II computer cost less than $500 to build, of which $350 was for components purchased from suppliers; and by 1990 Chrysler Corporation directly produced only about 30 percent of the value of its cars, whereas General Motors bought half of its design and engineering services from 800 different companies (Reich, 1989, pp. 93–94).

Nation-less Corporations

Is IBM Japan an American company or a Japanese company? Its work force of 20,000 is Japanese, but its equity holders are American. Even so, over the past decade IBM Japan has provided, on average, three times more tax revenue to the Japanese government than has Fujitsu.

Kenichi Ohmae notes in *The Borderless World* that "most companies in the Triad (Japan, The United States and Western Europe) are still financed by local debt and equity and serve local markets with locally traded goods produced by local workers. For them, nationality still has meaning. But for a growing population of firms that serve global markets or face global competition, nationality will disappear" (Ohmae, 1990, p. 10).

Robert Reich argues that as corporations are transformed into global webs, "the important question—from the standpoint of national wealth—is *not* which nation's citizens own what, but which nation's citizens learn how to do what, so they are capable of adding value to the world economy and therefore increasing their own potential worth" (Reich, 1991, p. 137).

New Kinds of Global Jobs

Reich argues that three broad categories of work, which correspond to the kinds of competitive situations American corporations are facing, are emerging in the world. The ability of these corporations to place themselves within this "new paradigm" will greatly affect the way in which Americans contribute to the coming global economy. He calls these three categories "routine production services, in-person services, and symbolic-analytic services" (Reich, 1991, pp. 175–180).

Routine production services involve the kind of repetitive tasks of labor-intensive industries upon which many of the international and multinational corporations built their empires by finding cheap labor abroad. These are high-volume operations that lack necessity for quick responsive changes; instead they are production processes that are labor intensive for products with a high degree of labor ingredients. Routine production services are found in both old, heavy industries, as well as in the new hi-tech software industries, many of which are exporting jobs to Hong Kong, Taiwan, and Singapore. In 1990, routine production jobs comprised about 25 percent of the jobs performed by Americans, and the number is declining.

In-person services are also routine, highly repetitive tasks, but they must be performed in person, rather than contributing to the manufacture of a product which is in turn sold worldwide. The immediate object of in-person services is the *customer* rather than the *product*. These jobs include retail sales workers, waiters and waitresses, hotel workers, house cleaners, taxi drivers, secretaries, and flight attendants. In-person services account for about 30 percent of the jobs performed by Americans.

Finally, the third job group Reich identifies is the **symbolic-analytic services**, which includes all "problem-solving, problem-identifying and strategic brokering." These "products" are data, words, and oral and visual representations. People in this category are research scientists, public relations executives, investment bankers, lawyers, and consultants, among others. Symbolic-analysts solve, justify, and broker problems by manipulating symbols. "They simplify reality into abstract images that can be re-arranged, juggled, experimented with, communicated to other specialists, and then, eventually, transformed back into reality." Symbolic analysts have partners and associates rather than supervisors and bosses. Their income depends more on quality than quantity, their careers are nonlinear, they often work alone or in small teams, and they may be located anywhere in the plant. Symbolic-analysts comprise no more than 20 percent of the American work force.

Reich notes that these three categories of workers account for *75 percent of the American work force subject to global competition.* The remaining 25 percent are composed of farmers (about 5 percent), government workers and workers in government regulated or financed industries like utilities, or workers in the military industrial complex, all of whom are sheltered from global competition.

In *The Borderless World,* Ohmae argues that the truly global company of the future will have multiple headquarters, global customers, global products, non-national globalized managers, a pluralism of values, and a management philosophy of constant improvement across competing and contradictory needs.

To achieve that, firms will need to be clear about their corporate visions and must instill their visions in managers and employees in a way that is inspirational, consistent, reinforced, and rewarded.

Any corporation that does not now have a 1995 vision of its global strategy, structure, and priorities will probably not be able to realign its resources, culture, and people quickly enough to meet the globally competitive challenges of the mid-1990s.

KEY PRACTICES AND TASKS FOR MANAGING COMPETITIVENESS

At the end of each chapter on the six global competencies, there will be a section to help you examine what practices and tasks you might undertake to develop your competency in that area. The outline for this chapter is included below.

Competence I: Managing Competitiveness

Definition: Ability to gather information on a global basis concerning global sourcing of capital, technology, suppliers, facilities, market opportunities, and human resources, and the capacity to utilize the information to increase the competitive advantage and profitability of the organization.

Action and Mindset: Driving for the bigger, broader picture

Personal Characteristic: Knowledge

As you can see from our definition, managing competitiveness really does mean driving for the bigger, broader picture. To be a manager in a global organization it will be necessary for you to constantly enlarge your horizon and scan your information sources and your world on a broader basis.

Global managers never stop learning, never have enough information, and are never satisfied with the current world in which they are operating. They are constantly looking over the horizon, not only for competitors, but also for opportunities. Here is a list of the kinds of things you can do now to increase your ability to manage your competitiveness globally.

Key Practices and Tasks

1. Set *critical success factors* (CSFs) for your organization or unit's global competitiveness and use these as a framework to filter global information for key trends.

    1.1 Determine the most important tasks to be done in your job to ensure that your function is managed well on a cross-functional and international basis.

    1.2 Use CSFs as a framework to search for and filter information on a global basis, which will affect your ability to be successful in the execution of your job responsibilities.

2. Establish *personal and organizational information systems* which scan globally for trends, best practices, and resources that provide new opportunities for increased competitive advantage and profit.

    2.1 Read professional and commercial publications that track your functional and industrial trends and practices on an international, rather than national basis.

    2.2 Join international professional associations and attend meetings and conferences that stress the global aspects of your job responsibilities.

    2.3 Search for the best practices in your job on a global basis, both within your organization and within your industry or profession.

    2.4 Develop one new idea each year to increase your productivity or your organization's competitiveness, the seeds of which you have obtained from outside your country.

3. Establish information processing systems that *deliver the right level information to the right people at the right time* for the most effective and timely decision making on a worldwide basis.

    3.1 Share information that is relevant to increasing your productivity or effectiveness on a global basis with others in your organization who could benefit from it.

    3.2 Ensure that people you manage or with whom you work abroad have the information they need to make as many decisions locally as possible to increase the quality of their decisions and their speed of response to local customer needs.

4. Conduct and update your *competitive analysis* on an ongoing basis to ensure that you are aware of what your key competitors are do-

ing on a worldwide basis, even if some activities may seem to be irrelevant to your current interests or priorities.

4.1 Track global merger and acquisition activity and foreign investment patterns of competitors and potential competitors.

4.2 Continually scan the global environment for potential competitors who could come from suppliers or customers who might want to vertically integrate, as well as for diversified multinational corporations who might look to expand through merger and acquisition in your industry.

5. Monitor *international trade, tariff, economic, social, and political changes* that may affect local, regional, or international competitiveness.

5.1 Read broadly in your industry and professional press and in popular literature about international social, political, and economic megatrends.

I hope some of these provide you with a roadmap of the kind of activity you can undertake immediately to broaden your global knowledge, information, and opportunity.

Managing competitiveness requires a manager to be curious and to be constantly attentive to the world and its changing social, economic, and political conditions. It is an engagement with life that can be vibrant and exciting for those involved.

You can see in Figure 3-5 how one sample of these elements translates into the global competency learning cycle (CLC) which was introduced in the last chapter.

You may start at any point on the learning cycle to extend your knowledge and competency to manage the competitive process. Many of the practices and tasks noted above have been used by people throughout the world as they begin to operate on a more global basis.

You have probably been involved with a "best practices" study in your functional area and industry. This is one of the ways to start to think more broadly and to expand your knowledge and value to your company. For the best results, however, you should try to conduct a best practices study on a global basis, searching through journals and articles that may give you a clue as to how corporations in Europe and the Far East are managing the area in which you are interested. This will not only make a more interesting and useful report, but it will also broaden your perspective and mindset to the bigger, broader picture.

FIGURE 3-5

Global Competency Learning Cycle (Managing the Competitive Process)

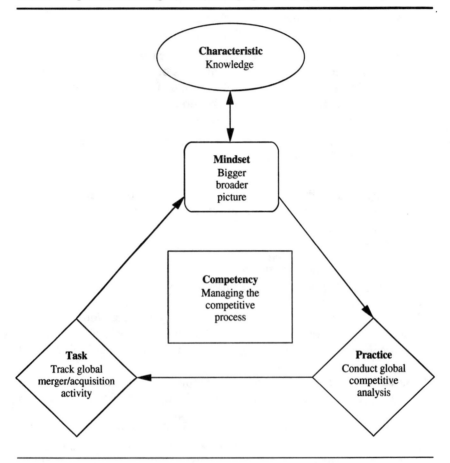

AFTERTHOUGHTS FOR GLOBAL MINDSETS

While all of the above is important in orienting yourself to some of the basic concepts in globalization, you should not forget the basic message of this journey—globalization is an infinite, not a finite game—and it is ultimately played out in the *execution* of strategy, rather than in its development.

Nevertheless, many of the strategies and corporate structural alternatives reviewed in this chapter form the basic business argument for international operations. Without an understanding of these issues, the development of a global corporate culture and globally oriented people exists in limbo—without context or purpose.

You should remember the quote at the beginning of this chapter, "The rules of a finite game are the contractual terms by which the players can agree who has won." This underscores the important role of strategy and structure in a global organization. Strategy and structure lay out some of the rules and guidelines for the game which, if followed, will allow you to win for a while.

But unless you are constantly redefining and reinventing the game and your global strategy, structure, and culture, you will not continue to win the infinite global game. In other words, there is no contract that spells out the rules of the global management game that are valid for more than a few nanoseconds.

Chapter Four

Managing Complexity

Finite players play within boundaries; Infinite players play with boundaries.

Carse, p. 12

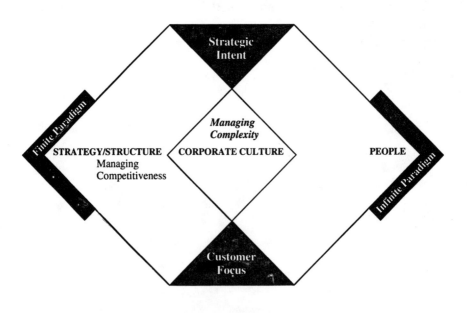

FORETHOUGHTS FROM A GLOBAL MIND

In the next two chapters I want to introduce you to the two keys to managing a global corporate culture. First there is the challenge of understanding and managing the complexity of global operations. And second, every global manager must be able to ensure that his or her organization has the *adaptability* to respond to continuous rapid change.

It should be apparent by now that a global business world is a more complex business world. It is more complex to comprehend and more complex to manage. Managing complexity is a focus of all companies and managers working on a global basis.

At first, many managers in newly globalized organizations believe that the complexity they experience is a result of the organization's not yet settling down. It is only after a period of years that many come to understand that this new complexity is not a passing phase, but is woven into the fabric of global operations and must be actively managed.

Much of the complexity results from inherent contradictions in the demands placed on a global organization. As you have seen in the last few chapters, global organizations must meet needs for global efficiency and local responsiveness, which often create tension over the allocation of resources.

The result of these many competing interests is increased conflict. There are not many organizations that deal effectively with conflict. It is always a learned art for both managers and corporate cultures. For this reason, it may be useful to begin with a discourse on cultural awareness as it relates to complexity. Americans have always found complexity difficult, not only because it retards action, but because it is usually accompanied by conflict.

To be a successful manager in a global organization you will need to learn how to deal with complexity, contradictions, and conflict, but from a different paradigm than that normally emerging from an American cultural model.

It appears that world diversity is here to stay. Global homogeneity was never a desirable vision—culturally, creatively, or philosophically. But now it has become clear that living with and managing diversity will be a central theme of the coming century. The explosion of ethnic identities in Eastern Europe and in the newly-independent republics of the former Soviet Union, the reassertion of the value of diversity in the United States, and the restatement of the values of fundamentalist religious concerns in the Middle East and middle America, all establish the management of diversity as a prime skill of the 21st century.

I have found in life that too many people with one perspective spend too much time denying the validity of another. The first lesson in global and cross-cultural management is that your own perspective is just one side of the elephant. To be a truly global manager, you have to be willing to crawl around the elephant, understanding how it looks from all sides, and be able to communicate and empathize with the people who are looking at it from the other side.

Furthermore, if you have any illusions about eventually moving the elephant in some purposeful direction in order to get through a swamp or over to a new green field for development, you will need to build a team of people who can push from every side and be motivated toward accomplishing something with the elephant's foot, ear, and left shoulder.

It is for this reason that a functional manager of any specialization—manufacturing, engineering, marketing, finance, or human resource development—needs to understand as many operations of the company as possible in order to work as part of an integrated cross-functional team contributing to the success of a global corporate effort.

The ability or inability to manage complexity, contradictions, and conflict has a deep cultural basis. It is entangled in Western and Eastern religious, philosophical, cognitive, and behavioral differences. For this reason, it might be useful to examine the cultural background of these phenomena before proceeding to a description of how they affect global managers and global organizations.

AMERICAN CULTURAL PREDISPOSITIONS ABOUT COMPLEXITY, CONTRADICTION, AND CONFLICT

Unpredictability is not comfortable for most Americans. We are used to applying the scientific method to determine correlations between nature and the future, weather forecasting being perhaps the most common example. Our cultural values have always stressed **pragmatism, action,** and **cooperation.** We see the lack of these as a failure on somebody's part. There are many areas of the world, however, where pragmatism, action, and cooperation are equally scarce, and where **complexity, contradiction,** and **conflict** reign as the normal state of affairs.

Complexity

North Americans have never been much for conspiracy theories compared to other cultures. Latin cultures and some of the cultures of Western and Central Europe, like France and Russia, have always attributed life's events to some dark set of conspiratorial forces that needed to be unraveled from an exceedingly complex explanation of how the world works.

Americans, on the other hand, have valued simplicity and straightforwardness. "What you see is what you get." An open, "tell it like it is" culture does not spend a great deal of time mired in complexity.

Likewise it has been important in the United States to be pragmatic and concrete. Emphasis upon doing rather than being was one of the earliest observations made by anthropologists about modern American culture

(Kluckhohn and Strodtbeck, 1956). Americans are action-oriented people who do not enjoy the intrigue of examining complex motives and situations the way the Russians do. And we certainly do not relish philosophical speculations about the world and the nature of life the way the French do.

As a result, when American managers face the competing interests found in global operations and the complexity of their expression in a range of cultures, their first reaction is to try to find ways in which "we can all cooperate together." Americans have an inherent belief in cooperation and fair play as the basic spirit of organizational life.

Much of the world, however, has developed in societies where families and fiefdoms fought to gain as much of the wealth of a society as possible. Sharing this wealth outside of one's own family is a foreign concept, just as it is foreign to think that one should be concerned about protecting the interests of foreigners. In these worlds, sophisticated ways have been developed to gather and keep the spoils of society and there are elaborate and many times unwritten rules about who gets what under what conditions.

This intrigue affects global business practices. It is often difficult for Westerners to know exactly who makes decisions in Japan and it is equally difficult to know what the criteria for decisions are. This in turn, creates problems in trying to negotiate or solve problems that may arise in business transactions.

Figuring out the complexity of global operations is a little like solving a crossword puzzle. One looks for clues and sometimes runs into blind alleys. This is a blow to many American managers who have climbed the corporate ladder demonstrating their ability to not only finish all puzzles, but to finish them on time, correctly, and with a profit.

Contradictions

Americans also do not deal well with contradiction. Our whole thinking pattern goes against holding two contradictory ideas at once. Since we are action-oriented, we seek to prioritize contradictory choices in order to determine how we can move forward. The emphasis here is not necessarily in determining what is right in a philosophical sense, but what is manageable and possible in terms of getting something done and moving forward. If forced to, Americans can accept that contradictions exist in life, but we are not anxious to dwell on them.

The exploration of basic contradictions, on the other hand, lies at the foundation of Eastern thinking. The Chinese philosophers saw life as two archetypal poles—yin and yang—between which there was continuous fluctuation creating a rhythm in the universe. Reality, whose essence they called Tao, was seen as a process of continual flow and change.

Eastern thinking is oriented toward flow and change rather than stability. In the Chinese view, *change is expected* as part of the natural dynamic of the Tao. When one extreme, the yin, has been reached, the flow starts back toward the other extreme, the yang. Nothing, however, is ever just pure yin or pure yang. There is always some combination of the two and there is *always movement,* because life's activities create new demands that swing the momentum back toward the end of the spectrum that is not in vogue.

This may sound familiar, because it is a pattern that also takes place in organizational life. How many times have you heard someone say after a reorganization to decentralize staff functions, "Don't worry, just wait five years until we have a new CEO and the staff functions will be recentralized again." Little did you know that they were just expressing ancient Chinese philosophy.

Some of the more globally oriented contradictions that managers face are noted below.

Efficiency	Responsiveness
Centralization	Decentralization
Competitiveness	Partnership
Differentiation	Integration
Comprehensiveness	Applicability
Control	Entrepreneurial chaos
Hierarchy	Network
Analysis	Judgment/Intuition
Cost	Quality
Individualism	Teamwork

Paul Evans and Yves Doz call these contradictions in global organizations "dualities." They believe that to manage global operations successfully, you need to understand the dynamic balance between these conflicting demands and the fact that neither column is inherently correct (Evans, Doz, and Laurent, 1989, p. 221).

In general, the right-hand column represents yin (integrative) activities, and the left-hand column represents more yang (dominant) activities. As we have noted before, the world appears to be moving from a yang to a yin paradigm. Certainly in the United States there is an emphasis on more cooperative, organic team-oriented values and the tough guy, male dominant, pistol-packing lone problem solver is becoming more of a metaphor for our mechanistic past.

While we, as pragmatists and problem solvers, prefer to develop a plan to overcome obstacles in order to move forward with the work that has to be done, we are increasingly encouraged to do this with the cooperation of others to ensure that their interests are included and that they feel represented in the final decision.

At the same time, we do not dwell easily or happily on these inherent contradictions in society, since we believe that personal, organizational, and social change are subject to our action. We tend to believe that all we have to do is get organized, and get going.

COMPLEXITY IN GLOBAL ORGANIZATIONS

Given these cultural predispositions, it should not be surprising that one common complaint American global managers have about globalization is that their work is more complex than it used to be. It is amazing how many of these managers spend extraordinary amounts of time trying to simplify their situations. Others live with a sense of unease that they are somehow failing when they are unable to reduce their work to the more simple formulae of the past.

Most experienced global managers, however, understand that complexity and contradictions are inherent in any global organization and that the task is not to eliminate them, but to manage the tension for creativity and innovation.

Peter Drucker, in *The New Realities* (1989), notes that the "fastest growing field of modern mathematics is the theory of complexity. It shows, with rigorous, mathematical proof, that complex systems do not allow prediction; they are controlled by factors that are not statistically significant" (p. 165).

"This has become known as the 'butterfly effect,' a whimsical, but mathematically rigorous (and experimentally proven) theorem, which has shown that a butterfly flapping its wings in the Amazon rain forest can and does affect the weather in Chicago a few weeks or months later. In complex systems, the 'climate' is predictable and has high stability; the 'weather' is not predictable and totally unstable" (Drucker, 1989, p. 166).

SOURCES AND METHODS OF MANAGING COMPLEXITY

Elliot Jacques and Stephen Clement note in their excellent book, *Executive Leadership: A Practical Guide to Managing Complexity*, that complexity in today's business world is "a function of the number of variables operating in a situation, the ambiguity of these variables, the rate at which they are changing, and the extent to which they are interwoven so they have to be unraveled in order to be seen" (Jacques and Clement, 1991, p. xvii).

The increased complexity that global managers face has three sources:

- Multiple objectives.
- Increased geographical scope.
- Conflicting interests of multiple stakeholders.

Let's take a look at each to understand the challenge it presents within a global organizational context.

Balancing Multiple Objectives

First, global management is complex because it involves the *simultaneous management of multiple objectives*. As Bartlett and Ghoshal point out, a global organization has three functions that must be managed simultaneously.

1. Its assets and resources are "widely dispersed, but mutually supportive" to achieve *global efficiency*.
2. The roles and responsibilities of various units are differentiated, but interdependent to maximize *national flexibility*.
3. Its knowledge and initiatives are linked throughout a worldwide learning capability that assures the efficient development and *diffusion of innovations* (Bartlett and Ghoshal, 1989, p. 157).

As we have discussed earlier, efficiency, responsiveness, and learning are three objectives that a global corporation must successfully manage if it is to survive. This is a much more complicated situation than that previously faced by international companies that could concentrate on only one of these objectives.

To manage these multiple objectives simultaneously requires the kind of coordinating mechanisms that we will describe in our next chapter on managing organizational adaptability through a global corporate culture. Bartlett and Ghoshal note, however, that American, European, and Japanese organizations have traditionally solved the complexity problem in three different ways (1989, pp. 160–165).

Americans have tended to use *formalization* through which they have established structures and impersonal systems and procedures to determine priorities among competing objectives. This has led to highly defined guidelines for managing worldwide decision making under conditions of multiple objectives and maximum complexity.

ITT is an example of a company that established its worldwide preeminence through the development of a wide-ranging set of management systems. Harold Geneen's management review meetings became legendary as formalized procedures established to determine the best decisions. Geneen's philosophy was to make careful and logical decisions on the basis of unshakable facts, then force the logic out into the open.

Forcing the logic out into the open may be less simple today than in the past. While different cultural patterns of thinking have always been present, the degree to which they have been considered important has never been as strong as it is today. One man's logic is another's irrationality. When one is running a more interdependent system, the logic that is forced into the open can be widely varying, based on differences in cultural perceptions and values.

The Europeans have taken a second approach to the simultaneous management of multiple objectives. They have depended less on formalization, than on *socialization*. Large multinational European-based companies like Shell, ICI, Philips, Unilever, and van Houten have over the years developed global mindsets in their managers through an extensive global socialization process of recruitment, selection, training, rotation, and development of a cadre of key international managers. They become versed in the corporate culture and are known and trusted by senior management, and they eventually become the glue that holds the organization together over time.

The major disadvantage of socialization is expense. The cost of rotating expatriates has increased dramatically in recent years, and the overhead associated with this approach has skyrocketed. There is also an assumption that this cadre of managers will remain with the corporation throughout the working life. While this is still more true of European companies than American corporations, the socialization process cannot be assumed to guarantee lifetime loyalty from employees the way it used to. As a result, many corporations are looking for other ways to ensure the integration of multiple perspectives through coordination councils, task forces, and international meetings.

A third method of managing multiple perspectives has been used by the Japanese. This relies on *centralization* of decision making. But centralization in the Japanese company has been highly dependent on the Japanese *ringi* decision-making process in which consensus is built from diversity.

This solution has a number of weaknesses. First, Japanese decision making, while inclusive of Japanese, tends to be exclusive of those who are not Japanese. While this centralized approach works well for companies managed by a totally Japanese staff, it is one of the reasons the Japanese have found difficulty in comanaging international operations.

A second problem with the centralized approach is that it is often expensive. Managers at the center are constantly juggling many different requests for information, guidance, support, and decisions. This results in a build-up of centralized staff resources, which can become burdensome and costly.

A final problem with the centralized approach is that it obviously creates a schism between the headquarters and the field. Subsidiary operations, or even more independent operations, chafe at the thought of having all important decisions centralized. They feel that their viewpoints are often not considered in global decisions. This leads to a sense of frustration, which can eventually affect international morale, productivity, and effectiveness.

It seems apparent that none of the three approaches to managing multiple perspectives—formalization, socialization, or centralization—is the total answer. Instead, a combination of the three for different businesses, different locations, and different functions must be developed.

Percy Barnevik, the maverick CEO of ABB, has found ways to overcome some of these dilemmas of centralization. With a global organization with 1991 sales of $28 billion, this is not a small organization. Yet the corporate headquarters in Zurich has only 140 people, five of whom constitute the global personnel department for a work force of 220,000 people spread through 20 countries (*New York Times,* March 2, 1992, p. D1).

Part of the reason Barnevik has been able to achieve this unusual corporate culture is that ABB is a recent combination of two corporations—Asea of Sweden and Brown-Boveri of Switzerland. As a result, the company has little entrenched culture, a short history, and no nationalist allegiances—three good keys to forming a global corporation that most organizations are not blessed with.

In his international acquisitions, however, Barnevik has applied the same philosophy of small corporate headquarters staff and tight, compact multidomestic operating units. When Barnevik purchased Combustion Engineering in Stamford, Connecticut, for example, he reduced the staff in the head office from 900 to 68, and the work force was cut in half.

Barnevik says, "you optimize globally, you call the shots globally and you have no national allegiances" (*New York Times,* March 2, 1992, p. D8). He has also created 1,300 legal entities and 5,000 profit centers in 65 small business areas combined into 8 larger business groups of $1 billion to $7 billion in annual sales.

This kind of decentralization has its obvious payoffs, but it is also an extreme form. According to Chinese philosophy, ABB may be in for a shock when the Tao starts to work against their polar solution, creating inefficiencies and disruptions as it starts its inevitable swing back across the universe.

Balancing Increased Geographical Scope

A second source of complexity in global management is the *geographical scope* of operations for which global managers are responsible. Any manager will tell you that as soon as you open an office, manufacturing, or distribution center in another geographical location, you have increased the complexity of your business. When you do this in foreign locations, with cultural, legal, and time differences, you have exponentially increased the number and range of challenges you face in accomplishing tasks, which at home would be routine.

Gareth Morgan, a Canadian management professor who has written an excellent book entitled *Riding the Waves of Change* (1988), has described the need for global managers to develop skills in what he calls "remote management," or what the Europeans call the "helicopter principle." The global manager hovers like a helicopter over an area of responsibility. If something goes wrong, the manager swoops down and corrects it, but the rest of the time, sits at a distance, letting the operation manage and direct itself.

Again, this entails a decentralized solution to the management of complexity. In fact, this is one of the central trends in global management. It is a tenet of faith with most global managers that you cannot manage local decisions centrally. While this was more possible in the past, the speed of today's changing markets and competitive conditions, combined with new consumer demands for speed and responsiveness is forcing all organizations to decentralize their decision making.

The key decision for global managers, as we have seen in the last chapter, is *what* decisions will be decentralized in *which* functional areas and within *what* kind of business structure.

Balancing Conflicting Interests of Multiple Stakeholders

Finally, all general managers know the constant balancing act of production versus sales or finance versus research. In global management these functional interests are compounded by national economic, social, and political interests that are often divergent from the primary concerns of the corporation.

Governments, labor movements, social activists, and international regulatory agencies all have interests in the operations of a global corporation. In addition, global customers, investors, financial markets, employees, and competitors are constantly scanning global business strategies and tactics to assess whether their policies and practices meet local priorities, values, and needs.

Global managers are beginning to understand that there is no easy *structural* way to overcome the complexity of global organizations. Instead, they are increasingly understanding that the only solution is *in their own minds*.

To achieve this requires extensive travel, reflection, and sensitivity to a wide range of interests. It is absolutely impossible to be a successful global manager sitting in your office. Every global organization expects its senior managers to travel constantly. This is the only way you can appreciate the problems and perspectives of people in multiple locations with diverse national interests and cultural values.

During my years in management, I spent 25 to 50 percent of my time either on the road or in face to face consultation with people from field operations, I spent another 10 to 15 percent reflecting on these discussions and writing think pieces that explored the implications of what I had heard for company policy. These papers were then discussed with senior management and a board from over 20 countries.

In the end, decisions were made, and not everyone was happy. It was impossible for someone to say, however, that they had not had a chance to state their views, and my own thinking was enormously influenced when I attempted to consolidate and balance very different and sometimes contradictory needs, feelings, and philosophies into a coherent policy. At the least, it was a good exercise in developing a more global mind.

So our three complexities have three solutions.

1. Balancing multiple perspectives—formalization, socialization, and decentralization.
2. Balancing geographic scope—remote management.
3. Balancing conflicting interests—mind matrixing.

These solutions however, are more directions than answers. As you will appreciate by now, the complexities of global management have no *final* solutions, only *processes* to deal with change.

SOURCES OF CONTRADICTION

F. Scott Fitzgerald wrote in *The Great Gatsby* that "the test of a first rate intelligence is the ability to hold two opposing ideas in mind and still hold the ability to function." There are many people who would agree with him, because they find it so hard to do.

Rosabeth Moss Kanter (1989), notes the following managerial demands, which seem increasingly incompatible:

- think strategically and invest in the future—but keep the numbers up today;
- be entrepreneurial and take risks—but don't cost the business anything by failing;
- continue to do everything you're currently doing even better—and spend more time communicating with employees, serving on teams, and launching new projects;

- know every detail of your business—but delegate more responsibility to others;
- become passionately dedicated to 'visions' and fanatically committed to carrying them out—but be flexible, responsive and able to change direction quickly;
- speak up, be a leader, set the directions—but be participative, listen well, cooperate;
- throw yourself wholeheartedly into the entrepreneurial game and the long hours it takes—and stay fit;
- succeed, succeed, succeed—and raise terrific children. [Kanter, 1989, p. 21]

This is a graphic statement of the demands that are placed on us these days. It is hard to think of *balance* when so many conflicting needs are hitting us at once. In fact, there will be a need to make *some* prioritizing decisions, merely to keep our sanity. The trick, of course, is determining which decisions can and should be made quickly and which ones should be allowed to flow toward their own, more creative solutions.

Evans and Doz (1991) note that global corporations cannot seek to maximize anything. Instead they must strive for balance as the key to success in global management. Dynamic balance, they note is a watchword in the management of global contradictions. It is manifested in such new terms as *glocal, multifocalism,* and *multidomestic,* which are creeping into descriptions of global corporations. Indeed, a new vocabulary is being invented to describe the kind of challenges that global managers face.

WAYS TO MANAGE GLOBAL CONTRADICTIONS

There are four different ways to manage the organizational contradictions that confront every global manager. These are global norming, policy flexibility, collective decision processes, and mindset reframing.

Global Norming

Many traditional European multinational corporations, as we have noted earlier, have managed global contradictions by establishing strong organizational norms of behavior—a strong corporate culture, in which they have attempted to supersede national differences and set a pattern for resolving the contradictions in global organizational life.

Indeed, the latest thinking about national cultural differences noted by Nancy Adler in her book *International Dimensions of Organizational Behavior* (1986), is that differences should be managed for synergy, rather than homogenized into a global corporate culture based on one national perspective.

The national motto of Indonesia is "Unity though diversity." This is truly a paradox, but one that is becoming an increasingly popular objective in our new world of multiculturalism. Global norming within this context appears to be out of line with the global flow. The answer to focus on is not content, but process.

What I mean by this is the norms set by a global corporation to manage complexity and diversity do not address the *content* of the differences, but the *way* in which the differences are considered and managed. In other words, new methods of conflict management, new forums for expression of diverse perspectives, new ways for self-managing teams to come to consensus—are all global norms that do not override different cultural values, but provide forms and methods for different values to be debated, considered, and agreed upon.

I am not suggesting that this is easy, and neither does Nancy Adler. One has to learn to *balance* the gains and losses from managing multiple perspectives in an open way. As Adler points out, however, diversity expands "ambiguity, complexity and confusion," which must be managed more effectively than without diversity. This is one of the reasons why managing complexity is a key competency for global managers to master and one of the reasons you need to develop your multicultural skills if you are to have creative solutions from your multicultural work force.

Policy Flexibility

A second method for managing contradictory tendencies in global organizations is by building flexibility into global policies. This flexibility should be in the nature of the policies themselves, as well as in their interpretation and application.

For example, according to Barnevik, ABB has three internal contradictions. They want to be global and local, big and small, and decentralized with centralized reporting. Barnevik states that the "only way to structure a complex, global organization is to make it as simple and local as possible" (Taylor, 1991).

To achieve policy flexibility ABB has developed a flexible matrix organization that allows the businesses to be optimized globally, while maximizing performance on a geographic basis. The business area manager for power transformers sits in Mannheim, Germany, and manages the strategy for a business with 25 factories in 16 countries with global revenues of more than $1 billion. He is a business strategist who determines mix and allocation of resources across all units.

ABB Norway, with its headquarters in Oslo, has a transformer company which, while policies on resources are set in Mannheim, has complete control over policies concerning labor negotiations, bank relationships, and highlevel contacts with customers.

Collective Decision Processes

A third way of managing contradictions is by establishing forums in which differing perspectives can be thrashed out. One of the best companies with a collective decision process is Procter & Gamble.

P&G works to ensure that emergent interests gain legitimacy within the organization through global councils and other forums in which divergent opinions get aired. They then allow access to the company's information resources and communications channels so that these views can have a wider hearing. And finally, if peoples' views are felt to be germane, they are given access to the final decision-making process.

Mindset Reframing

Talcott Parsons, the well-known Harvard sociologist, founded social systems theory in 1956 when he and his co-author, Edward Shils, developed a comprehensive theory of social action that attempted to integrate all levels of systems, from the intrapersonal, to the personal, interpersonal, group, community, nation-state, and global community.

Systems thinking has now been a part of the Western world for more than 50 years, but many Americans are just beginning to understand its applications to social sciences, in addition to computer science. Indeed, the turn to systemic thinking at the senior management level has been nothing short of spectacular.

Lee Bolman and Terrence Deal, in their excellent work, *Reframing Organizations* (1991), outline a shift that they feel must take in managerial thinking, which is very similar to the position we are taking in this study; that is, managers must move from the rational, analytic, left-brain approach to dealing with complexity to an holistic, intuitive, right-brain emphasis (see Figure 4–1).

FIGURE 4-1
Expanded Managerial Thinking

How Managers Think	*How Managers Might Think*
1. Managers often have limited views of organizations (for example, many attribute most organizational problems to the defects of various individuals and groups).	1. They need a holistic framework that encourages inquiry into a range of significant issues; people, power, structure, and symbols.
2. Regardless of the source of a problem, managers often choose rational and structural solutions: rational discourse, restructuring, facts, and logic.	2. They need a palette that identifies a full array of options: bargaining as well as training, ceremony as well as reorganization.
3. Managers have often been taught to value certainty, rationality, and control, and to shun ambiguity and paradox.	3. Managers need to become more creative and more willing to take risks in response to the dilemmas and paradoxes of organizational life. They need to focus on finding the right questions as much as the right answers, on finding meaning and pattern amidst clutter and confusion.
4. Leaders often try to change organizations by finding the one right answer and the one best way; they are stunned by the turmoil and resistance that they thereby generate.	4. Leaders must be passionately committed to their principles but also flexible in understanding and responding to the events around them.

Source: Lee Bolman and Terrence Deal. *Reframing Organizations,* 1991, p. 18.

The major mindset reframing occurring today in global management is the shift from functional to total systems management and the move from provincial to global analyses. If you are part of a global corporation, or want to be a global manager, you will need to "think systems"—not in the sense of management information systems, but in the sense of the global social, economic, and political systems and their effect on your global business and management system.

CONFLICT MANAGEMENT AS A KEY TO MANAGING COMPLEXITIES AND CONTRADICTIONS

It should be apparent by now that conflict is unavoidable in global organizations. As a result, the way in which a global organization manages its many specialized interests and the conflict that ultimately ensues will be a crucial factor in its global competitiveness.

Evans and Doz report that in sixty global companies they studied, the key top management task was "maintaining a dynamic balance between key opposites." They note that in these organizations "dualities should be viewed not as threats to consistency and coherence, but as opportunities to creative organization development, for gaining competitive advantage, for organizational learning and renewal" (1990, p. 224).

All observers agree that reorganization to avoid conflicts is not the answer. It is also clear that with increasing complexity and trade-offs, it is naive to think that a global organizational structure can establish a global way of approaching problem solving and conflict management.

If conflict cannot be reorganized away and cannot be avoided through socialization, formalization, or centralization, how then do corporations deal with this problem? There are four basic methods.

Legitimizing Conflict

The first challenge of any global corporation is to find a means of legitimizing conflict as a positive part of its culture. INTEL has its "push back" norm, in which everyone is encouraged to push back against any new idea until it has proved its reliability, consistency, and relevance. In this model, people are rewarded for constructively challenging old and new ideas in ways that improve them. It is a delicate balance, obviously, between testing new ideas and creating an adversarial atmosphere that demotivates people from raising new initiatives. Rewards have to be offered both for putting new ideas forward and for pushing back and testing assumptions and validity of new thinking.

Other companies legitimize conflict by encouraging diversity in policy development. Some require more than one option for all decisions. Others structure decision-making procedures so that all relevant units, businesses, or functions must voice an opinion on given issues.

Whatever the method, every successful global company must create a cultural norm that legitimizes conflict, views it as a creative dynamic necessity for organizational innovation, change, and learning, and rewards people who not only raise conflicting views, but work to find viable, successful resolutions for competing interests to move the organization to new levels of success.

Creating Company Integrators

When the frequency of complex decisions reaches the point where it can strain normal decision-making channels, top managers often delegate responsibility to specific levels of management who become responsible for decision arbitration.

Ericsson, the Swedish manufacturer of telecommunications equipment, has used this approach extensively through marketing vice-presidents who, located in each of the 40 countries in which Ericsson has operations, arbitrate issues between local country interest and centralized product divisions—transmission, switching, telephone, and accessories—all of which are located in Sweden.

These integrators have "matrixed minds" and are sensitive to the needs of the business from various viewpoints. They are able to be multifocal in their approach and are committed to ensuring that both points of strategic advantage—local responsiveness and global integration—are explicitly examined and balanced.

Ideally, these people have interpersonal, cross-cultural, and group skills to enable them to facilitate decision making among differing positions. In the end, however, they must also have the power and clout and be supported by senior management in making final decisions that they recommend, if they are unable to reach an arbitrated solution.

Using Temporary Coalition Management

Perhaps the most favored approach to managing contradictions is through temporary coalition management (Prahalad and Doz, 1989, p. 175). In this approach, *ad hoc* teams are created to conduct studies and make recommendations on key issues where there are contradictory organizational needs.

Task forces, committees, projects teams, working parties, and study groups are common methods of achieving recommendations on difficult issues. Ultimately, however, these groups will make little headway if the members are not supported by a corporate culture that values diversity of thinking and explicit management of conflicting ideas.

Holding Global Forums

The last method used by many companies to manage conflict is some form of annual or semiannual global planning retreat or policy conference where the key stakeholders from throughout the business come together to examine the directions, policies, and priorities for the company.

These geographically representative forums, with accompanying product and functional representation, are the arenas in which major business issues are aired and all competing viewpoints are heard. The way in which final decisions are made will vary from one company to another. Some use such forums for making decisions, others use them as a means of presenting a variety of ideas to senior management before a decision is taken by the top.

When I was president of AFS we used to have three regional meetings each year leading up to our annual board meeting. With 60 countries and their constituencies involved, gaining some semblance of agreement on organization directions and priorities was not an easy task. The three meetings, held in Europe in September, the Americas in October, and Asia in November for one week each gave those of us from the international headquarters a chance to discuss and debate the policies and directions of the organization prior to the board meeting.

After the meetings, we prepared policy papers for the board members from 20 countries. These were circulated in December and January to all countries who then had an opportunity to comment on them, either directly by writing to headquarters or indirectly through any of the board members, who would be meeting at the end of January for three days to deliberate the directions and goals for the organization.

Every three years, a World Congress was held with representatives from every country to discuss the plans and priorities of the organization for the next three years.

While these global forums were held in a not-for-profit organization, similar forums are used in for-profit corporations. Grace Cocoa, a global speciality food company producing 10 percent of the world's cocoa powder for industrial uses, in 1991 brought its top 50 managers from around the world together in Holland for a week in order to build their common corporate culture and determine priorities and directions for the future.

The four conflict management methods we have discussed are a few of the ways in which global corporations are today trying to deal with the challenges of complexity and contradictions. There will be many more approaches created in the future.

The following lessons emerge from our discussion.

1. Conflict is friendly and leads to better solutions.
2. Conflict has to be managed or it becomes unhealthy and destructive.
3. The best use of senior management time is to establish a pattern for conflict management that ensures that the best decisions are made by the best people at the right levels.

In the end, the words of Jim Carse perhaps say it all when one examines the best way to manage complexity, contradictions, and conflict—"finite players play within boundaries; infinite players play with boundaries."

KEY PRACTICES AND TASKS TO MANAGE COMPLEXITY

This has not been an easy road and you're probably tired. Let me suggest some tasks and behaviors that may be helpful in determining what you can do about the issues we have discussed in this chapter.

Competence II: Managing Complexity

Definition: Ability to identify, analyze, and intuitively manage complex global relationships that affect personal and organizational effectiveness.

Action and Mindset: Balance of contradictions

Personal Characteristic: Conceptualization

Key Practices and Tasks

1. Manage *relationships that are simultaneously cooperative and competitive* such as strategic alliances, headquarters-field relations, and functional, geographic, and product matrices.

    1.1 Analyze which aspects of cooperative/competitive relationships should be cooperative and which need to remain competitive, and compartmentalize your information, decision making, and operations accordingly.

2. Look for *contradictions and paradoxes* in your work and rather than trying to eliminate them, determine how they can be managed for richer decisions.

    2.1 In situations of generic conflict between functions or interests, use the conflicting positions as a check and balance system to ensure the best decisions.

    2.2 Learn to manage and feel comfortable with conflict in order to ensure that you do not prematurely close off decisions that could lead to better solutions, because of anxiety over differences.

3. Use *intuitive* as well as analytical skills to assess the "feel" for the information gathered and the direction of things.

    3.1 Be willing to make decisions without adequate information.

    3.2 Learn to trust your sense of things rather than waiting for all the facts to make a decision for you.

    3.3 If your intuitive skills are not strong, find people who are and bring them around you so they can influence your decision making.

4. Look for *balance* and inclusion in problem-solving activities.

    4.1 Find ways to include multiple stakeholders in decisions through power sharing, rather than excluding them through power plays.

    4.2 When something seems straightforward and clear, examine the opposite perspective to see whether it has any merit or provides an opportunity to do something innovative and unexpected that could provide competitive advantage.

Managing complexity requires thinking skills and conflict management skills, on both a conceptual and interpersonal level. *All* global organizations are more complex than domestic organizations, and they experience much more conflict as a result of the diversity of views and perspectives that must be brought to bear in decision making.

This complexity and conflict in turn requires managers who are simultaneously able to see the validity of conflicting viewpoints while making decisions that reflect the best interests of the organization (see Figure 4–2).

FIGURE 4–2
Global Competency Learning Cycle (Managing Complexity)

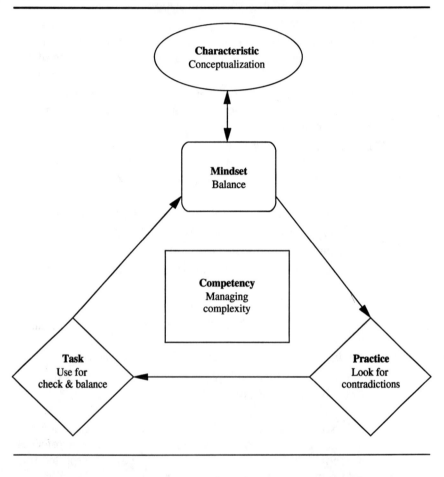

AFTERTHOUGHTS FOR GLOBAL MINDSETS

In conclusion, I want to leave you with two authors' answers to the issue of complexity. The first is Peter Vaill, professor of management at George Washington University, who has written an excellent book entitled *Managing as Performing Art*. In it, he addresses complexity in what he calls "Satchmo's Paradox," named after the great jazz trumpet player, Louis Armstrong.

Armstrong once said, "If you have to ask what jazz is, you'll never know." Some people will maintain that this is equally true in certain aspects of international cross-cultural relations. In order to overcome it, Vaill maintains, we need to "unlearn" what we know so that we can remember what it was like not to know it and then try to teach it to someone who never knew it (if you know what I mean). **One of the challenges of developing a global mindset is to discover how to "unlearn" what you know, so that you can help others to learn** (if you know what I mean).

On the other end of the spectrum in advice about life and complexity is Robert Fulghum, author of *All I Really Need to Know I Learned in Kindergarten* (1988).* He has a wonderful set of observations that apply to managing in a complex global world.

Share everything.
Play fair.
Don't hit people.
Put things back where you found them.
Clean up your own mess.
Don't take things that aren't yours.
Say you're sorry when you hurt somebody.
Wash your hands before you eat.
Flush.
Warm cookies and cold milk are good for you.
Live a balanced life—learn some and think some and draw and paint and sing and dance and play and work every day some.
Take a nap every afternoon.
When you go out into the world, watch out for traffic, hold hands and stick together.
Be aware of wonder. Remember the little seed in the Styrofoam cup: The roots go down and the plant goes up and nobody really knows how or why, but we are all like that.
Goldfish and hamsters and white mice and even the little seed in the Styrofoam cup—they all die. So do we.
And then remember the Dick-and-Jane books and the first word you learned—the biggest word of all—LOOK. [p. 7]

---

*Copyright © 1986, 1988 by Robert Fulghum. Reprinted by permission of Villard Books, a division of Random House, Inc.

*Chapter Five**

Managing Organizational Adaptability

Culture . . . is an infinite game. Culture has no boundaries . . .
for this reason it can be said that where society is defined by its
boundaries, a culture is defined by its horizons.

Carse, p. 52 and 59

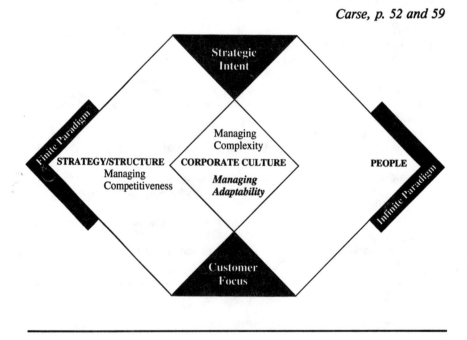

---

*Portions of this chapter have appeared in "Going Global from the Inside Out," *Train-*
ing and Development Journal, November 1991.

FORETHOUGHTS FROM A GLOBAL MIND

In a global environment, volatile political and economic factors and unstable competitive and customer patterns demand continuous organizational change. The constant reorganization of resources, technologies, marketing, and distribution systems, and human networks becomes part of the business itself.

The decision to develop a global organization brings dramatic new changes and learning requirements for everyone associated with it. A basic shift often takes place as the organization moves from a classic control model of management to one that is characterized by highly adaptive and temporary operating systems, and decision-making processes that are entrepreneurial, rapid response, and risk oriented.

This is not only complex, as we saw in the last chapter, but also demands a great deal of flexibility—both personally *and* organizationally. **Your skill as a global manager in dealing with complexity and adaptability constitutes the two keys to your organization's ability to survive in global competition. To do this, you must know how to manage a global corporate culture that can be responsive to constant change.**

A global corporate culture is the glue that keeps a highly decentralized and matrixed structure together. If strategy and structure are necessary but not sufficient conditions for success in a highly volatile world, then corporate culture must form the *process* through which the *structure* of your organization breathes and engages in *flexible, adaptive* behavior.

This brings us to the heart of the contradiction that you must deal with as a global manager—the simultaneous management of structure and process.

If corporate culture is not structure and not pure process, then from a systems perspective what is it? It is structured process. That is, it is fundamentally process, not structure. *But it is process that is structured in a way that allows it to be monitored, measured, and modified.* TQM and methods for continuous improvement are examples of structured process. They are process driven, but in a way that allows them to be monitored, measured, and modified based on changes in the environment. We will examine this in Chapter 8 on personal and organizational learning.

This is the structural-functional interpretation of the role of corporate culture in global organizations. Here's another way to think about it.

If global corporations are faced with constant change, but can't respond by changing their structure because it's too rigid and fixed, then there needs to be another part of the organization that *is built to respond to change.* This *can be* the global corporate culture. I stress *can be,* because if your corporate culture is not specifically constructed to play this role and is not managed for that purpose, it can become the organization's greatest barrier, rather than its greatest asset in responding to changes in the environment.

As you can tell, we are moving away from safe left-brain territory into the more fluid and dynamic challenges of global management. The next few chapters may become a little bit more confusing, less specific, and seem to be more out of control than our discussions on strategy, structure, and complexity. As we proceed from here, there will be more speculation, less experience, and fewer guidelines than in the beginning, because we are approaching greater and greater uncertainty in our exploration of globalization, as well as in the nature of globalization itself.

A recent review of globalization activities in nine major multinational corporations revealed that the major problem they faced was not developing a global strategy, but developing the global organizational capacity to implement their strategy. It was estimated that top managers spend less time in decision making (3 percent) than in finding the problem (48 percent) and the process of implementing solutions (49 percent) (Marsick and Cederholm, 1988, p. 5).

This is not news to anyone who has been working with large-scale change in multinational corporations. As one IBM manager I worked with said, "understanding corporate culture is like trying to get your arms around a 2,400 lb marshmallow!"

A recent McKinsey study revealed that most corporations today, domestic and international, believe that correct strategy formulation constitutes only 20 percent of organizational success. The remaining 80 percent lies in strategy implementation, which is becoming increasingly difficult in a world of constant change.

There is growing evidence that the lack of an integrated global corporate culture has inhibited many American corporations in their attempt to implement their global strategies. ITT, GE, and Corning Glass Works have all experienced difficulties competing with Japanese and European firms in recent years for reasons that have been identified as a lack of speed in response, a lack of flexibility in organizational structure, and a lack of capacity to transfer technology to the right place in a timely fashion.

Each of these failures is a failure of implementation, not strategy. Failure of implementation invariably involves failures of organizational capacity. Failures of organizational capacity are directly related to corporate culture.

GLOBAL CORPORATE CULTURE

The development of a global corporate culture is for most corporations the last step in the integrated approach to globalization described in Chapter 3. It is not just a matter of doing business internationally or even having subsidiaries abroad. **Developing a global corporate culture involves forming the integrating values, mechanisms, and processes that allow a company to successfully manage constant change in a competitive marketplace.**

Most companies begin their globalization effort with changes in strategy and structure and some initial training of people for intercultural assignments. But when a company becomes global in its research and manufacturing operations, as well as its marketing and distribution activities, it eventually confronts the issue of whether its entire corporate culture, not just its strategy and structure, is in sync with the demands of global competition. Peter Drucker, in an interview in *Business Month* in May 1989 noted that "many large multinationals do not have a global culture, because nobody in top management has ever worked overseas" (p. 51). Developing a global corporate culture, by contrast, transforms a corporation and its management into an entity where it is difficult to discern a single country bias—from the executive suite to the lowest or most critical level of the organization.

In a global corporate culture there are no longer privileged areas for a home nationality—by product, people, or function. As *Fortune* magazine characterized it, "in a world without walls, a company without a country has an undeniable edge" (Stewart, 1990, p. 68).

But international corporations can only "decompose" their structures, as Kenichi Ohmae calls it, if they have a deeply and universally held set of values to put in its place (Ohmae, 1989, p. 46). All organizations need some form of structure within which to operate. If this structure is not physical, then it needs to be based on shared vision, values, and norms of behavior; that is, a strong corporate culture.

What are the elements of a global corporate culture? What are the competitive advantages? What are some examples of companies who have global cultures? What can be done to develop a global corporate culture in your company? These are the issues addressed in this chapter.

MANAGING IN A GLOBAL CORPORATE CULTURE

We will divide the elements of corporate culture according to those that affect basic management activities. In this way, we can personalize the globalization process so that you, as a practicing manager, can identify with the kinds of changes that you will need to make in your day-to-day management operations if you are to align your global corporate culture with your overall strategy and structure.

The three activities we will consider here are old in conception, but new in interpretation—they are planning, organizing, and controlling. Staffing, which is the fourth key area for managing a global corporate culture, will be considered separately in Chapter Eight. Leading, the fifth area, will be addressed in the next chapter on managing multicultural teams.

Planning

Five planning activities affect your global corporate culture. These are:

1. A globally inspiring mission.
2. A global corporate vision.
3. Global information sources and systems.
4. A system of resource allocation that is perceived to be globally fair and equitable.
5. Decision-making criteria that reflect global and local values.

Let us briefly examine each.

Globally inspiring mission.   It is easier said than done to create a mission that is inspiring to people from many different cultural backgrounds and many different social, political, and economic circumstances around the world.

One manager's inspiration, "to eliminate cholera from the world" may be inspiring for people living in abundant post-industrial societies, but may be a nightmare for other managers in the same corporation living in countries plagued by overpopulation and lack of adequate food.

Global missions must be tested against many different social, political, and economic circumstances. One reason it is so difficult to achieve a culturally acceptable global corporate mission is that a mission statement is the connection of a corporation to the values of a society and its workforce. A global corporation by definition operates in many different societies with a multicultural workforce. This means that its mission must be stated in a way that is attractive to the greatest number of people from the greatest number of cultural, social, economic, and political backgrounds.

One of the difficulties for global organizations—especially not-for-profit and public sector organizations based on volunteer support—is that if they decide to revise a mission that has been carefully developed over many years on a multinational basis, they may find themselves faced with resistance from a global volunteer population.

There are, indeed, very few global values on which all people in the world can agree. Peace and children appear to be two of the more popular ones, which is the reason UNICEF and the American Field Service (AFS) international student exchange program have gained such broad volunteer bases around the world.

Global corporate vision. The basic difference between mission and vision is that **a mission speaks to the purpose of the organization and a vision describes what the corporation will look like in achieving its mission.** It is somewhat easier to have an agreed-upon global corporate vision from a cultural perspective, but not from a power perspective. Global corporate visions usually involve matters of structure, authority, and resources—all of which involve power, status, and personal ambitions. Forming a global corporate vision, therefore, is a complicated process involving sophisticated visioning and equally sophisticated global negotiations with all the power figures who are needed to achieve the vision.

Ben Tregoe, the founder of Kepner-Tregoe, has said that "the last thing a company headed in the wrong direction needs is to get there more efficiently" (Peak, 1991, p. 33). In recent years, global managers have found that global corporate visions, to be headed in the right direction, must encompass greater numbers of people. These visions have also become increasingly dependent upon suppliers and customers, as well as internal stakeholders. Managers in global organizations are discovering that all boundaries need to be broken, all stakeholders revised, and all power-sharing processes and methods reviewed to develop a global vision.

Global information sources and systems. As a manager in a global organization involved in planning, one of the first things you become painfully aware of is the need for more and better information about global social, economic, and political conditions. For most global managers, global scanning becomes an obsession. Some global managers become paralyzed by the lack of adequate information, or become blind-sided by inadequate scanning of a broad enough range of variables.

The first step as a manager in a global corporation, therefore, is to review all your information sources and make sure that you are scanning on a worldwide basis, as well as across many different functional, business, and technological areas. Only then will you be able to develop an adequate plan for your company.

A fair and equitable system of resource allocation. Perhaps one of the most difficult and contentious aspects of a global corporate culture—

and of global management in general—is the development of a fair and equitable system of resource allocation. It appears to be almost impossible to have everyone's agreement about the way in which financial, human, and other resources are allocated.

One of the most common methods of dealing with this problem in the financial area is through transfer pricing. This practice involves the development of a financial formula in which different parts of a production process result in different income credits being awarded to different geographical locations, depending on their contribution to the overall value of the finished goods or services. While the concept is great, agreeing upon the amount of value added by each part is often a time-consuming negotiating process.

There are many other methods that global companies have devised to ensure that there is enough perceived fairness in the system. But there are also instances in which the consensus around resource allocation breaks down so severely that managers become fixated on negotiating their own internal power relationships to the detriment of their customers, their financial viability, and their ultimate survival.

In other words, on this issue it is possible to commit corporate suicide through paying more attention to internal power relations than to customers (see Myer and Zucker, *Permanently Failing Organizations,* 1989).

Decision-making criteria with global and local values. Not only does the allocation of resources need to be seen as fair and equitable, but the decision process through which the allocation of resources is determined also needs to be seen as taking into account local as well as global values.

While all of this may seem to be just an exercise in democratic decision making, there is increasing evidence that such sensitivity to local as well as global values is good business as well as good politics. The representation of diverse values, opinions, and perspectives is one of the rich assets of a global corporation, needed to ensure a better strategy and a more thorough analysis of all options. The big trick is to establish a means for polling these diverse views and negotiating a final decision that cannot, by definition, equally incorporate all concerns.

The fact is that many companies ignore diverse perspectives, because they have not yet developed the global corporate cultural norms for managing diversity and the inevitable conflict that accompanies it. **During the years ahead, you will increasingly see that successful global companies have developed a means for managing a global diversity of opinions, perspectives, and values in a way that enriches strategy and contributes to more creative and competitive operations.**

Organization

We have discussed the structure of a global corporation, but have not discussed its organization. They are two different issues. The structure is *where* functions are placed; the organization is *how* they are coordinated.

There are four specific aspects of organization that affect global corporate responsiveness. These are:

1. Clear levels of authority and responsibility.
2. Formal and informal networking and integration mechanisms.
3. Global-functional and cross-unit coordination councils.
4. Global corporate meetings and conferences.

Let's examine each of them.

Clear levels of authority and responsibility. It is critically important that authority be clearly designated within roles and responsibilities that are equally clear. One of the worst mistakes made by many global managers is to assume that people will somehow interpret their roles, responsibilities, and authority for themselves.

Percy Barnevik, ABB Chairman, points out that clarity of roles, responsibilities, and authority in a complex matrixed global corporation is critical in allowing it to respond effectively to changes in the corporate environment.

This is particularly true of the vertical delegation of authority and responsibility between global centers and local operating units. It is equally true of geographic, functional, product, and business organizations that may be matrixed in different ways in different functions in different businesses in different products in different parts of the world.

One of the greatest failings of newly globalized corporations, especially those with a matrix structure, is that they do not think through how their structure will *operate* on a global basis. As a result, they fail to develop the *policies, procedures,* and *mindsets* necessary to run the organization globally.

The first step in ensuring an effective global organization is therefore to clarify roles, responsibility, and authority for as many issues as possible. For those issues where no clear definition can be reached on a continuing basis, some form of decision making to allow for conflict needs to be put into place.

Formal and informal networking and integrating mechanisms. One of the formal mechanisms used for networking and integrating global corporations is management rotation and training.

Through global career pathing and frequent changes of responsibility and location, managers of global organizations develop a global perspective and at the same time become acquainted with people from throughout the world. This informal networking facilitates global decision making, especially at times when speed is essential and knowing the person at the other end of the line 10,000 kilometers away is imperative.

Global-functional and cross-unit coordination councils. Another organizational mechanism to ensure global coordination of conflicting opinions, needs, and ideas is the continual use of global-functional and cross-unit coordination councils.

Grace Cocoa holds global operations and commercial meetings from all their plants to examine the total company's needs on an ongoing basis. It also has a global seven-member executive committee comprised of a people from five countries representing all divisions. This group meets quarterly to review overall company strategy as well as to coordinate month-to-month operations.

Philips, in the face of intensifying Japanese competition needed to improve its consumer electronics coordination among its independent national organizations. It created a World Policy Council that included key managers from strategic markets around the world. Through this council, Philips co-opted country support for company decisions about product policy and manufacturing location.

At IBM Europe, country CEOs are autonomous in their country subsidiaries, but also sit on a pan-European board. This glocal structure achieves coordination across the company's European operations.

These kinds of coordination councils and other forms of international cooperation means more travel. Many managers who have worked in international or multinational organizations are used to taking a business trip to their territory or headquarters once a year. These are the people who many times fail to understand that when you form a global organization, the amount of travel necessary to keep its disparate parts together increases geometrically. Frequent global travel is not an option to be eliminated during budget crunches, but a necessity to keep the organization in coordinated, competitive condition.

Global corporate meetings and conferences. Any successful global corporation, if it is to develop and sustain an integrated global corporate culture, needs to have a range of global meetings and conferences involving people from throughout the corporation.

Ideally, on an annual basis, it should go one level lower than any normal decision-making groups or committees. In other words, if you have quarterly meetings of your vice-presidents from various areas of the world, then you should have an annual meeting of vice-presidents and directors.

The first reaction of many managers is that the travel cost cannot be justified. The second thought, if they are thinking, is that a global corporation cannot stay in business in a fast-changing environment without updating and coordinating not only the executive group, but also the senior operating people responsible for ironing out the day-to-day misunderstandings that inevitably occur in global operations.

In the end, we all must accept the fact that the decision whether there are or are not adequate resources for effective coordination of a global organization is not a matter of money, but of vision and priorities.

Control

The final building block of a global corporate culture is the means and methods for recognizing and rewarding the behavior and performance seen as contributing to the overall objectives and philosophy of the corporation.

Every management textbook ever written about corporate culture notes that *corporate cultures are not established through visions and mottos, but through a reward and recognition process.* This process must acknowledge performance, which is consonant with the corporation's values, philosophy, vision, mission, and direction. If these aspects of corporate life are out of line, the corporation will not perform to its potential.

There are four areas in which this reward process is applied in global corporations. These are:

1. Reward systems incorporating quantitative and qualitative data.
2. Globally consistent and culturally sensitive performance measurement for managers.
3. Measurement systems to encourage continuous improvement.
4. Globally consistent business unit measurement and reward systems.

Let's review each of them for a moment.

Quantitative and qualitative data for performance review.   Given the complexities of global corporations with many rotating or matrixed boss/subordinate relations, it is becoming increasingly important to include qualitative, as well as quantitative data in performance reviews.

This is a time-consuming and difficult process and one that has not been well developed in many corporations. Investment banks and other companies that have flat, de-layered organizations with shifting project teams use qualitative peer feedback. This is because many times supervisors have not had enough contact with an employee to adequately evaluate performance at year's end.

The same situation is true for many managers in global organizations. They may report to someone who is on the other side of the globe or to several people in several parts of the world. To accommodate this, performance appraisal systems can be electronically operated through coded channels to allow people to have input from various points in the world without getting bogged down in paperwork.

Globally consistent and culturally sensitive performance review standards and processes. Another difficult area in conducting individual performance reviews in global corporations is the cultural bias of the typical American performance review process. There are many cultures, like France for example, where senior managers above a certain level are simply not subject to annual performance reviews. There are others, like Indonesia, where performance reviews do not involve face-to-face discussion between a supervisor and employees, but instead are done through a third party or some other impersonal mechanism to prevent loss of face.

A major challenge for global corporations is to incorporate performance appraisal systems that are sensitive to these cultural differences, yet are also perceived as valid and equitable in their measurement of employee contribution to the total organizational achievements.

Most companies who have done this successfully have been very clear about their global corporate values and have allowed local variety in process, while requiring consistency in content.

Measurement systems to encourage continuous improvement. Total quality management and the Japanese concept of Kaizan have etched the idea of continuous improvement into the corporate mindsets of many of the world's largest corporations. Whether TQM takes hold in operations as a long-term methodology depends on the corporate culture of an organization.

In a global corporation that is process driven, however, continuous improvement is an important means of monitoring and improving processes, and therefore corporate effectiveness. As such, it must be an integral part of a global corporate culture.

There is not enough space in this brief review to examine the elements of Demming's 14 principles, which could be applied to global corporations. For a global manager, however, it would be a useful exercise to ascertain the relevance of implementing a continuous process improvement program for a global corporate culture.

In any case, successful global corporations, if they are to compete head-on with the Japanese, will need to take into account the fact that their competition will be operating on a philosophy of continuous improvement that will impose a hard competitive stance over the long haul. Any global manager who believes that it is possible to establish a product niche and sit on it without constant adjustment and improvement will be doomed to fall victim to the higher quality or lower cost of a global competitor.

Globally consistent business unit rewards.   Individual recognition and reward is one aspect of managing a successful global culture. Equally important, however, is the basis upon which business units are evaluated and rewarded and the degree to which the processes and standards are considered consistent and equitable among units on a global basis.

This is a rather complicated situation that rests on perceived as well as actual contributions to the corporate bottom line. It goes without saying that without the correct definition of profit centers and the right financial policies for allocation, accounting, and control, there will be constant warfare between business units over their perceived and real contributions, both to corporate profit as well as corporate overhead.

The definition of financial units and accounting standards for a global organization can be one of the main methods of avoiding painful misunderstandings, jealousies, and time-wasting meetings, debates, and arguments. Financial transparency or something like it must be an objective of global corporate finance departments in order that illusions of contributions and misunderstandings about the real cost structure of global operations can be prevented or filtered out.

A chief financial officer who understands her or his role as a developer of the global corporate culture, as well as a chief financial strategist and controller, is one of the most important assets that a global corporation can acquire.

Developing a global corporate culture with appropriate management practices depends heavily on changing the individual attitudes and skills of executives, managers, and employees in the organization. Without a change in people's mindsets, the best vision or global strategy will never get off the ground.

THE COMPETITIVE BENEFITS OF A GLOBAL CORPORATE CULTURE

One competitive advantage of a global corporate culture lies in the *flexibility to shift from local to global strategy when necessary to blunt a competitor's attack*. It is relatively easy to adjust a global culture to local needs, but it is much more difficult to adjust a locally responsive culture to global needs.

Philips, the Dutch-based electronics giant, has been constantly frustrated in its attempt to overcome its multinational localized bias. Despite the fact that Philips has technological superiority over the Japanese in a number of areas, it has been unable to transfer and distribute the technology quickly enough to be competitive in the right markets. It has lacked the strategic coordination and the global corporate culture to facilitate this.

Explanations given for Philips' failure are all too familiar. They include some suggestions that those who developed the product were too distant from the market; others felt that there were barriers between research, development, manufacturing, and marketing that led to delays and cost overruns. Still others suggested that since worldwide subsidiaries are not involved in new product development, they are not committed to distributing new products that do not appear to be tailored to local demands.

By contrast, Matsushita Electric Company, Philips' rival in worldwide electronics, has built global leadership through the development of a corporate culture that overcomes these shortcomings. Matsushita has three characteristics of its corporate culture that allow it to be successful. First, it gains the input of subsidiaries into management processes; second, it ensures that development efforts are linked to market needs; and third, it manages responsibility transfer from development to manufacturing to marketing (Bartlett and Ghoshal, 1988, p. 3).

A globalized corporate culture can facilitate a longer-term corporate view. To use an analogy developed by McKinsey & Co., large, globally integrated corporations are more "farmers" than "hunter-gatherers" (Bleeke and Johnson, 1989, p. 67).

Global hunter-gatherers identify the newest product resulting from the most advanced technology or latest fad and travel the globe trying to sell it in the best markets. The result is short product life cycles and a high overhead marketing effort, which is in constant change and adjustment. On products with high margins in introductory phases of their product cycle, this can be a profitable strategy.

Global farmers, on the other hand, build long-term stable customer relationships and sell more mature dependable products over a longer period of time. A global corporate culture, with a series of checks and balances internationally, tends to shift corporations toward developing and maintaining relationships rather than hunting-gathering products. This is because globalization encourages global efficiency and innovation, but not at the cost of being unresponsive to local long-term needs and relationships.

To become global farmers, managers must have a highly refined understanding of the world, good global scanning skills, a sharp instinct for generic business strategy, and a deep sensitivity to cultural, social, economic, and political differences around the world.

Ericsson, the Swedish telecommunication company, appears to be everyone's choice as a model global corporate culture. It has done the best job of managing the need for global integration and local responsiveness, while developing excellent strategic coordination mechanisms. Three characteristics stand out:

- An interdependence of resources and responsibilities among organizational units through mandatory sharing of resources, ideas, and opportunities.
- A set of strong cross-unit integrating devices.
- A strong corporate identification and well-developed worldwide management perspective.

By changing responsibilities, shifting assets, and modifying relationships between various geographic, product, and functional groups, Ericsson has built a diverse organization in which multiple perspectives exist not only within the decision-making process, but within the global managers themselves.

These diverse viewpoints, combined with a fluid structure, are complemented by a set of interunit integrating devices that form the core of the global corporate culture. The three most critical aspects of the Ericsson's corporate culture that enhance global competitiveness are:

- A clearly defined and tightly controlled set of operating systems.
- A people-linking process employing such devices as temporary assignments and joint teams.
- Interunit decision forums, particularly subsidiary boards, where views can be exchanged and differences resolved.

These three elements provide the infrastructure necessary to manage diversity and ensure effective and timely decision making. Its systems have been constructed to facilitate worldwide coordination, rather than central control.

All of this requires good interpersonal relations on a worldwide basis. For this reason, temporary interunit transfers between headquarters and subsidiaries, as well as between subsidiaries, lie at the heart of the people equation. Ericsson's transfer process is much more intense than the normal, however. It often transfers a team of 50 to 100 engineers and managers from one unit to another for a year or two.

Ericsson's conflict management forums tend to be in active board meetings (both headquarters and subsidiary) during which differences between headquarters and local subsidiaries are thrashed out with input from people with a wide range of perspectives and backgrounds.

Summary of Competitive Benefits of a Global Corporate Culture

We have discussed many aspects of a global corporate culture and its role in enabling global organizations to adapt to constant change in their environment. Let's take a minute to summarize some of the major benefits that have been noted in this chapter. A global corporate culture provides the following.

1. *Strategic, competitive flexibility*—the ability to move between global and local strategies in a flexible and timely fashion.

2. *Clear methods for conflict management*—the development of a system for balancing and managing the conflicting interests that are an inherent part of global operations.

3. *Clear methods of information processing and resource allocation*—which enables better and faster decision making at the appropriate point of authority.

4. *World-class executive talent*—that has been seasoned throughout the organization and represents the best human talent worldwide. As a result, the company can make better judgments and can experience better coordination and implementation of strategic directions.

5. *A compelling mission and vision*—that creates not only organizational loyalty, but also speeds decision making, because priorities and values are clear and authority can be delegated in a network, rather than hierarchical structure.

With these benefits in mind, it is clear that the steps to create a global corporate culture should be high on the agenda of any large multinational corporation. Human resource managers have an important role to play in developing and implementing global corporate strategies. Hopefully some of the steps outlined here will provide a framework for action to enhance your organization's competitiveness in the global marketplace.

KEY PRACTICES AND TASKS FOR MANAGING ORGANIZATIONAL ADAPTABILITY

The following is a list of the practices and tasks that you as a global manager can undertake in managing organizational adaptability.

Competence III: Managing Organizational Adaptability

Definintion: Ability to appropriately centralize and decentralize decision making for various businesses, functions, and tasks to provide the quickest, best, and most coordinated decisions and actions on a global basis, and to develop and dissolve temporary teams and mechanisms to deal with environmental changes.

Action and Mindset: Trust process

Personal Characteristic: Flexibility

Key Processes and Tasks

1. Review your current corporate culture against the list outlined earlier. Determine *which corporate policies, procedures, systems, values, and practices facilitate or hinder the development of your global operations* within a three- to five-year strategy and structure.

    1.1 Clearly restate your three- to five-year business strategy in terms of its implications for your global operations and your global corporate culture.

    1.2 Compare your corporate culture today against your global business strategy to determine where you need to make adjustments to ensure adaptability to future competitive and market demands.

2. Determine *which decisions should be centralized* for coherency and efficiency and *which decisions should be decentralized* for local responsiveness by business, function, and task.

    2.1 Research practices in your industry and function concerning centralization and decentralization of various policies, practices, and tasks.

    2.2 Analyze your managerial area to decentralize as many marketing, sales, and customer-oriented operational decisions as possible, while retaining central control over general policies and operational areas such as finance and research where technology or practices can provide policy coherence and/or cost efficiency.

3. Develop a *global strategy and structure that is fixed,* but a *global corporate culture that is process driven and flexible* to changing world conditions through the use of global task forces, temporary decision committees, regional coordination groups, and global integrators.

    3.1 Look for opportunities to make your job and function as flexi-
    ble as possible by establishing annual or semiannual cross-
    functional reviews and building in feedback loops on your
    performance from internal and external customers on a global
    basis.

    3.2 Look for extraordinary individuals who seem to have an ability
    to see many sides of an issue and use them for global trouble-
    shooting and analysis, regardless of their full-time position and
    responsibilities.

    3.3 Ensure that your reward systems and criteria are re-enforcing
    the global cultural values and behavior that you want to see in
    your unit.

4. *Benchmark* your business and operational policies, procedures, and
practices against European and Japanese competitors. Determine
what changes need to be made to achieve world-class status.

    4.1 Examine the global business and operational practices of your
    global competitors and suppliers.

    4.2 Incorporate one new idea each year from a global competitor
    or supplier into your operations.

The management of global corporate culture could well be the most
important task of a global manager. Herein lies the manager and the organization's capacity to respond to the rapid changes that affect the organization's survival and growth in the environment on a global basis.

To be a successful manager of global corporate culture, one must be
willing to occasionally break all rules, be addicted to change, and *"thrive* on
chaos," as Tom Peters would say.

In Figure 5–1, you can see how your ability to manage a global corporate
culture comes together within the CLC.

It is becoming clear to observers of corporate cultures and management
practices that Japanese and European firms put much greater thought over
a much longer period of time into developing global corporate cultures and
human resources than do companies in the United States.

Much of the U.S. human resource community is far behind in its understanding of globalization requirements and the development of appropriate
technologies to deal with them. But the blame must be shared by corporate
leaders themselves, who have been reluctant to commit the needed resources
to the task in advance of the need.

The lack of well-developed global corporate cultures is a strategic weakness that American corporate leaders and human resource professionals
need to address as soon as possible. The time has come for an integrated

FIGURE 5-1
Global Competency Learning Cycle (Managing Organizational Adaptability)

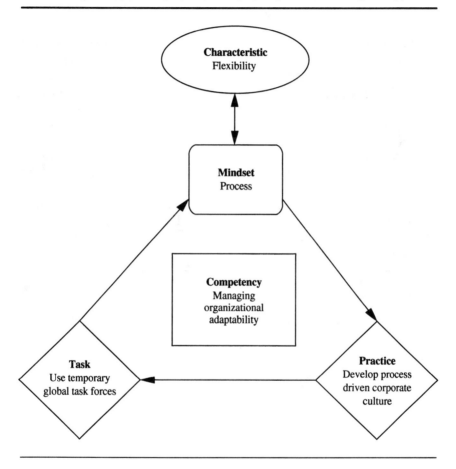

effort to ensure that Americans will have the management and cross-cultural skills necessary to compete on a global basis.

AFTERTHOUGHTS FOR GLOBAL MINDSETS

The world leaders in aligning global corporate strategy and structure with culture and practices are old European firms such as Philips, Shell, and ICI and new, global, Japanese firms such as Matsushita, NEC, and Toyota. In the United States, Motorola, General Electric, and 3M are leaders in globalizing their corporate cultures, but all admit to the need to monitor and improve their practices constantly.

One reason many organizations find this aspect of globalization so difficult is that the international management literature does not provide much guidance. As noted earlier, due to different professional boundaries and restrictions, business school professors, corporate culture consultants, and cross-cultural experts have failed to assist corporations in achieving an integrated approach to globalization. One of the best books in this area is by Evans, Doz, and Laurent, *Human Resource Management in International Firms* (1990).

Many of the procedures, systems, and practices necessary for a global corporate culture were noted in the list outlined previously, but many of the practices are unfamiliar in management training and development programs. Academics, consultants, and human resource professionals must further document the best practices in these areas and develop appropriate educational technologies to help international executives gain more global skills and attitudes.

Chapter Six

Managing Multicultural Teams

No one can play the game alone. One cannot be human by oneself. There is no selfhood where there is no community. We do not relate to others as the person we are; we are who we are in relating to others.

Carse, p. 45

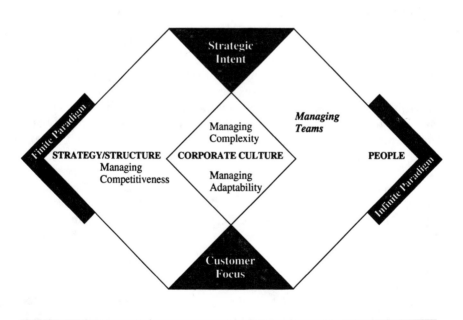

FORETHOUGHTS FROM A GLOBAL MIND

By now you probably sense how important teamwork is to developing an effective global corporate culture and to global management in general. Just as the management of complexity is the interface between strategy/structure and corporate culture levels of organization, the management of teams constitutes the interface between the corporate culture and the individuals within the organization. Whether the integrating and coordinating units are global meetings, cross-unit councils, cross-functional project teams, or matrixed business unit/country management policy groups—teamwork is essential.

The central operating mode for a *global* enterprise is the creation, organization, and management of *multicultural* teams—groups that represent diversity in functional capabilities, experience levels, and cultural backgrounds.

The fourth key to success for you as a global manager is to understand how to organize and lead multicultural teams; how to deal with issues of collaboration and cross-cultural variance; and how to develop processes for coaching, mentoring, and assessing performance across a variety of attitudes, beliefs, and cultures. This requires the ability to effectively lead and direct a diverse group of people, many of whom have values, beliefs, behaviors, business practice standards, and traditions that are likely to be culturally different from your own.

In this sense, the requirements of a manager in a global organization extend well beyond traditional management practices, to reflect sensitivity to cultural diversity and understanding of different—and sometimes conflicting—social forces. You will often be required to operate in an unfamiliar and uncomfortable organizational setting. This will demand enormous personal flexibility, as well as sensitivity.

Within the architecture of cross-cultural teams, global managers recognize and focus on the subtle requirements for organizational loyalty and commitment, despite the presence of different cultural values and beliefs. At the same time, they manage in the context of continuous change and diversity.

We are approaching territory that has been intuitively managed for many years. While some recent research and theory has been developed on comparative management practices in different countries, there remains a large gap between the needs of managers to understand the intercultural subtleties of multicultural team management and the state of the art in the applied behavioral sciences.

In this chapter you will find the fundamental elements necessary to understand and lead a multicultural team. In general, this is an area ripe for further study and definition in the 1990s. It is also an area in which you will need to combine some substantive knowledge about different cultures and their predispositions, combined with an attitude of patience and openness. This means that you may have to experiment with new behavior that is more sensitive and open to unexpected reactions of bosses, colleagues, and subordinates from different cultures who may operate on totally different assumptions about leadership, communications, problem solving, and decision making.

Dealing with the unknown within a small group, however, is good practice for what lies ahead in the next two chapters as we examine the third level of our integrated approach to globalization—people. People in *teams* (Chapter Six), people dealing with *uncertainty* (Chapter Seven), and people *learning* from their experience (Chapter Eight) form the heart of this third level of global management.

Multiculturalism is a force that has rocketed through the world with staggering speed. While it has long been festering in the Middle East, Asia, and Africa, it has exploded in Yugoslavia, the republics of the former Soviet Union, and Eastern Europe in the last few years in a way that brings unease to diverse American campuses and questions to an American workplace that will be increasingly multicultural during the years ahead.

Diversity in the American workplace and multiculturalism in international enterprises both contain the need to compare, contrast, and understand cultural differences in a new way; a way that does not melt and homogenize, but recognizes and employs differences for cultural synergy and creativity. Something that is easier said than done.

IMPORTANCE OF TEAMS
IN A GLOBAL ORGANIZATION

Effective, efficient, multicultural teams are the key to future global competitiveness and work force motivation and management. Self-directed teams are critical to quality improvement; cross-functional teams are important for customer service and product development; and multicultural teams are necessary for the success of global enterprises.

Behind much of this emphasis on teamwork is a realization that a better educated work force wants to take more responsibility for their work and accomplishments (Carnevale, 1991). With decentralization and de-layering, it is also clear that authority and responsibility will devolve on people throughout the world who are the closest to the customer, and at the same time are able to operate in a multicultural environment.

One executive in a recent Conference Board report on global teamwork noted:

> We have over 75,000 employees and $8 billion in sales, 40% of which are from the international arena. Almost all goods sold overseas are produced overseas. We are extremely broad based in terms of products—we sell 55,000 different products.

FIGURE 6-1
Teamwork in Global Organizations

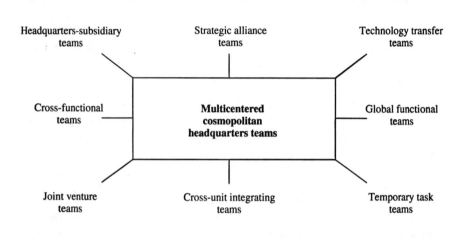

Adapted from Gross, Turner, Cederholm, "Building Teams & Global Operations." *Management Review,*
June 1987, p. 32.

We are in niches—we have small unit sales in many area that are related in terms of
process technology. This makes global teamwork essential. [Schaeffer, 1990, p. 5]

The cosmopolitan management team is becoming a familiar site in global
organizations. Whirlpool International's management committee is made
up of six people from six different nations. IBM prides itself on having five
different nationalities represented among its highest ranking officers, and
three among its outside directors. Four nationalities are represented on Unilever's board, and three are on the board of Shell Oil.

In Figure 6-1, we have identified nine types of teams important for effective global management (see Gross, Turner, and Cederholm, 1987).

Briefly, the purpose of each of these teams is the following.

Multicentered cosmopolitan headquarters teams are developed from
top management to oversee strategic directions for various parts of the
business on a functional, product, or geographic basis.

Headquarters-subsidiary teams are formed to ensure effective representation, coordination, and integration of glocal interests.

Strategic alliance teams are created as part of new cooperative/
competitive strategies to share development costs, technological advances, and proprietary approaches for global competitiveness.

Technology transfer teams are formed to transfer organization innovations from one geographical location to another.

Cross-functional teams are developed to coordinate company programs such as quality improvement or customer service across functions.

Global functional teams are created to coordinate strategies, policies, and procedures on a global basis for commercial, finance, administration, operations, or human resources.

Joint venture teams are formed to manage the start-up and ongoing operation of new enterprises with a foreign partner.

Cross-unit integrating teams are created to coordinate strategies and plans between operating divisions or different businesses within the same global company.

Temporary project teams are formed for temporary tasks usually involving the study, research, and communication of special issues throughout the corporation.

These nine specialized teams are *in addition* to the normal workplace implementation teams, which in many global corporations are multicultural. Many of these teams, as we have discovered already, are critical to the functioning of a global corporate culture that can integrate and coordinate the conflicting interests of complex global operations.

It is imperative that you, as a global manager, feel comfortable leading a multicultural team if your organization is to be successful in the global marketplace. It is also imperative that these multicultural teams have some training and development.

3M Company has had experience in multicultural team building through their EMATS (European Management Action Teams) program. While the program experienced some difficulties getting off the ground in 1988, the company put a transnational training program "Leadership for Growth" into place that brought together 350 European 3Mers for two different rounds of training in 1989 and 1990.

UNDERSTANDING MULTICULTURAL TEAMS

All teamwork has its challenges. Blending the needs, interests, backgrounds, and styles of people from different functions, disciplines, and businesses is not an easy task. Accomplishing this within a multicultural context, with differing assumptions, values, and beliefs about management and group behavior, can be awesome.

To assist in sorting out the various elements of multicultural team management and leadership, we have developed a formula, which while complex, is comprehensive. After we have explained its various elements, we will work to operationalize it, so that it does not become a skeleton in the burial ground of comprehensive, but unusable ideas.

The formula consists of the following elements.

$$MTL = f(PS \times FC \times CC \times NC \times SPD \times STD \times ETF)$$

Multicultural Team Leadership is a function of:

PS = Personal Styles of team members

FC = Functional Cultures of team members (e.g., finance, engineering, marketing)

CC = Corporate Cultures of the company, division, or unit represented by each team member

NC = National Culture of each team member

SPD = Stage of Professional Development of each team member

STD = Stage of Team Development

ETF = Effectiveness of Team Functioning

It is obvious that no one person can be concerned about all of these variables at the same time, but they provide a good checklist of issues to be considered when teams are experiencing difficulty working together. As a manager in a global organization, you should at least be familiar with the various factors, so that you can diagnose the cause of problems you may face in multicultural teams.

One of the best methods for understanding how teams function is an off-site team-building meeting. In this situation, the team leader or outside facilitator helps the team assess the degree to which these different factors may affect the team's operations. To do this, models, instruments, and exercises can be applied to each of the variables in the formula. Let's review these to gain an understanding of how each factor can be approached for more effective teamwork.

Personal Styles

There are a multitude of ways to assess personal styles, but one that has been highly effective is the Myers-Briggs Type Inventory (MBTI). This brief test, based on the lifelong insights of Carl Jung, can be self-administered and is an excellent way to open a team-building meeting.

The purpose of the MBTI is to assess the way in which people access and process information—two critical aspects of team functioning. Jung determined archetype personal styles based on the interaction of the following four sets of preferred actions.

Extrovert (E)   .... Introvert (I)

Sensing   (S)   .... Intuitive (N)

Thinking (T)   .... Feeling   (F)

Perceiving (P)   .... Judging   (J)

People *access* information through sensing (S) or intuiting (N) information from their environment. Sensors tend to take in more detailed information by using their eyes, ears, nose, and touch to make contact with the environment. Intuitives (N) are more big picture people, looking for patterns, systems, and a sense of *gestalt* in the world around them. As a result, both S and N type personalities can read the same information or have the same experience, but will perceive different things. This can greatly affect a team's functioning, since for example, an S may be looking for empirical data upon which to base decisions, while an N may be looking at strategic directions.

Second, once people have accessed information, they *process* it in different ways. Thinking people (T) tend to analyze the information they have accessed to determine what should be done in a particular situation. Feelers (F), on the other hand, will tend to classify information against a set of beliefs and categorize it as good or bad, right or wrong. These beliefs may be based on experience, upbringing, or religious and philosophical systems. One can see, however, that the *criteria* used in decision making will be different between a T and an F. This can greatly affect interpersonal relations and team functioning.

With these four variables, there are four basic archetypes—NT, NF, ST, and SF. Each of these people see the world differently, not because of cultural differences, but because of differences in *personal styles* that are related to personality.

The application of the Jungian archetypes to team functioning holds that all four basic personal styles should be present in each team for a balanced effort. Teams with only intuitives will excel in determining strategic direction, but may not have any idea how to get there. Likewise, sensors may have all the data, but may not know or care where it leads. Thinkers will have everything analyzed, but may miss the moral aspects of decision making. Feelers may be clear about what is right and wrong, but may not understand how to communicate the results of a decision in a way that thinkers will understand and follow.

The other variables (extrovert-introvert) reflect whether people look to ideas (I) or other people (E) to verify their impressions about what direction they should take. Introverts march to their own drummer and enjoy time by themselves to reflect. Extroverts develop synergy through people and prefer to work in teams. Extroverts are energized by people. Introverts are sometimes exhausted by people.

Perceivers (P) are open to all possibilities. They hesitate to come to closure on decisions, because they want to take in more data to ensure that all angles have been covered. Judgers (J), on the other hand, want to make decisions and move on to the next topic on the agenda.

This P/J category can have a great effect on team functioning as a P prefers to think decisions through thoroughly, while a J is action oriented. A J without a P rushes to conclusions, sometimes in the wrong direction, and a P without a J procrastinates in making decisions.

While it would not be useful to try to make every multicultural team a group therapy session, it is important that team members and leaders have some idea of how to distinguish cultural factors from personality factors in team functioning. The MBTI provides one method that is reasonably easy and nonthreatening.

These few observations on the Myers-Briggs personal styles inventory do not do it justice. Our purpose here is not to be comprehensive, but merely to provide one overview of how personal differences affect multicultural team operations. (For more information on Myers-Briggs profiles, see Keirsey and Bates, *Please Understand Me,* 1984.)

Functional Culture

There has been some correlation between the MBTI and certain functional cultures, because the requirements of various functional cultures tend to attract people with certain personal styles.

CEOs, for example, tend to be ISTJ, ESTJ, INTJ, or ENTJ due to the need to analyze problems, make decisions, and be action oriented. Many highly creative entrepreneurs, on the other hand, are INFP who can allow things to remain open-ended and do not rely on others for advice and counsel. R&D types are often ISTP, involved in detail and allowing for long, open-ended inquiry.

Sales people are often ESTJ or ESFJ who are concerned about what others think and are looking to close sales to obtain revenues. Marketing people, on the other hand, are usually NPs who enjoy looking at the larger strategies of market targeting and the creative process of probing for the right message.

In addition to personal style, functional cultures also have their own norms of behavior, values, frameworks for analysis, and tests of significance. Marketing, finance, personnel, manufacturing, engineering, and design will emphasize different aspects of policy decisions brought to a cross-functional team. This is one reason that cross-functional teams are now becoming such a rich source of information and creative decision making (and conflict!).

The importance of cross-functional teams has been a cornerstone of TQM and customer-focused quality. During these attempts to ensure that customers are served in a seamless fashion that responds to their every need, many organizations have run into the strong differences in functional cultures—their perspectives, values, and priorities.

Global cross-functional management can build on the early experiences of TQM and examine the ways that the movement has found for coordinating these very different perspectives. There is a great deal of synergy to be gained from TQM and globalization when they are considered as complementary forces in an organization.

Corporate Culture

While national cultural differences have been documented for many years, the concept of corporate culture, first brought to the public's attention in a *Business Week* cover story in 1980, is not that old. This was followed quickly by four books that popularized the concept; Ouchi's *Theory Z* (1981), Pascale and Athos's *The Art of Japanese Management* (1981), Deal and Kennedy's *Corporate Cultures* (1982), and Peters and Waterman's *In Search of Excellence* (1982).

By now, it is generally accepted that different corporations have different values and ways of operating. This is true of different corporations *within* a national culture, and, as we will see, it is certainly true of different corporations in different countries.

In the last two chapters, we examined some of the characteristics of *global* corporate cultures. This is a new breed of corporate culture that is still evolving. Other types of corporate cultures, such as those discussed by Ouchi and Peters and Waterman, are more well defined.

With the exception of Edgar Schein's excellent work, *Culture and Organizational Leadership* (1989), most corporate culture books have not borrowed from the anthropological literature, but have developed their own typologies for examining corporate traditions, mission, vision, values, and behavior.

As Schein states, "I have found no quick, reliable way to identify cultural assumptions." Corporate culture methodology, which can easily uncover basic cultural assumptions and values, remains as difficult as obtaining a quick and simple overview of national cultures and their impact on management.

For our purposes, however, the corporate cultural dimensions noted in Figure 6–2 provide one workable overview of the subject, which can be applied to any organization—domestic or global.

These three dimensions—organizational image, shared values, and management behaviors—conform to the way in which many national cultures view themselves. As we will see, people from different national backgrounds perceive themselves differently and have different values and norms of behavior.

Corporate culture continues to have some mystery about it and many managers are unsure how to approach it. If you are one of these, hopefully this chart, plus our discussion in the last two chapters will provide some comfort in dealing with this important part of globalization.

National Culture

With exception of some early empirical work by Bernard Bass, the literature that has examined national cultural differences, (Adler (1986), Christopher (1983), Davis (1971), Gibney (1982), Hall and Hall (1987), Moran and Harris (1991), Hofstede (1980), Joynt (1985), Kras (1989), Lawrence (1990), Mole (1990), Muna (1980), Pascale and Athos (1980), Ronen (1986), Terpstra and David (1985), Webber (1969), and Weinshall (1977)), has provided little attempt to systematically examine the effect of national differences on multicultural team functioning. Most of the literature is anecdotal, providing no *framework for analysis*, which can be helpful to managers of multicultural teams.

The best attempt to examine the management implications of national cultural differences on management is Geert Hofstede's seminal empirical research project entitled *Culture's Consequences* that was published in 1985 and updated in his 1991 work, *Cultures and Organizations*. It contains an overview of four major cultural variables across 40 countries and examines their implications for managerial differences.

Other recent research is beginning to reveal considerable differences in the way in which nationalities approach basic management activities. For example, as can be seen in Figure 6–3, Andre Laurent of INSEAD has discovered that there are very different expectations of managers across 12 cultures.

As can be seen, Nordic and Anglo-Saxon cultures prefer an open leadership style, in which managers can admit that they do not know all the answers, but will be happy to find out an answer and get back to subordi-

FIGURE 6-2

Corporate Culture Survey Dimensions

Organizational Image

Customer Focus: The extent to which the company is concerned with providing quality service; searches out feedback to maintain quality; employees feel a personal sense of responsibility for customers.

Environmental Awareness: A concern for events outside the organization in terms of the competition and technology that affects the workplace; they can adequately determine the effect of new services.

Excellence of Performance: The extent to which a high standard is set internally; cares about the quality of work; and employees care about doing their best.

Organizational Pride: The positive feelings of employees for their organization. People feel they are members of a superior company. Their association brings them prestige.

Organizational Mission: Where the purpose and philosophy are being clearly communicated; are clear-cut and reasonable; worthwhile to society; and related to their work.

Shared Values

Innovation, Change, and Creativity: The extent to which value is attached to developing new ideas in spite of resistance or lack of resources. Encourages risk taking, and people are not punished for new ideas that don't work out. Rather, they are encouraged to reexamine such failures to learn from their mistakes.

Value of People: Being supported and committed to employee development; a company strong in this area views its people as a major asset to be developed, cared for, listened to, and supported.

Egalitarianism: The degree to which all employees are treated the same, regardless of level or function; employees feel highly valued and interact with each other on a first name basis.

Bias for Action: The commitment of an organization to the timely accomplishment of important tasks; problems are attacked with energy and resolved; procedures are streamlined in the interest of ease; employees know how to find resources to get their jobs done.

Competitiveness: Reflected in the degree to which people are asked to work independently toward the achievement of common goals. In strongly competitive organizations people do not share or exchange information, engage in win-lose competitions, and are not responsive.

Trust: The amount of confidence shared by management and employees that they will work in a fair and predictable manner. Please have a favorable view of each other's actions and are not responsive.

Policies and Procedures: The degree to which the formal organizational systems reinforce the activities and behaviors necessary. In a strong company, employees understand why policies exist and feel they facilitate getting their work done.

Rewards and Incentives: The degree to which a company believes individuals should be recognized for performing in the company's interest. A strong company believes in providing monetary incentives as well as acknowledgment of those who do a good job.

Management Behaviors

Teamwork: Products and services result from team effort, and managers support extensive cooperation and interaction among employees.

Leadership: The ability of managers to articulate and motivate employees. Leaders help others succeed, follow up on delegated responsibility, and communicate effectively.

FIGURE 6–2 (concluded)
Corporate Culture Survey Dimensions

Communication Patterns: Open and frequent communication is considered vital; information is transmitted; people have the facts necessary to do their jobs. The grapevine is not depended upon to get the work done.

Conflict Management: The degree to which the company is committed to solving personal as well as professional problems in an open, honest and caring fashion. In a strong company, people listen, discuss differences, and work out constructive solutions.

Camaraderie: The value placed on employee gatherings for the purpose of developing their sense of identity with each other. These include nonwork activities as well as recognition ceremonies and retirement parties.

Balanced Decision Making: the way in which organizations approach the process, acting in a deliberate, logical and rational fashion as well as spontaneous and subjective manner depending on needs.

Accountability: The organization's process of holding people responsible for accomplishing assigned tasks. Employees are clear about their responsibilities, have agreed upon performance objectives, and received periodic and clear feedback on the accomplishment of these objectives.

---

nates. Japanese, Indonesian, and French managers, on the other hand, expect their leaders to have at hand precise answers to the questions their subordinates may ask.

Ten years before Hofstede's empirical study, I worked with Kluckhohn and Strodtbeck's cultural assumptions and values to develop a theoretical framework for integrating comparative management perspectives with differences in cultural values, beliefs, and patterns of thinking.

I called it a model for cultural-managerial analysis (CMA). It grew out of my doctoral dissertation, which was based on research I conducted in a rain forest hospital in Ghana. While it still remains to be fully developed, the basic thesis is outlined in Figure 6–4.

This framework provides an overview of the relationship between the major cultural factors—perception of self, perception of others, perception of the world, and patterns of thinking—and three management activities that most affect multicultural team performance—planning, organizing, and leading.

The assumption is that most cultural differences are reflected in differing perceptions and different patterns of thinking. One example of differences in the way in which cultures perceive the individual is illustrated in Figure 6–5.

The concentric circles represent different levels of information needed by workers in high-context cultures and low-context cultures (Hall, 1976). The higher the context, such as Japan, the more circles of information people need to work together. It is therefore much more important that you spend

FIGURE 6–3

National Differences in Expectations of Managers

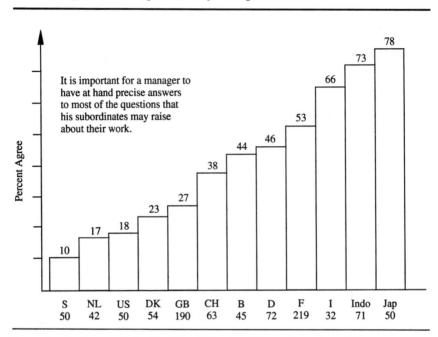

Source: Based on Laurent, Andre. The Cultural Diversity of Western Conceptions of Management. *International Studies of Management and Organization*, Vol. XIII (No. 1–2), Spring–Summer 1983, 75–96

FIGURE 6–4

A Framework for Cultural-Managerial Analysis

Management Activity \ Cultural Factor	Perception of Self	Perception of Others	Perception of the World	Patterns of Thinking
Planning				
Organizing				
Leading				

time with managers from the Far East, Latin America the Middle East, and even certain parts of Europe, like France, providing information about yourself and your background before people will work with you.

FIGURE 6–5
Different Levels of Information Needed for Work Relations

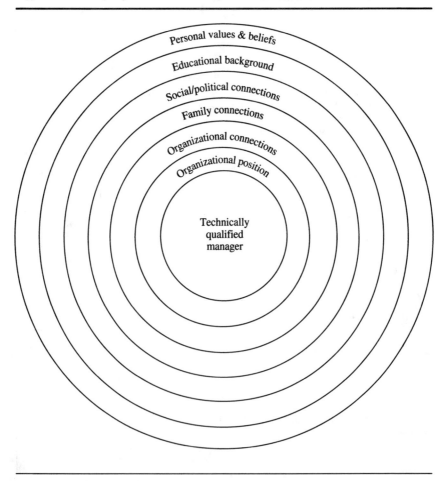

The lower the context, like in the United States, the less information people need. Many American managers have said that all they need is someone who is technically qualified (center circle); they don't have to love people to work with them.

When examined systematically, one can posit a pattern to the kinds of influences cultural differences can have on management. This is represented in Figure 6–6.

FIGURE 6–6

An Application of the Framework for Cultural-Managerial Analysis

Management Activity \ Cultural Factor	Perception of Self	Perception of Others	Perception of the World	Patterns of Thinking
Planning			XX	XX
Organizing	XX	XX		
Leading	XX	XX	XX	XX

Planning activities, for example, are very much affected by people's perception of the world and by their thinking patterns. Organizational structures, on the other hand, are affected by how people see themselves and their relationship to others. Leadership, as one might expect, is the most complex aspect and is affected by virtually all cultural variables. Figure 6–7 contains a list of some of the management areas that can be affected by cultural differences in perception and thinking patterns.

Finally, in Figures 6–8, 6–9, and 6–10, cultural variables are crossed with planning, organizing, and leading activities to suggest which cultural factors might affect each management activity.

As we have noted, most planning activities tend to be affected by beliefs about the world and patterns of thinking. Time horizons of plans, for example, are greatly affected by the time perspectives held by people in different cultures. Americans tend to be oriented toward milestones and deadlines, because they generally can control their environment and affect their own success.

In many African, Latin American, and Eastern European countries, however, people are less able to affect the world around them due to the lack of infrastructure or experience in managing environmental factors. The lack of adequate telecommunications, for example, severely reduces the productivity and extends the time it takes managers to operate in most of Eastern and Central Europe. The assumptions these managers have about the time it will take to accomplish something will, therefore, vary considerably from an action-oriented American.

Likewise, thinking patterns can be dramatically different. Risk taking is one area in which there are very different ideas, again, based on experience and assumptions about control. In general, Americans are moderate risk takers. In Russia, however, many people do not have any experience to judge the degree of risk involved in a deal. As a result, they often propose very

FIGURE 6–7
Managerial Activities Affected by Cultural Differences

I. Planning
   • Nature of organizational objectives
   • Time horizons of plans
   • Quantification of objectives
   • Flexibility of plans
   • Planning methods
   • Type of information collected
   • Amount of information needed for decision
   • Application of scientific method
   • Risk taking/change attitude

II. Organizing
   • Centralization of authority
   • Work specifications
   • Span of control
   • Staff/line relationships
   • Nature of job description
   • Formal role relationships
   • Committee use
   • Informal organization
   • Flexibility to structural change

III. Leading
   • Leadership role
   • Decision-making procedures
   • Communication style
   • Motivating techniques
   • Delegation of authority
   • Coordination activities
   • Subordinate development philosophy
   • Problem-solving methods
   • Negotiating styles
   • Conflict management methods

FIGURE 6-8

Cultural-Managerial Analysis Planning

Planning Activity \ Cultural Factor	Perception of Self	Perception of Others	Perceptions of the World	Patterns of Thinking	Language	Nonverbal Behavior
Nature of organizational objectives			• Availability of valued "good" • Role of providence • Happiness • Hard work • Man/nature relations • Role of religion	• Application of scientific methods • Systems thinking • Cause and effect assumptions		
Time horizons of plans			• Time orientation			
Quantification of objectives			• Time measurement	• Level of abstraction		
Flexibility of plans				• Cybernetic thinking		
Planning methods			• Providence	• Problem/solving rationale • Cause/effect assumptions • Reasoning patterns		
Type of information				• Problem/solving rationale • Level of abstraction • Reasoning patterns		
Amount of information needed for decision				• Risk taking • Cybernetic thinking		
Application of scientific method				• Scientific methods • Cause/effect assumptions		
Risk taking/change attitude			• Change attitude	• Risk taking		

high-risk ventures without a context within which to understand the degree of risk or gauge an American's response.

Organization is also affected by culture. The cultural factors most affecting organizational preferences have to do with the way in which people perceive themselves and their relations with others.

The best example of a difference in this area is the relationship between individualism and group identification. Americans and many other Anglo-Nordic cultures tend to be quite individualistic and egalitarian. There is great emphasis on individual freedom and a preference for informality.

More group-oriented societies, like Japan, or more formal cultures, such as France, prefer more structured organizational relations, less informality and, in the case of Japan, much less emphasis on the individual. The group in Japan, and rules and regulations of formal hierarchy in France, define a person's place within a larger context. The individual is part of a larger system and is treated according to position, rather than his or her personal needs and desires.

It should be obvious by now that culture can greatly affect management. It is also obvious that when people come together in global organizations and multicultural teams, the chance of some confusion and misunderstanding based on cultural differences can be quite high.

As a manager or member of a multicultural team, these issues will not only affect how you plan and organize your work. As we saw earlier in Andre Laurent's research, these differences can also affect the expectations that people have about your leadership style and effectiveness. Some of the leadership activities subject to cultural interpretation are outlined in Figure 6–10.

While this framework has not been tested empirically and needs further development, it points the way toward a more systematic understanding of the relationship between culture and management. With further development, this can become one of the many new tools global managers can use in their management of multicultural teams, as well as their interaction with staff, joint ventures, customers, and suppliers on a worldwide basis.

Stereotyping and Cultural Analysis

A word should be said about stereotyping, because it is a very misunderstood concept. Many people resist putting labels on themselves or others, whether it is an interpretation of personal styles as in MBTI, or a description of national cultural behavior as in the last section. These people either personally resist being put in boxes or feel that it is unfair and inappropriate to put others in boxes.

FIGURE 6-9

Organizing Cultural-Managerial Analysis

Organizing Activity / Cultural Factor	Perception of Self	Perception of Others	Perceptions of the World	Patterns of Thinking	Language	Nonverbal Behavior
Centralization of authority	• Individualism	• Authority structure • Status				
Work specialization	• Activity • Motivation					
Span of control	• Self-esteem	• Authority base				
Staff line relationships		• Authority base				
Nature of job descriptions	• Activity • Motivation	• Role flexibility				
Role of formal relationships	• Age/sex • Individualism	• Social relations • Relationship between sexes • Communication style • Activity				
Committee use		• Authority structure • Opinion expression				
Informal organization		• Communication patterns • Intermediaries				
Flexibility to structural change	• Cultural self-awareness	• Role flexibility				

FIGURE 6–10
Leading Cultural-Managerial Analysis

Cultural Factor / Leading Activity	Perception of Self	Perception of Others	Perceptions of the World	Patterns of Thinking	Language	Nonverbal Behavior
Leadership style	• Cultural self-awareness • Activity • Motivation • Self-esteem	• Communication style • Role flexibility • Social relations				
Decision-making procedures	• Individualism • Age	• Opinion expression • Authority structure				←
Communication styles	• Cultural self-awareness • Age	• Relationship between sexes • Social relations • Authority structure			• Verb structure (2nd person singular)	• Hand gestures • Facial expression • Posture and stance • Interdistance • Touching
Motivating techniques	• Motivation	• Work/play		• Cybernetic thinking		• Eye contact • Smell • Voice tone • Time symbolism • Timing/pauses • Silence
Delegation of authority	• Age/sex • Individualism	• Authority structure • Group member				→
Coordination activities	• Activity	• Communication patterns		• Cybernetic thinking		→

FIGURE 6–10 (concluded)
Leading Cultural-Managerial Analysis

Cultural Factor / Leading Activity	Perception of Self	Perception of Others	Perceptions of the World	Patterns of Thinking	Language	Nonverbal Behavior
Subordinate development philosophy	• Age/sex • Self-esteem	• Humanitarianism • Group membership	• Nature of man • Change attitude	Cybernetic thinking		➡
Problem-solving methods				• Problem-solving rationale • Cause/effect assumptions • Level of abstraction • Application of scientific methods • Reasoning patterns • Systems thinking • Cybernetic thinking		
Negotiating style		• Status • Work/play • Intermediaries • Communication patterns	• Problem-solving rationale • Cause/effect assumptions • Level of abstraction • Application of scientific methods • Reasoning patterns • Systems thinking • Cybernetic thinking • Risk taking			
Conflict management methods		• Status • Work/play • Intermediaries • Communication patterns • Social relations • Communication style				

There are obvious pitfalls to generalizations. Any extreme use of a paradigm to characterize the behavior of others *all the time* will obviously lead to false assumptions. The idea of generalizations, on the other hand, is to describe the *most likely* response of people over time, based on samplings of individuals and groups.

Anthropologists describe this as "value orientation," or the "preferred way" of thinking or acting by the *majority* of a particular population. Thus, we talk about Japanese as group oriented and Americans as individually oriented. *This does not mean that there are no individually oriented Japanese or group-oriented Americans.* It simply means that the *majority* of Americans tend to be individually oriented and the majority of Japanese group oriented.

Figure 6–11 provides a graphic representation of the generalizations made in cultural analysis. This graph, which represents feelings in the United States concerning the relationship of man (in the generative) and nature reveals that while the majority of Americans may feel control over their environment, there are obviously many who do not and others who believe that it is important to establish harmony with one's environment.

Obviously, many of the underclass in American cities feel very little control over their environment, as do many rural poor in the United States. These people, unsure whether they will be able to get through another day or another week, either due to the harshness of inner city life and dangers of crack-filled streets, or because of the unpredictability of floods and droughts, do not represent the dominant American profile of people who are involved in life planning and career development.

Likewise, there are a growing number of people in the United States who feel that while America has the technology to cut through mountains, exploit timberland, and create products that destroy the ozone layer, man must at some point acknowledge the need to live in harmony with nature, even when the technology is available to control certain aspects of the environment. The environmental movement in the United States is still not the dominant American profile, but it is gaining ground as a significant value orientation of the American people.

Generalizations are necessary in dealing across cultures and differences. People need to be able to contrast their own behavior with others so they can explain and predict the likely reaction they will encounter if they behave in a particular way.

To reject generalizations because of their misuse would be foolish. It is therefore incumbent on all of us who engage in theory building and the description of group behavior *to acknowledge that individual differences can always transcend group norms.*

FIGURE 6–11
Stereotyping and Cultural Analysis: Man's Relationship to Nature

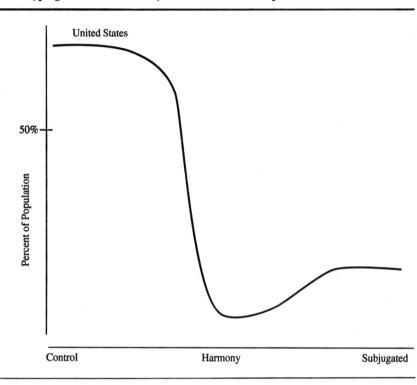

Stages of Team Development

All groups develop over time. Many managers are not aware that their teams are affected not only by external events and internal operations, but also by the subtle changes as the group has experience with one another.

A useful, simple theory on group development, which we referred to in Chapter 2, was created by Tuckman (1977). He characterizes four stages of group development that are experienced by all groups, but may be manifested differently by groups in different cultures (see Figure 6–12).

In the *forming* stage, teams work through questions of identity and control. Who are we? What are our roles and responsibilities? Who's in charge? What will be the power coalitions in the group that will affect decisions?

In the *storming* stage, personal, cultural, and other differences in the group play out as the group begins to function and encounter difficulties.

FIGURE 6-12
Stages of Team Development

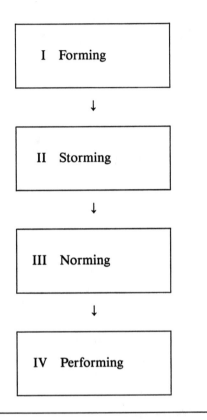

During this critical stage the team must find ways to manage diversity and conflict constructively so that these differences do not block its ability to function.

In the third phase, *norming,* the team develops its own norms of behavior, which are a composite of the differences represented by all team members. If the team works well, the new norms should facilitate the team in achieving their objectives.

In the final stage, *performing,* the team puts all its resources together toward accomplishing its mission. When operating well, it is not hampered by issues of internal functioning and is able to devote the majority of its energy toward the task at hand. When this happens, we say we have a fully functioning group.

If groups do not face up to the realities of the first three stages, they will not be able to reach stage four. Many teams become fixated on an earlier stage of development and continue to replay issues of forming (purpose, roles, and responsibilities), storming (power struggles/cultural misunderstandings), or norming (priorities or criteria and methods for decision making). In these cases, every problem the group faces seems to push it back to the same old issues.

Effective Team Functioning

There are a wide range of tests and questionnaires that teams can take to test their perceptions of team effectiveness. In general these questionnaires are self-administered by team members. Their purpose is to gather information concerning how members see the team functioning on the following kinds of factors:

1. Shared goals and objectives.
2. Utilization of resources.
3. Trust and conflict management.
4. Shared leadership.
5. Control and procedures.
6. Interpersonal communication.
7. Problem solving and decision making.
8. Creativity.
9. Evaluation and rewards.

There are many variations on these items, plus more sophisticated simulations and activities to help teams understand the causes of their operational problems. The best source for more information is the two volume *Encyclopedia of Team Development Activities* edited by J. William Pfeiffer (1991). (It is available from Pfeiffer & Company in San Diego, California.)

Stages of Professional Development

Finally, it is clear that various team members are always at different stages in their professional development. The leadership style adopted by a multicultural team leader will also need to take into account the different needs of group members for support or delegation of responsibility.

FIGURE 6-13
Situational Leadership Matrix

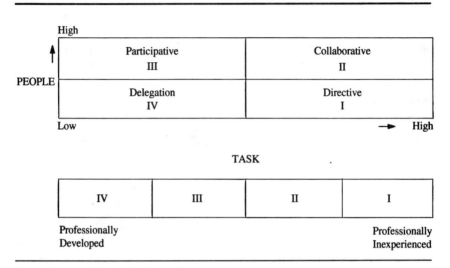

Source: Hersey and Blanchard, 1976, p. 45

One of the best frameworks for understanding leadership style under different staff and environmental conditions is Blanchard and Hersey's situational leadership theory. Figure 6-13 provides an overview of its main elements.

In this model, a leader changes his or her leadership style depending on the external situation as well as the amount of professional experience and competence of the team.

Leaders may be highly directive (I) in times of crisis or when there is a great deal at stake. They may be more collaborative (II) when there is time to consult with others to get their input for a decision which, in style II, is still made by the leader.

In situations III and IV, the leader turns over authority to make decisions, either to a group in which he participates (III) or to an individual or team to whom he delegates (IV).

The less experienced the team and/or more urgent the need for a decision, the more directive the leader will need to be. The more experienced the team members and/or more time available for a decision or action, the more a leader can delegate responsibility to team members.

Such a view of leadership, however, is culturally dependent. In cultures where leaders are expected to have the answers to all the questions their subordinates might ask (as we saw earlier in Andre Laurent's study), participative leadership may not be appreciated at any time.

Many workers in more stratified and hierarchical societies such as those in Asia and Latin America feel their boss loses face if he tries to be too much like the worker. In these cultures, all people have their place and should accept the roles society has assigned to them. If not, all those associated with them, including their subordinates, may lose face when a superior acts in a way that is not in accordance with his position.

GUIDELINES FOR DIAGNOSING THE EFFECTIVENESS OF MULTICULTURAL TEAMS

These seven variables constitute all the dimensions that need to be considered in leading multicultural teams. The formula can be used in team-building meetings to check factors affecting teamwork. Various elements and instruments can also be used independently to diagnose specific interpersonal or group problems.

When forming a multicultural team or facilitating the development of such a group, however, it is best to begin as one would with monocultural teams until there is a problem that appears to have a cultural basis. While cultural differences can be important, many multicultural teams function very well due to similarities in professional and educational background, corporate socialization, and current interests and objectives.

One of the mistakes that many intercultural specialists have made over the years is to assume that cultural differences were the *primary* driving force in multicultural interaction. Many observers have found, however, that most multicultural teams are driven *first* by personal factors and issues of team development such as roles, responsibilities, power, and conflict.

Differences in national culture, while important, are usually secondary. When they are present as a source of team difficulties, they often involve differences in thinking patterns that affect problem-solving and decision-making styles, differences in leadership expectations, and differences in conflict management styles.

Many multicultural teams have also found that these differences are most pronounced during periods of stress. One way to test a multicultural team's effective integration is to place them under stress with stakes that affect their personal future. Any differences that exist will probably surface. This is particularly true if the team is tired, suffering from jet lag, or suffering from any other physical adaptation to the local culture.

The mistake made by many managers is not that they leap to cultural solutions from personal differences, but that they do not know enough about cultural differences to determine whether or not they are a factor. For this reason, the work of Hofstede, Laurent, and Rhinesmith holds new hope for increasing the understanding and capacity of global managers to lead their multicultural teams more effectively.

To return to our earlier promise to ensure that this chapter can be used operationally, there are a few guidelines that can be applied to multicultural team analysis. When developing or diagnosing a multicultural team, a manager or facilitator should use the following order in examining potential team difficulties.

1. *Personal styles*—to what extent do personal differences create conflict or inefficiency?

2. *Stage of team development*—are people clear about roles, responsibilities, power, and how to manage differences and conflict?

3. *Effective team functioning*—where are there problems in team problem solving, communication, and decision making? Are the team norms of behavior well developed and understood? Are these norms functional or dysfunctional to team operations?

4. *Stage of professional development*—are there problems created by team members overreaching their development stage or others assuming too much competence on the part of inexperienced members?

If difficulty is encountered in any one of these four areas and an answer does not appear to be found in any one of the theories applied to these issues, then it is important to look at the three sources of potential underlying cultural differences. It should be stressed, however, that this is usually a secondary, rather than primary area of analysis, since the majority of problems that multicultural teams face are similar to any other team.

5. *National culture*—are there differences in perception of self, others, the world, patterns of thinking, language, or nonverbal behavior causing problems?

6. *Corporate culture*—are there differences in corporate values and interests, or norms and styles of behavior creating difficulties?

7. *Functional culture*—are there differences due to different functions or professional disciplines?

With these seven areas for diagnosis, it is likely that a multicultural team leader, member, or facilitator will be able to determine the source(s) of ineffective team operation, which is the first step toward correcting it.

The objective of the exercise is not just to gain a better understanding of multicultural teams, but to lead and develop teams that are flexible, mobile, adaptable, and able to solve complex problems anywhere in the world.

As Robert Reich notes, "creative teams solve and identify problems in much the same way whether they are developing new software, dreaming up a new marketing strategy, seeking scientific discovery, or contriving a new financial ploy." They are horizontally coordinated, and because problems and solutions cannot be defined in advance, formal problem-solving meetings are less important than frequent communications and interaction, which provide creative solutions to "creative problems" (Reich, 1991, p. 88).

KEY PRACTICES AND TASKS FOR MANAGING MULTICULTURAL TEAMS

Multicultural team leadership has its challenges, but it also has its rewards. You may have become slightly intrigued by the prospect of working effectively with people from many cultures. This may be one of the most exciting aspects of becoming a global manager.

Some of the personal mindset, characteristic, competence, practices, and tasks associated with effective multicultural team leadership are outlined below.

Competence IV: Managing Multicultural Teams

Definition: Ability to manage teams that represent diversity in functional skills, experience levels, and cultural backgrounds with cultural sensitivity and self-awareness, which uses differences for creative innovations, while managing conflicts constructively.

Action and Mindset: Value diversity

Characteristic: Sensitivity

Key Practices and Tasks

1. Learn and use an understanding of the basic *dimensions of cross-cultural behavior* and their impact on managerial style and organizational functioning.
   1.1 Read management literature that describes how managers in other cultures manage their work and their people.
   1.2 Apply management ideas from other societies to your own unit to improve its productivity and/or effectiveness.

FIGURE 6-14
Global Competency Learning Cycle (Managing Uncertainty)

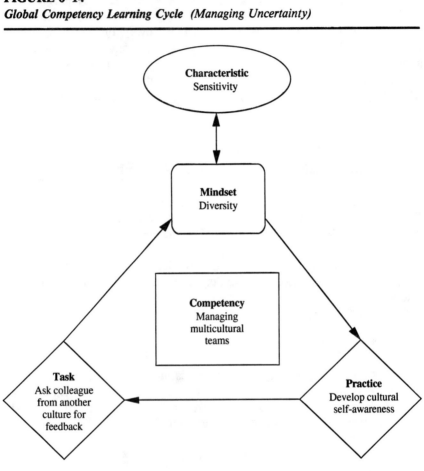

2. Develop *cultural self-awareness,* which allows you to contrast your own culture with other cultures to allow flexible movement from one culture to another.

    2.1 Read books that describe the cultural perceptions, values, and behaviors of people from your culture and become aware of the biases you bring to your job as a result of your national background.

2.2 Ask a colleague from another culture to give you semiannual feedback on how your management actions are seen from his or her cultural perspective.

Along with flexibility, cross-cultural sensitivity is the second most often mentioned desired characteristic of a global manager that I have encountered in my interviews of chief executive officers and senior managers from global organizations around the world. Its relationship to our fourth key competence is shown in the example of the global competency learning cycle in Figure 6–14.

Developing cultural self-awareness is probably one of the most important practices that global managers can undertake. It's critical for the management of multicultural teams. Unfortunately, most international organizations are curiously reluctant to provide adequate cross-cultural training to any but a few managers who are being transferred overseas as expatriates.

The truth is that a successful global organization must provide cross-cultural exposure and develop cross-cultural sensitivity in *all* its managers, whether domestic or international, so that they are able to work with other parts of the organization around the globe with whom they are interdependent, not to mention working with global customers, suppliers, and competitors.

AFTERTHOUGHTS FOR GLOBAL MINDSETS

There are several things you can do to develop a better understanding of multicultural teamwork.

1. Read the two books by Harris and Moran, *Managing Cultural Diversity* and *Managing Cultural Synergy* (1987) for an overview of the influence of culture on management activities and some understanding of various management perspectives in different regions of the world.

2. For better understanding of the effect of culture on Western Europe and EC 1992, read *Mind Your Manners* (1990) by the British journalist John Mole.

3. To gain the best understanding of American culture and its effect on your life, read Edward C. Stewart and Milton Bennett, *American Cultural Patterns* (1991).

4. To further understand the unfolding challenges for management in Eastern and Central Europe, look at *Behind Factory Walls* (1990) by Paul Lawrence and Charalambos Vachousticos.

5. For one of the most penetrating examinations of what makes Japanese process management a success, read *Kaizen* (1989) by Imai.

6. Make an agreement with a global manager in another part of your organization from a different country to meet at least twice a year to discuss the influence of culture on your work together and within your company.

7. The next time you are on a multicultural team, think about the cultural, personal, and team development issues outlined in the formula in the early part of this chapter. You will discover yourself getting much more out of the team meetings than the substance of the discussions—and growing personally richer in the process.

8. Remember the "Lessons from Geese."

As each goose flaps its wings, it creates an 'uplift' for the bird following. By flying in a V formation, the whole flock adds 71% more flying range than if each bird flew alone.

Lesson: People who share a common direction and sense of community can go further and get where they are going quicker and easier because they are traveling on the thrust of one another.

Whenever a goose falls out of formation, it suddenly feels the drag and resistance of trying to fly alone, and quickly gets back into formation to take advantage of the 'lifting power' of the bird immediately in front.

Lesson: If we have as much sense as a goose, we will stay in formation with those who are headed where we want to go.

When the lead goose gets tired, it rotates back into formation and another goose flies at the point position.

Lesson: It pays to take turns doing the hard tasks and sharing leadership with people, as with geese, who are interdependent with each other.

The geese in formation honk from behind to encourage those up front to keep up their speed.

Lesson: We need to make sure our honking from behind is encouraging—not something less than helpful.

When a goose gets sick or wounded or shot down, two geese drop out of formation and follow it down to help and protect him. They stay with the goose until it is either able to fly again, or dies. Then they launch out on their own with another formation or catch up with the flock.

Lesson: If we have as much sense as geese, we will stand by each other like that. [Anonymous]

Chapter Seven

Managing Uncertainty

The rules of the infinite game must change in the course of play.

Carse, p. 11

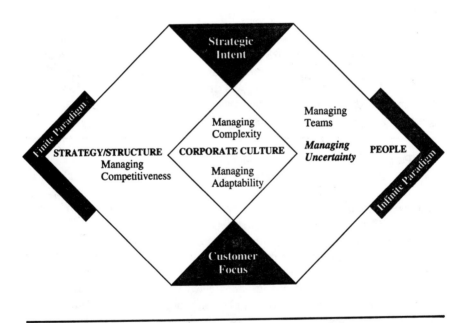

FORETHOUGHTS FROM A GLOBAL MIND

Continuous change—not stability—is the dominant influence in global business activities today. This demands not only new skills, but also new comfort zones for you as a global manager. Your traditional role of making order out of chaos is shifting to one of continuously managing change and chaos in ways that are responsive to customers and competitive conditions.

The idea that change—not stability—will be the regular and understood frame of reference for your life may constitute a *major paradigm shift* for you. Taken further, it means that you probably will need to learn to feel differently and gain comfort with ambiguity. For some managers, it means they must change their self-concept and even their determination of self-worth.

This change in self-concept and self-worth emanates from the fact that most of us have grown up believing that we were good managers if we could demonstrate control over the range of situations that confront us. When was the last time you had to assure your boss that everything is under control? Probably not too long ago.

Well, in this new world, "under control" is going to have to have a new meaning for you and your boss. If you apply the old paradigm, you are going to have constant feelings of inadequacy and failure and you may well be focusing on the wrong levers to ensure the long-term health of your organization.

Managing uncertainty can be a deeply threatening personal experience. In this chapter we will summarize the accumulated impact of the preceding chapters and examine what it means for your feelings about yourself and your work. In the next chapter we will discuss the HRD implications of our learnings to determine what they may mean for preparing managers like yourself to operate in an increasingly uncertain global arena.

"Permanent white water"—that's how one author describes our current time of turbulence and uncertainty (Vaill, 1989, p. 1). As many global organizations appear to be on the brink of spinning out of control, some managers are asking if they are trying to manage chaos, instead of change.

James Carse, our guide through this journey, maintains that "the rules of an infinite game must change in the course of play." If we see global management as an infinite process of continuous improvement and change, we will need to move beyond the rules of a finite, fixed management philosophy and be open to constant change and revision in the way in which we do things. Control, in the old sense of planning, organizing, and *controlling,* is probably no longer an appropriate way to think about management.

Let's break this down into some concepts and practices that will help you work effectively as a global manager in this new constantly changing world.

Peter Vaill, in his description of white-water rafting, comes closest to describing the control challenge facing global managers today. "Things are often only very partially under control, yet the effective navigator of the rapids is not behaving randomly or aimlessly. Intelligence, experience and skill are being exercised, albeit in ways that we hardly know how to perceive, let alone describe" (1989, p. 2).

White-water rafting is perhaps the best way to think of your responsibilities as a global manager. Your world, as we have seen, is complex, requires constant adaptation, and involves the management of teams from many different cultures. In such a world, things are often only very partially under control. At the same time, you are exercising your intelligence, experience, and skill to keep your organization from tipping over.

At this point it is important to note that there is a critical difference between *a lack of total control and a sense of helplessness*. White-water rafting places the right emphasis on the use of skill and ability to maintain equilibrium within a flow beyond control. Remember our earlier reference to *wu-wei*, the Chinese nonaction in a desire to follow the "constant flow of transformation and change."

Learning to go with the flow is a fundamental part of global management. Learning not to be swept uncontrollably into dangerous or life-threatening waters, however, requires the global management *skills* we are discussing in this book.

UNCERTAINTY AND GLOBAL MANAGEMENT

Vaill quotes Ralph Siu (1980) who has fantasized a game he calls Chinese baseball. "It's just like American baseball, except that when the ball is in the air, anyone is allowed to pick up any base and move it—anywhere!" This is a game, says Vaill, that "no one knows how to play" (1989, p. 8).

While global management may at times feel like Chinese baseball when you first approach it, there are obviously ways to play the game that can increase your chance of succeeding. We have been discussing many of these in our previous chapters.

Don Schon, in the *Reflective Practitioner,* suggests the lack of clarity, which international managers face in their work, results in situations that managers describe as "the swamp" (Schon, 1983). He observes that people frequently depend on technical rationality to solve problems, while most problems in the swamp call for more right-brain, intuitive, action-learning approaches.

Marsick and Cederholm note a similar pattern, which they describe in the following manner:

> International managers struggle with their judgment over problems that increasingly fall outside the realm of the right answer into this grey area of 'the maybe,' 'the probably' and 'the likely.' To formulate the problem correctly and implement a solution when working internationally, managers must frequently depart from comfortable cultural norms. [Marsick and Cederholm, 1988, p. 6]

Of all the competencies we are examining, the management of uncertainty is perhaps one of the most difficult to understand and deal with. If you turn to a dictionary, you will see why managing uncertainty has its challenges. Here are the words associated with uncertainty in the *Random House Dictionary of the English Language.*

- not clearly or precisely determined; indefinite; unknown
- vague; indistinct
- subject to change; capricious, variable, unstable
- ambiguous; unreliable; undependable
- dependent on chance or unpredictable factors
- unsteady or flickering; of changing intensity

This is an accurate characterization of the way in which many managers in global organizations describe their world. The constant feeling among many new global managers I have worked with is that things are not clearly or precisely determined, that everything seems ambiguous, unreliable, and undependable and that it seems like their former work, which was knowable and manageable, has suddenly become unknowable and unpredictable.

Ralph Stacey, in his excellent new book, *Managing Chaos,* talks about the need for managers to face the unknowable. He writes:

> This new approach is disturbing because it means accepting that you really have no idea what the long-term future holds for your organization . . .
>
> The new approach is about sustaining contradictory positions and behavior in organization . . .
>
> The new approach is about positively using instability and crisis to generate new perspectives, provoking continual questioning and organizational learning through which unknowable futures can be created and discovered . . .
>
> The new approach faces reality and accepts the consequent increase in levels of anxiety as necessary for creative activity . . .
>
> This is perhaps the chief contradiction of all—the structures and behaviors necessary for stable normal management have to coexist with the informality and instability of extraordinary management which is necessary to cope with the unknowable. [Stacey, 1992, pp. 17–18].

If it is any consolation, this is a common feeling. And it is a common feeling not only of global managers, but of *many* managers trying to deal with increased complexity and uncertainty in the world. McCaskey (1982) noted a wide range of sources of ambiguity for all managers in his study, *The Executive Challenge: Managing Change and Ambiguity.* Among the most common is a lack of confidence about understanding what the problem really is, what is really happening, what we want, who is supposed to do what, how to get what we want, and how to determine if we have succeeded.

This description, in turn, is related to some larger issues that many thoughtful writers from Peter Drucker to Tom Peters have been writing about (Drucker, 1980, 1989 and Peters, 1988). This sea change occurring at the end of the 20th century many observers believe is of a magnitude that occurs once every couple of hundred years. Without getting too far off course, let's take a minute to understand some of the bigger, broader picture within which our current discussion of global management is embedded.

PHYSICS AND GLOBAL BUSINESS STRATEGY

Fritjof Capra, in his seminal work *The Turning Point* notes that at the beginning of the 20th century, physicists began extending their understanding of Newtonian physics to the atomic level (Capra, 1982, p. 48). In the process, they discovered something quite shocking. The classical Newtonian laws that had explained so much observable physical activity for over 200 years became obsolete almost overnight. Two new principles challenging Newtonian physics that are relevant to our current investigation of global management are Heisenberg's uncertainty principle and the recent evolution of chaos theory.

Uncertainty Principle

In 1927 Werner Heisenberg, a German physicist, discovered what he called the uncertainty principle. This states that the position and velocity of an object cannot be measured exactly at the same time, even in theory.

For example, in wave theory, every particle has a wave associated with it. The particle is most likely to be found in that part of the wave where its undulations are most intense or uncertain. There is a continuous uncertain reaction between the particle and its wave, and, as one is stabilized the other becomes more unstable. An accurate measurement of one, therefore, involves a relatively large uncertainty in the measurement of the other. In global management, there are many instances that follow the same uncertainty. Market forces and currency fluctuations in particular are at no time precisely measurable, because they are constantly changing based upon a continuous exchange of currency and economies, 24 hours a day. We have the illusion of knowing exchange rates only because convention has established that at a certain time each day, each country's central bank fixes the rate of exchange as a result of the day's trading.

In investment banking, sophisticated mathematical formulations drive the equity derivatives business, as mathematicians, physicists, and computer scientists combine with traders in New York, London, and Tokyo to try to calculate on a split second basis the movement of hundreds of variables that affect the particular buying or selling of financial instruments now and in the future. Hedging, futures, listed options, SWAPS, as well as sophisticated alterations of complex global portfolios are done through extensive mathematical calculations to determine the best method and time to make a trade.

While the Wall Street mavens do very well in reducing uncertainty, they do not eliminate it. Their work, however, is important, because they are using advanced mathematical formulations and computer programming to search for patterns in complexity that otherwise appear to the laymen to have no patterns. While, as Heisenberg has stated, this can never result in absolute certainty, it does result in more certainty than would otherwise be observable. Therein lies their competitive edge in global money management.

Chaos Theory

Our Wall Street example brings us to a second recent development in mathematics that affects our understanding of uncertainty.

Ralph Abraham, an experimental mathematician at the University of California at Santa Cruz, and others in mathematics have founded a branch of mathematical vibration theory based on chaos. Their basic finding is that the Newtonian formula that allows one to establish laws, which are at the same time explanatory and predictive, is no longer true in complex systems. Instead, chaos theory deals with complex phenomena whose course cannot be determined by timelessly valid laws. In other words, complexity that is beyond the rules of a finite game.

George Soros, one of the most successful investors in the history of Wall Street, maintains that in this world of chaos and complexity, events follow a path that is irreversible and unreplicable. They are therefore unknowable in advance and unpredictable according to some rules of the game. Soros also maintains, in his theory of reflexivity, that one of the factors making the world unknowable is that as participants, we are constantly changing the world that we are observing. He maintains that not only is the world complex, but complexity is compounded by our own thinking (Soros, 1991, p. 159).

Predictability and uncertainty are, to a certain extent, a function of the level of analysis. If you are concerned with predicting detailed behavior and events, you must narrow your area of focus until you have reached a certain level of reliability. This, for example is the problem in social science research. In order to have a level of significance, reliability, and consistency in their findings, social researchers have to narrow their research question to a very small subject, like "Under what conditions do Mexican managers find adjustment to Japanese business dinners problematic?"

The broader you proceed in your inquiry, the less reliable and predictable will be your results and the greater will be your uncertainty. Thus, if we tried to answer the question, "Under what conditions do global managers find it difficult to adjust?" we would be left with a level of uncertainty that could not be scientifically provable and predictable.

I have often characterized this dilemma as a paradox in which the level of statistical significance attainable in applied social scientific research is inversely related to the significance of the problem for an operating manager. In other words, it is hard to reliably prove anything that is truly important to global management, because of the complexity of the environment within which we must operate as global managers.

Chaos theory, however, maintains that there *are* patterns that flow from disorder, which can be used in understanding the larger transformation of systems, even if one cannot accurately predict their change in detail. It is this drive for the bigger, broader picture, looking for the megatrends, that constitutes one of the critical skills necessary for managing uncertainty. Let me elaborate a little further.

The level of uncertainty is affected by our expectations. **One of the fundamental messages of this book is that to be a global manager you have to recalibrate your assumptions about certainty, simplicity, and control.**
Ralph Stacey notes:

> In everyday business life managers have to answer questions . . . in a world that is quite clearly characterized by stability and instability, predictability and unpredictability, regularity and irregularity, contention and consensus, intention and chance. The world they face is intertwined order and disorder. When we try to explain what is going on and design actions flowing from those explanations, we almost always approach the task from the perspective of order. In doing so we greatly under-emphasize the role of disorder. [Stacey, 1992, p. 29]

Stacey believes that there is too much emphasis in management today on stability, regularity, predictability and cohesion. He believes that this is a misplaced emphasis. Instead, he believes that managers should stress the management of "bounded instability", as he calls it. Bounded instability is a state in which behavior has a pattern, but it is irregular. He contrasts this with explosive instability, in which behavior and systems go completely out of control and sometimes self-destruct.
Stacey writes:

> **Chaos** is the name that scientists have given to this border area (between stability and explosive instability) . . . It is also known as strange or fractal. Chaos, in its

scientific sense, is not utter confusion. It is not explosive instability. It is constrained instability; a combination of order and disorder in which patterns of
behavior unfold in unpredictable but yet similar, familiar, yet irregular forms
[Stacey, 1992, p. 63].

You need to shift your paradigm to look at the bigger, broader picture and
to look for megatrends and stress fractures on a global basis. If you refocus
on this broader picture, with less expectations of finding rules and more
expectations of finding the next flow in the evolving global environment, the
less you will be concerned about uncertainty, because you will not *expect*
certainty—if you get what I mean.

All these observations underscore a new paradigm that includes chaos as
a natural part of change. Just as the limits of Cartesian and Newtonian thinking have been reached in physics, the idea that everything relevant to successful
management is knowable and controllable must also be abandoned.

Many change formulae over the years have stressed change as a process to
be controlled through the application of principles of management science.
In such instances, these people have viewed chaos as something beyond
control. In this, as in the other complexities of global management, the
answer is not either/or, but the simultaneous management of both views—
some of which are in control and some of which are out of control.

The idea that management needs to clearly juxtapose those things that
are out of control with those that are in control has its roots in World War
II. Management as a science had only been recognized for a decade and the
war was, to a certain extent, the first ultimate test of this new management
science. The challenge, in a way, was to wage a war in a way that was in
control. The postwar era left little doubt that if management was well applied, things could be held in control.

Capra notes that to transcend classical models, scientists will "have to go
beyond the reductionist and mechanistic approach as we have done in physics, and develop holistic and ecological views" (Capra, 1982, p. 49). This
means an increase in complexity and uncertainty that ultimately leads to the
reintegration of the natural sciences and the humanities. In turn, it reveals
our ultimate dependence upon people—their intuition and judgment—
which is the focus of this chapter of our book.

SEEING CHAOS AS A
USER-FRIENDLY ALLY FOR CHANGE

If you think managing chaos is an oxymoron, you must admit that managing change is also in today's world. The difference between the two is that
managing change gives a *false* sense of control, whereas managing chaos, or

bounded instability as Stacey calls it, more accurately describes the need to stay with a process that is fundamentally beyond our control.

Vaill notes that *"comprehension* of what is going on in an organization" and *"control* of what is going there are the unique things that the manager is supposed to bring to the system" (Vaill, 1989, p. 77). He believes, however, that the global manager's capacity to do this is history.

An old world manager who today tries compulsively to use linear-logical, cause-and-effect thinking to understand dynamic, integrated holistic systems is, in Vaill's term, a *technoholic*. This person is also *irrelevant* to the kinds of managerial skills necessary for successful global leadership in the 1990s. Remember, in 1983, Shell conducted a survey of how long business organizations survive. This revealed that corporations live about half as long as individual human beings. The chances are that your organization will die before you do (Stacey, 1992, p. 18).

New Management Paradigms

Three paradigms have characterized Western management in the postwar period (see Evans, Doz, and Laurent, 1990, pp. 222 ff).

In the 1950s and 1960s, the major management concern lay in organizational *structure* as the world tried to restore itself to order after a devastating world war in which vast social, political, and economic systems were destroyed.

During this time the environment was relatively stable after the crushing dislocations of the 1930s and 1940s and attention in the new management profession turned to *systems* to maintain stability. Management processes such as planning, organizing, budgeting, and information systems and performance appraisal systems became tools for stabilization.

In the 1970s and 1980s a new management metaphor was developed with attention turning to human relations and establishing *fit* and *consistency* between people and organizations, and organizations and their environment. Instead of structure, the emphasis turned to strategic management, customer-focused quality, and job design.

All of these approaches are very left-brain and rational. They are attempts to focus on a less complex strategy. But global managers are confronted with a different world. The typical global manager must manage many changes at once. Each, in turn, is in a different phase of the change process. The complexity of this world results in more chaos than change and means that sometimes some things will need to be allowed to be out of control in a way that is seen as healthy and normal.

In the 1990s, the change from a mechanistic to an organic metaphor has begun the paradigm shift that will enable managers to better understand the systemic role of chaos in organizational life. This is one of the reasons Peter Drucker has described the 1990s not as an evolution, but as a sea change from the decades that have gone before (1989).

This new age is characterized by *flexibility* instead of order, *de-layering* and *networking* superseding structure, *teamwork* replacing the individual, *cooperation and strategic alliances* in order to compete; and *developing people* who can live in turbulent, complex, and highly volatile environments rather than planning, organizing, and controlling their lives and the world around them.

As a result, we need a new paradigm for understanding global management in an information society. The old illusion that change can be managed in a way that should always include some element of control must be smashed if global managers are to learn the art of change in a complex world.

Soviet Lessons on Managing Chaos

Mikhail Gorbachev was perhaps the foremost leader in recent years who tried to manage change that was out of control. He did this not as much due to his philosophic predisposition as due to his realization that his situation was beyond control. Any attempt to control the change process in the former Soviet Union, would, in effect, have been a step to reinforce the established order.

This is a critical point. There are situations in *transformational* change when any attempt to control the change process, in effect, leads to a reinforcement of the present order. When organizations and societies become so rigid in their hierarchy and bureaucracy like the Soviet Union did, only radical, transformational white-water change will shake the old structure out of power. A strategy evolves that allows synergistic forces in the system to work toward unknown, but dynamic change.

The complexity of change in Russia, while extreme, has certain similarities to situations faced by managers of diverse global businesses. Oddly enough, Russia (which brought us the vision of managing *every* aspect of complexity through central planning) is now providing one of the most vivid demonstrations of the inadequacy of that method. In fact, if anything, Russia of the early 1990s is a magnificent experiment in the art of managing chaos in its transition to another yet to be determined form.

Ralph Stacey, in his excellent book on *Managing Chaos,* describes the challenge of managing change in Russia today. He writes:

> . . . A preoccupation with order, stability and consistency in all time frames damages management creativity and the ability to cope with the unknowable. When

the future is unknowable you cannot install techniques, procedures, structures or ideologies to control long-term outcomes. . . . They key question is not how to create stable equilibrium organizations, but how to establish sufficient constrained instability to provoke complex learning. It is through complex learning that businesses manage and create unknowable futures [Stacey, 1992, p. 208].

In this process, Gorbachev as manager was a master at managing on the edge of control. For the most part, his interventions were timed not to *control the uncontrollable, but to focus and delineate the boundaries of chaos.* His miscalculation in 1991, which led to the August coup, was the result of setting transformational forces in motion and then trying to manage the boundaries with the old processes (Communist Party, KGB, military, and central bureaucracy), rather than allowing new processes, as well as a new structure to evolve to enable the system to self-manage. *There is a subtle, but significant difference between focusing on control and preventing disintegration* by focusing on bounded instability. The latter is one of the arts of global management.

Gorbachev understood that he was really not in control in the traditional sense. He allowed natural chaotic forces in the system, like political and economic entrepreneurs, to force change in ways that could not be planned. Gorbachev, like many leaders of global corporations, established certain directions, if not a vision, from which the change process was let loose for the system to work out in its own dynamic, decentralized manner.

Yeltsin, on the other hand, is an entrepreneurial revolutionary. He is even *more* willing to throw the system out of control than Gorbachev. This is one of the reasons he has been able to initiate the price reform that Gorbachev was always reluctant to undertake. There are lessons to be learned by global managers from Russia's attempt to move from a *structural bureaucracy* to a *dynamically responsive entrepreneurial enterprise.* One of the scary aspects of this change in the Soviet Republics is the lack of managerial skills among managers to operate in a decentralized environment. This makes a radical decentralization of the economic and political system very risky. It would be equivalent to decentralizing a global corporation with a group of country national managers who had only managed in public bureaucracies.

On the other hand, if Gorbachev had waited to implement radical economic reforms until all managers were trained to operate decentralized, market-driven enterprises, there would never have been reform. Which was exactly Yeltsin's point and the reason he put pressure on Gorbachev from the very beginning to move, even in the face of uncertainty and additional chaos.

In such a case, one has to *force change by creating bounded chaos* without letting it slip into volatile, destructive chaos. In such a situation, managers and enterprises make their own way and survival of the fittest becomes the watchword.

It is clear that many global corporations and managers face a similar, if somewhat less daunting challenge. What is required is the ability to operate from both a left-brain and right-brain perspective, alternating between flow and control. There are few change theories that have recognized this need for contradictory and alternating phases.

A FLOW-CONTROL THEORY OF ORGANIZATIONAL CHANGE

About 45 years ago, one of the founders of the group dynamics movement, Kurt Lewin, formulated a way of describing the change process. He said that people and organizations go through three stages of change.

The first stage involves *unfreezing*. During this time a person or organization has to come to terms with the fact that something is wrong with the current situation and that change is needed.

The second phase, *moving,* requires overcoming the personal and organizational inertia of the past and present. It also involves overcoming resistance to change from people and systems that have vested interests in current patterns of behavior.

The third phase, *refreezing,* acknowledges that no change is permanent until it has been installed. This means that reward systems have been retooled to reward new behavior supporting the change, and there is sufficient success and satisfaction with the new behavior so that the person or organization considers it to be the normal way of operating.

These easy words unfreezing, moving, and refreezing, in use now for over 40 years, have proven to be deceptively simple. The terms are so basic they lead one to believe the process is easy.

We have spent the last 40 years refining these three stages of change and have discovered that, in fact, they constitute a rather complex and difficult process that has meant the difference between life and death for many organizations.

From my own experience in managing corporate change, I have developed an approach that is a combination of left- and right-brain thinking. Like Gorbachev's and Yeltsin's approach, it acknowledges that there are certain aspects of change that can be managed, and others that cannot. The result is a change theory that is on the one hand chaotic, creative, and out of control and on the other hand rational, observable, measurable, and in control.

I call this approach the flow-control theory of change. It is built on four basic principles.

• *The Principle of Unmanageable Reaction*—people need to get used to new ideas, so all change has periods that are not under control, but subject to chaotic, unpredictable, and unmanageable reactions.

• *The Principle of Trustable Process*—during these times, leaders need to trust the process and allow the unmanageable, unknowable, and unpredictable aspects of change to play out in ways that may be far more helpful to the goals of change than anything that could be planned, managed, or controlled.

• *The Principle of Constant Reinforcement*—at the same time, change will not move forward unless there is consistent and continual pressure applied to break down barriers and reinforce and reward new behavior.

• *The Principle of Consistent Attention*—as a result, any leader who is serious about change must make time every day, every week to concentrate on the change process, either engaging in an active intervention or analyzing when no action is the best means to facilitate change.

Six phases of change transpire from these four principles. They are the following.

Stage	Phase	Action
I. Unfreezing	1. Awareness	Letting go (Flow)
	2. Interest	Taking charge (Control)
II. Moving	3. Acceptance	Letting go (Flow)
	4. Experimentation	Taking charge (Control)
III. Refreezing	5. Adaptation	Letting go (Flow)
	6. Installation	Taking charge (Control)

As you can see, these six phases are equated with the three stages identified earlier. Within each of these stages, we have formulated one phase that is out of control (flow) followed by a phase that is in control (control). The result is an alternation of letting go and taking charge. It is important to note that the first step in each stage involves flow, or letting go. **This means that any manager who is unwilling or unable to let things go out of control will more than likely fail to either initiate or sustain significant change.**

Global managers need to learn to manage both flow (letting go) and control (taking charge) as two different aspects of change to successfully manage their complex, geographically diverse organizations.

Let us examine each phase of the flow-control change theory to see how the dynamic operates.

Awareness of Chaos

Many organizations do not survive because they discover too late that change is needed. There are many cases in the international arena such as ITT's ill-fated attempt to operate in European competition with Ericsson and GE's lack of ability to convert it's consumer products group in the face of competition from Matsushita.

Farquahar, Evans, and Tawadey have identified change as evolving from certain trigger events. They cite Jan Carlzon's restructuring of SAS as an example of a crisis-oriented trigger, whereas David Kearn's restructuring of Xerox is a noncrisis trigger (Evans, Doz, and Laurent, 1989, pp. 33–56).

To develop an awareness of the need for change requires an understanding and acceptance of the concept of chaos. Since chaos is always present as a destabilizing force to the current order it can be viewed as a precursor of change and a friend to anyone interested in change. If change is something that must be tended to on an ongoing basis, then chaos is friendly to change-oriented people.

If we do not accept this first basic principle of change, we will have little hope of proceeding through the next stages of change.

Organizational Interventions to Develop Awareness.   Seeing chaos as user friendly is not easy. But it is a critical shift for anyone interested in facilitating change. Gareth Morgan, in *Riding the Waves of Change* (1988), speaks of the search for the "fracture lines" that will signal directional changes for the future.

The identification of these fracture lines in a chaotic environment is one organizational intervention that senior global managers can take to anticipate sea changes, which may affect the long- or short-term interests of the business. In a retreat setting, or in ongoing global scanning, managers can be guided to look for opportunities not in what is evident, but in strategic fracture lines where cracks that could signal wholesale change in the future are evident.

These fracture lines can signal both danger and opportunity, but if a global organization does not have an active search process, they are likely to go unidentified until some rupture brings them to the open in a way that could be highly disruptive to the organization.

Interest in Change

Once a potential for change has been identified, the organization needs to respond in a more logical, left-brain manner. Many times the first step is to call the need for change to people's attention in a way that develops their interest. Oddly enough, many managers assume that when other managers and staff are aware that the organization is in trouble, or faces an unusual opportunity, they will be interested in doing something about it. Sadly, experience has shown this is not always the case.

Frequently, people become aware of a trend that is negatively or positively affecting the organization, but believe that outside forces beyond their control are the cause. As a result, they may struggle against these forces, rather than examine the forces that are reinforcing or inhibiting the change and orient their behavior in this direction. If, in fact, organization change is spurred by chaotic forces that by definition are beyond control, this means that there needs to be a new definition of the kinds of factors that should be examined by leaders and managers to determine the need for organizational change.

To develop real interest in organizational change, employees must feel that the change is meaningful to them. Farquahar (1989) talks about the need to "sell the crisis" before it actually hits the bottom line. Marks and Spencer, an extremely successful British retailer, is an example of a company which, although it attempted an abortive move into the international market, found the process helped its employees see the need for change in other areas in order to maintain their industry leadership (Evans, et. al., 1989, pp. 39–40).

Organizational Interventions to Develop Interest. One well-known method that can be used to plan and manage change is a force-field analysis. In this process, people are encouraged to analyze change by listing all the forces inhibiting a desired change on one side of a line, and all the forces reinforcing the change on the other.

These forces are weighted according to their estimated strength of influence. This is represented by the length of the line drawn to represent each force. The basic premise of a force-field analysis is that more progress toward change will be made more by overcoming the areas of least resistance than by reinforcing the forces for change. Experience has shown that reinforcement often leads to an equal and opposite force against the change process. Old Newtonian laws are still valid—even in organizational life.

Acceptance of Chaos

Once an awareness of chaos has been developed, strategic fracture lines have been identified, and force-field analyses have been conducted, managers need to accept the fact that there are some things that will not be immediately controlled. In fact, there may be some things best left unattended.

I first learned this lesson during a short assignment with the U.S. government. I asked the State Department desk officer in charge of Soviet affairs for policy guidance concerning how much we wanted to tell the Soviets about managing change. The answer I received was a classic State Department response, but perhaps more insightful than they are usually given credit for. The answer was, "We have studied the issues and determined it is best not to have a policy on this matter at the current time."

This is the practice of *wu-wei* discussed in Chapter Four. Believe it or not, State Department personnel, of all people, may be masters at managing change through accepting the fact that at certain times no policy is better than some policy as one waits to see how factors beyond our control play out.

Organizational Interventions to Stimulate Acceptance of Need for Change. It is difficult to get people to let change go after they have done their force-field analyses and begun to concentrate on how to manage various inhibiting factors. On the other hand, force-field analysis acknowledges that there are certain forces that may be too strong to tackle and that it is better to wait them out.

It also acknowledges that action to reinforce existing trends may lead to equal, but perhaps unpredictable counterforces. Implicit in all of this is an acknowledgment that the process of change is managing those things which can be changed, while not managing those things that can't be changed and having the wisdom to know the difference, to paraphrase a well-known proverb.

In this case, the best organizational intervention to stimulate acceptance of chaos is to identify those factors that are subject to managed change and those that are not. It is also important during this phase in the change process to note things that will *not* be changed.

Change creates enough resistance from people who have a reason to be threatened without creating resistance among people who think erroneously that somehow they are next on the hit list. Better to identify areas where no change is anticipated and line these people up as allies for the changes that will have to occur.

Experimentation with Change

This fourth phase marks a change from interest to action. After an organization has become aware of the need for change, analyzed forces operating for and against the changes needed, and accepted what can and cannot be changed, it needs to experiment with a variety of ways to implement the changes needed.

Phase four emphasizes new behavior needed to work on the forces that can be affected by action. To build commitment to change requires opportunities for people to behave differently and to become personally involved in the change process in a way that is meaningful to them and can give them a sense of satisfaction.

As a result, this phase of the change process needs to be planned, developed, and implemented in a very logical fashion in order to ensure that the organization begins taking corrective action for the problems identified.

Organizational Interventions to Encourage Experimentation. The major method used by most organizations to encourage experimentation is training. Whether the subject is globalization, quality, or customer service, training programs have evolved as a mainstay of organizational change.

In addition to training, the formation of action-research-learning teams has become a critical method for managing change in organizations. Teams are mutually supportive, but can also be highly entrepreneurial units when well managed. On a global scale, as we saw in Chapter Five, teams can be the key to organizational synergy, creativity, and innovation.

Within all of this, the corporate culture needs to be supportive of change projects. Rewarded behavior has often been as critical in allowing organizations and individuals to experiment with new forms of behavior. In other words, permission needs to be given for experimentation in new directions, which may eventually solve the challenge the organization is facing.

Adaptation to Chaos

The best planned and executed training programs do not result in behavior changes exactly according to the theories and practices advocated during classroom time. Instead, people must be encouraged to adapt what they have learned to their own circumstances so as to make it relevant and meaningful for them.

The adaptation process also acknowledges that there are elements of chaos in every back-home situation which must, in turn, be allowed for. The rules of the game are in constant change especially when one changes geographical, functional, or product locations in a global organization. Allowances have to be made for local adaptation of global theories, practices, and mandates.

Organizational Interventions to Assist in Adaptation.   The variety of managerial tasks in a global corporation fall into three categories—control, change, and flexibility.

Corporations that successfully adapt to change understand that structure is not the ultimate answer and it is impossible to restructure one's way to success on a global basis. If the answer is anywhere, it is building in the capacity to manage change and maintain flexibility in the face of environmental volatility (Prahalad and Doz, 1989, p. 170).

Examples of this are the use of human resource management at Ciba-Geigy and Ericsson's use of strategic framing to create variety and breadth in decision making. Many global organizations have spent much time on technology transfer (ITT, NEC, and Ericsson) and other methods of ensuring that centrally developed ideas are adapted to local needs. Many have realized in the process that technology needs to be adapted to the different cultures of the world.

In addition to technology transfer training, international task forces and global-local task teams can many times work on adaptation procedures that can improve global ideas for local application. When done within a glocal team, lessons learned at the local level can be fed back to the global level to modify future global initiatives.

Installation of Change

Finally, for any change to become aligned, installed, or embedded in a corporate culture, it must be consciously and consistently reinforced over time.

At times it is necessary to even destroy the old culture in order to embed new values, norms, and behaviors. Olivetti has developed its own approach to the management of a major change program. It can be summarized as "fire, hire and build a new culture" (Evans et. al., 1990, p. 40).

For other organizations, this so-called second wave of change, is a longer process, anchored in the organization's systems and procedures. This change strategy is most often directed toward middle management, and, as in the case of SAS, it takes a longer time to implement than the Olivetti philosophy.

Rewards are important throughout all phases of the change process, and especially in the installation phase. The only way that people will move from one phase to the next is if they have a positive, reinforcing experience that allows them to feel good about their new behavior.

Organizational Interventions to Assist in Installation of Change. No change takes place in isolation. All change is a complex renegotiation of the structure and processes that hold certain kinds of behavior in place. As a result, it is impossible to talk about installing change in an organization without talking about its corporate culture and the degree to which a corporate culture hinders or is friendly to the change that is being implemented.

In most instances, changes of any magnitude affect an organization's corporate culture and create the need for a very persistent and long term program of change directed at values, attitudes, and behaviors. This is a very control-oriented, left-brain phase of the change process and its operation needs to be highly analytical and rational.

This last phase entails not merely encouraging people to behave differently, but also changing the information systems to ensure that they have the information they need for the new behavior and ultimately changing the reward systems to ensure that they are recognized for their new behavior. Only in this way will behavior change be installed and become the new routine behavior.

The ultimate catch-22, however, is that no behavior in the global organizations of the 1990s can become routine again. Instead, there needs to be consistent scanning for new threats and opportunities to start the process all over again to create a new organizational change that will lead through the next six stages.

NEW MINDSETS FOR FLOW MANAGEMENT

George Bernard Shaw once observed that all progress depends on unreasonable men. He argued that reasonable men adapt themselves to the world, whereas unreasonable men persist in trying to adapt the world to themselves.

The *real* human resource challenge in globalization is the development of right-brain, intuitive skills through which global managers develop the personal mindsets and behavioral capacities to operate in this uncertain global world—what I have chosen to call flow management.

The basic thesis of this book has been that the world is becoming more complex and less predictable, requiring organizations that are more complex and less predictable, therefore requiring managers that are able to deal with complexity and ambiguity.

Charles Handy, in his seminal work *The Age of Unreason* notes:

> . . . we are now entering the Age of Unreason, when the future, in so many areas, is there to be shaped by us and for us—a time when the only prediction that will hold true is that no predictions will hold true; a time, therefore, for bold imaginings in the private life as well as public, for thinking the unlikely and doing the unreasonable. [Handy, 1990, p. 5]

Flow dominant management requires managers who have five basic characteristics:

- The ability to feel comfortable with ambiguity.
- The capacity to see uncertainty as opportunity.
- The desire to view things differently.
- The ability to translate opportunity into concrete products, services, strategies, and structures.
- The ability to see the potential obsolescence of all products, services, strategies, and structures.

Let's look into each of these a little further.

Comfort with Increased Ambiguity in Decision Making

Global management is more complex because one faces the challenge of managing increased ambiguity in decision making. This results from being exposed to many more variables and broader issues that often have philosophical, moral, and cultural dimensions, as well as business considerations. This makes the decision process more ambiguous.

To attack this problem, global managers scan differently. They track additional factors in their decision making. They are sensitive to different interests and needs. And in the end, they must be clearer than ever about their purpose, priorities, and vision in order to make the decisions that are in the best interests of the corporation.

The irony of all of this is that *the more ambiguous a situation becomes, the simpler and clearer need to be the criteria for decision making.* Jimmy Carter is the best example of a recent global leader who made the mistake of dealing with complexity with complex criteria.

Carter was undoubtedly one of the brightest presidents of the United States. He was extremely analytical and thorough in his decision making. In fact, he was so thorough that he found himself accused of inconsistency, because for each problem he would conduct an exhaustive analysis in which he would become buried in detail, reaching conclusions which at times were contradictory to the last conclusion he reached on a similar issue.

Part of this dilemma is what I call the *decision-ascendancy principle*. According to this, the higher one goes in an organization, the more complex are the decisions and the less available is the necessary information to make the decision. Judgment and clarity of vision therefore become much more critical factors than at lower organizational levels.

This is not an odd phenomenon if one thinks about it. At lower levels of an organization, the information necessary to make a decision is generally available if one has the skills and abilities to access and properly analyze it. When the weight of evidence for a decision after analysis is 70 percent to 30 percent, lower levels of management can make the final decision.

But as one progresses up through an organization, the decision-ascendancy principle begins to enter in. The information available for analysis and action becomes more sparse, the judgment factor increases and middle managers begin passing decisions up, because they do not want to take the risk or they do not have the authority to make decisions in which the choice is not clearly supported by data and analysis.

By the time decisions reach the top of a corporation or the top of a government, the evidence is many times 51 percent in favor and 49 percent against a particular decision. It is then that the decision-making process moves from analysis to judgment. And judgment depends on clarity of vision, principle, and purpose, not on level of information and detailed analysis.

One should not assume, therefore, that the management of ambiguity requires just a little more data information or analysis to come to a conclusion. Managers who take this path are waiting for the tough decisions to be made for them by the information available. Tough decisions are not made for you—you have to make them.

Uncertainty as Opportunity

Traditional management philosophy has rewarded managers for closing off uncertainty. We have stressed probability analysis, moderate risk taking, and risk analysis for loss prevention as key behaviors for which we recognize and compensate our managers.

The ability to see uncertainty as opportunity is being tested today throughout Eastern and Central Europe as hundreds of Western lawyers and accountants pore over early market, technology, and political risk reports indicating a variety of uncertain horizons in the region. The future development of Eastern and Central Europe is not being fought out on their territory as much as it is in the offices of Western corporations worldwide, where the struggle continues between left brain and right brain for investment and trade opportunities full of uncertainty and risk.

As a result, we find that there are two kinds of companies investing in these uncertain areas. The first are small entrepreneurial, wholly-owned companies where an individual or family can decide to risk personal funds. The second are large corporations where the CEO is strong enough to offset the natural and responsible caution coming out of the staff legal and financial departments.

Desire to View Things Differently

With all the talk about paradigm shifts, we often stress ability, rather than desire. It is perfectly possible that many people do not shift their paradigms, not because they are unable to, but because they have absolutely no desire or motivation.

Motivating people to shift their world view, as Joel Barker writes in *Discovering the Future,* is one of the most fundamental aspects of leadership. The great leaders of the world like Churchill, Lincoln, Martin Luther King, and Gorbachev have been people who could motivate others to change their paradigm. They have accomplished this either because of a view of a better life or from an understanding of the pain associated with continuing their current view.

Daryl Connor, president of ODR, Inc., and a specialist in change management notes that "pain management" is one of the greatest reasons why people are willing to change their thinking and their lives. In fact, he and some other researchers believe it is impossible for the vast majority of people to change significantly without a sufficient amount of pain being associated with their current state to drive them to seek an alternative.

One of the assumptions behind all management training and development is that we can educate people to adopt new worldviews through the pull of new possibilities rather than the push of pain. In fact, this is an implicit assumption behind much of HRD, not only in management training, but also in coaching, counseling, and consulting. While there is no simple answer to the push/pull approach to perceptual and behavioral change, it would seem that a balanced perspective is key. This means that we should continue to try to find pedagogical paradigms and methods that will attract people to new ways of viewing the world, while at the same time developing pain indicators that might assist in pushing change in the direction necessary.

Making Opportunity Actionable

There are thousands of opportunities that present themselves to people every day. Of these, there are hundreds that are seen by a majority of the population. Of those that are seen, however, there are relatively few that are actually turned into products, services, strategies, and tactics to become new opportunities for service, profit, or change in the world.

To make opportunity actionable, global managers have to first view change as friendly, look beyond the chaos of the moment to the opportunities being opened by instability, and then move swiftly and decisively to act on intuition in a way that turns these opportunities into concrete products or services. This requires a combination of right-brain intuition, left-brain analysis, and right- and left-brain action, which is seldom found in the general population, but which must be a prime quality of global managers.

Global opportunities often do not provide the luxury of detailed analyses to reduce risk and increase the chance of success. Instead, global managers must seize opportunities and move at a faster and harder pace than those managers who enjoy taking their time, examining all the angles, and feeling comfortable that all their down-side risks are covered. This is not a game for the timid.

Drumming Obsolescence out of Order

On the other side of the equation, a global manager must not only be able to seize opportunity from chaos, but should also be prepared to drum obsolescence out of order. There are many organizations operating in the international arena who go out of business because of their obsession with past traditions, past ideas, and past successes.

Effective global managers understand that durability of global products and services needs to be measured in months, rather than years. The number and speed of global competitors, combined with global scanning information systems, means that any new product success is immediately spotted by the competition and, if there is a good market for it, the chances are that someone will be there with an alternate choice within a very short time.

As a result, effective global managers understand that their most vulnerable products and ideas are those which have been successful over the long haul—these are prime candidates for obsolescence through erosion of market share to an aggressive competitor.

An effective global manager does not assume that the normal state of the world is a long-term cash cow. Instead, he or she is constantly analyzing what is winning today to determine its vulnerability tomorrow.

Anticipating future needs, seizing new opportunities, living with ambiguity, seeking new paradigms, and drumming obsolescence out of order are all aspects of global mindset right-brain activity necessary for effective global management.

KEY PRACTICES AND TASKS FOR MANAGING UNCERTAINTY

Below is a list of some of the practices and tasks you can engage in to develop a better feel for managing uncertainty.

Competence V: Managing Uncertainty

Definition: Ability to manage continuous change and uncertainty on a personal and organizational level, ensuring that an adequate blend of flow and control are achieved, which enables the organization to be responsive to changes in the environment in a timely fashion.

Action and Mindset: Flow with change

Personal Characteristic: Judgment

Key Practices and Tasks

1. Work with *continuous global change,* rather than stability as the norm and learn to navigate in perpetual white water.

   1.1 Analyze what aspects of your job are subject to outside change, which should be reviewed for change from the inside and what the shelf life of your policies, practices, and procedures should be to remain relevant to changes in your industry and profession.

2. Create *new opportunities out of change and chaos,* rather than trying to re-establish the old order.

   2.1 Examine the changing conditions around you for new products, policies, practices, or procedures that can increase your personal, professional, or organizational efficiency and/or effectiveness.

3. Manage *change as a cyclical process* of taking charge and letting go, flow and control, using right-brain as well as left-brain thinking skills.

FIGURE 7–1
Global Competency Learning Cycle (Managing Uncertainty)

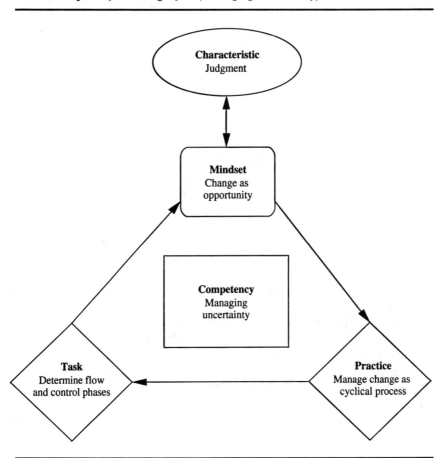

3.1 Determine which phases of change must be controlled and which phases must be left alone for their own development, thereby resisting the tendency to manage the change process through continual control.

Some of these factors are related to the global competency learning cycle as shown in Figure 7-1.

This will be a new world. Most of us today derive security from structure. But if you think about it for a moment, a democracy derives security from process—like due process and the free market. Our problem is that for years we have identified security with organizational structure and as a result we have not spent much time feeling comfortable with organizational process. As we have noted throughout this work, however, global corporations are more process than structure. Global managers, therefore, must feel as comfortable with process as with structure.

AFTERTHOUGHTS FOR GLOBAL MINDSETS

This exploration of the management of uncertainty has one central message—as global managers we can no longer depend on rules, or even traditional left-brain knowledge. Instead, our ability to succeed will be based on judgment that is developed by broadening our perspective and trusting people, organizations, and organizational processes from time to time to go out of control, in the traditional sense. **Any global manager who is afraid to occasionally let go will be doomed to be left behind, concentrating on control, while the world—and opportunities—flow away.**

This kind of flow-driven global organization with flow-comfortable managers by definition will need to be a learning organization. Learning derives from process, not from structure. To play infinite games, global managers must be open to constant learning from playing with organizational process. This process, as we have seen in our earlier discussions of global corporate culture, allows global organizations to be resilient, flexible, and adaptive to changes in the environment. Ultimately, this process-oriented paradigm is the formula for success—as a global organization and as a global manager.

Chapter Eight

Managing Learning

Because infinite players prepare themselves to be prepared for the future, they play in complete openness. To be prepared against surprise is to be trained . . . to be prepared for surprise is to be educated.

Carse, p. 23

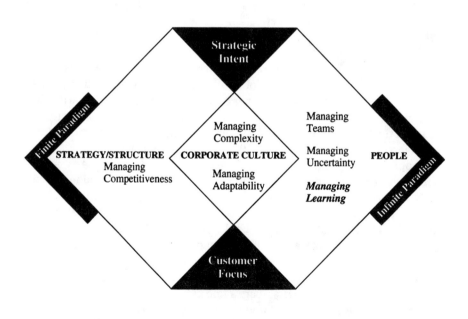

FORETHOUGHTS FROM A GLOBAL MIND

As we come to our sixth and final competence, managing personal and organizational learning, it should be no surprise to you that human resource managers throughout the world are challenged by how to help their man-

163

agers grow, adapt, and thrive in the kind of global organization we have been describing.

Most people are beginning to realize that the 1990s are ushering in a new time in which the complexities, uncertainties, and challenges we have been describing will increasingly become part of *every* manger's life. This will be true whether you reside here in the United States and operate nationally or travel globally in search of markets, capital, technology, facilities, and skills.

Personal adaptation to the changing conditions, cultures, and operating requirements of global enterprise represents a significant and largely unfunded training need. Development of global managers in most American businesses has been *ad hoc,* rather than systematic and there is a great need to develop a more orderly movement toward the mindsets, competencies, and practices of effective global management.

Whatever the challenges, it is clear that you as a manager in a global organization will have to manage accelerated change in your life and in the life of your organization. As a result, finding the time and methods for personal and organizational reflection and learning will be critical to your fulfillment and the success of your organization.

The management of global learning, on a personal and organizational level, has been developed in only a few forward-thinking companies. Many of the attitudes and skills for global adaptation can be provided in well-structured learning and training experiences. But complete growth will come only when training and personal on-the-job experiences are integrated to reflect a thoughtful, institutionalized development process. For most global managers, that process can and will be a lifelong journey.

People are, after all, the ultimate answer to global success. And in globally savvy organizations, the human resource function is becoming increasingly important. It may even be that one of these days there will be a chief HRD officer with the CEO, COO, and CFO to run global organizations. In this case, the chief HRD officer could be responsible for developing the global corporate culture and global human resources necessary to achieve the strategic business objectives of the organization.

If you are an HRD manager, this chapter will state the challenge for you in the globalization effort. If you are a line manager, we will show you where you may want to invest some time and resources in yourself and others in your unit to develop the competencies necessary to keep your division or company relevant for the years ahead.

We have been discussing the mindsets and competencies managers need to operate effectively on a global basis. It is one thing to identify and describe these areas and quite another to develop them. Let's consider what an integrated plan for developing managers to operate successfully in a global organization would look like.

CORPORATE GLOBALIZATION AND GLOBAL COMPETENCIES

If you recall our discussion in Chapter One on the evolution of corporations from domestic to global, and our discussion in Chapter Two of the mindsets and competencies needed for global management, it becomes apparent that there are different degrees of global competencies needed at different stages in global organization development.

The movement from domestic to global leadership involves a transition not only in geographic focus, but also in attention to process over structure, seeking out change rather than defending against it, creating chaos rather than avoiding it and moving to a more free-flowing, open, integrated systems mindset that stresses adaptability of both people and global corporate culture.

Shifting from a domestic organization to a global corporation is not just a matter of strategy and structure, but culture and people. This involves a fundamental change in style, as well as substance. In fact, style—global style—*becomes* substance in producing a competitive edge for the company.

Let's briefly examine each of the six competencies we have been considering within the context of moving from a domestic to global organization.

Managing the Competitive Process

Managers of domestic organizations, as we have noted, tend to focus on domestic market trends and resources. It is important, however, that they also look for global competitors and suppliers if they are to protect themselves from loss of market to an unexpected foreign competitor.

Managing the competitive process expands geographically as one moves from domestic to export, international, multinational, and global. Each level requires broader scanning, better and more expanded knowledge and a greater familiarity with the industry on a global basis.

Managers must press for the bigger, broader picture and increase their knowledge of more and more factors in more and more world regions. The more global their organizations become, the more global managers have to learn in each of the six global competencies.

Managing Complexity

Conceptual skills, in addition to technical knowledge, are required for managing complexity. Left-brain analytical and right-brain intuitive skills enable managers to explore broader and broader contexts.

While many managers of domestic organizations are also complaining about increased complexity, it is clear that organizations on an international, multinational, or global track simply multiply the number of variables that need to be considered in a strategic plan or operational decision.

Managing Organizational Adaptability

The TQM movement and customer-focused emphasis of the last decade have stressed the need for organizations to be customer responsive, even on a domestic basis.

Customer responsiveness, however, becomes more demanding and requires greater flexibility when managers are dealing with customers in a variety of countries on a variety of continents.

Not only are the customers more varied, but the special interests of governments, unions, and other stakeholders increase the need for adaptable, decentralized, responsive corporate cultures.

It is an interesting paradox that the larger and more geographically global a corporation becomes, the more bureaucratic it can become. Successful global managers, therefore, must learn the strategy and tactics of managing centralization and decentralization and temporary teams in a way that enables increasingly far flung organizations to continue to be customer driven—in many countries at once.

Managing Multicultural Teams

As we have seen, multiculturalism, whether in the form of domestic diversity or global diversity, will be a major management challenge of the next century. The management of diversity is therefore a skill necessary for *all* managers, whether domestic or international.

At the same time, there are differences. Managing domestic diversity is in some ways more difficult, because it often involves greater confrontation and conflict and is more stress producing. In my experience managing diverse teams, both domestically and internationally, I have found that the skills and abilities necessary to manage domestic diversity are more complex personally and emotionally than those required to manage multicultural teams. For this reason, I am not an advocate of trying to deal with domestic and international diversity in the same way, and especially not through the same training methods. **While some of the concepts may be transferable, the difference between domestic diversity and international multiculturalism is that the former is ultimately about power and the reallocation of opportunity and resources, while the latter is about working with people across differences in cultural perceptions, thinking patterns, and modes of operation.**

I believe, therefore, that multicultural team building in the international arena is more likely to involve people who are fundamentally working toward the same objective, but with different styles of preferred behavior. In such instances, it is generally easier to work out misunderstandings than to deal with the shifts in policy, authority, and responsibility necessary to meet domestic diversity issues.

Managing Uncertainty

The management of change and uncertainty is also a preoccupation of managers today, both domestic and global. Like the management of complexity, this area does not require a different kind of competence as one moves from domestic to international, as much as it requires *more* of the same.

There is no question that because of the increased scope, complexity, and uncertainty of global versus domestic management, global managers must have a better feel for the balance necessary in making decisions and must make greater attempts to ensure that their judgments are as broadly informed as possible.

The management of uncertainty on a global basis, therefore, requires processes that allow for a diversity of opinions to be expressed and for the management of decision making in a way that allows multiple stakeholders from many different parts of the world to feel that they have been consulted and listened to.

The decision-making process, therefore, becomes more complex and the answers more uncertain. Managers must prepare themselves personally and organizationally to deal with this uncertainty by preparing for different decision time lines and by ensuring that they are operating more out of the perceiving than the judging side of their Myer-Briggs personal style.

Managing Personal and Organizational Learning

Preparing people and organizations with the appropriate mindset and skill level is a challenge at all levels of corporate development. As we all know, people's ability to change, grow, and develop are what makes or breaks a company's ability to move through various stages of development.

Personal and organizational learning must therefore come together. They must be managed together and considered together. In my experience, this ultimately comes to a question of leadership and corporate culture. If a president establishes personal and organizational learning as a value, the organization will develop a culture that reinforces and supports this. If leadership does not provide time and incentive for reflection and review, then the organization and its people will not pursue these initiatives.

The best way to ensure that personal and organizational learning is built into an organization is through management retreats, team building, and a good global human resource development system that selects, orients, and develops people to operate within a global context.

From the preceding observations, it should be evident that the HRD function is critical to the success of a firm's globalization effort. The development of a sophisticated global strategy and structure, as we have often said in this guide, is a good starting point. But until the right people have developed the appropriate mindsets and competencies, a globalization effort will never get beyond the executive suite. Let's see what an integrated global HRD program would look like to begin to develop the mindsets and competencies we have been discussing.

TWELVE HUMAN RESOURCE PRACTICES FOR DEVELOPING GLOBAL MANAGERS

When examining the range of mindsets and competencies we have outlined in this book, it becomes clear that all aspects of a human resource management system must be used in developing effective global managers.

Almost every study of global corporations has concluded that without an integrated and forceful human resource function, the talent and mindsets necessary to manage these new complex organizational forms will not be developed and the organizations will fail.

Unfortunately, my experience in consulting with many globalizing companies has revealed that in more cases than anyone would like to admit, the human resource professionals have not been adequately prepared for their new global responsibilities. A second concern is that even where there are far-thinking people, many CEOs still have not realized that the key to global success is not strategy and structure, but culture and people.

The thoughts below, therefore, are not just for HRD professionals, but for *all* global managers. We will examine 12 components of an effective global HRD strategy, which is an integral part of the corporate culture glue that holds a global organization together. These are:

1. Global sourcing.
2. Assessment and selection.
3. Global orientation centers.
4. Global mindset education.
5. Global business training.
6. Cross-cultural management training.
7. Culture and language training.
8. Multicultural team building.
9. Staff exchanges and network development.
10. Relocation transfer, mentoring, and re-entry.
11. Career pathing.
12. Performance management.

Too often we have automatically assumed that the major contribution HRD can make to developing global managers is a series of training programs to expand awareness, add knowledge, or develop new skills. We often have done this because it is easy to find an expert who claims that he or she has some relevant knowledge or skills that can be transferred to increase executive effectiveness.

In Figure 8-1, we begin to see how an integrated strategy might be used to develop various mindsets and competencies for global managers. It is immediately evident that a multipronged approach must be used, because some of the competencies and mindsets must be present in selection, while others can be developed by education, and still others must be developed over time through experience.

Let's see how each of these play out in real life policies and practices.

Global Sourcing

Acceptance of global sourcing as a key element of a global HRD function is one of the first changes that managers have to make in the transition to global corporations.

Multinational corporations have for many years seen themselves as the penultimate achievement in international human resource policies, because most of them have had a philosophy of staffing all national operations only with nationals from that country.

This philosophy has been seen as a far-reaching advance from the international corporation that staffed most of its senior executive overseas posts with expatriates, usually from the home country. Procter & Gamble, after

FIGURE 8–1

Mindsets, Competencies, and Twelve HRD Practices

Competency (C) / HRD Practice	Competition	Complexity	Adaptability	Teams	Uncertainty	Learning
1. Global Sourcing	M					
2. Assessment/ Selection		M	M	M	M	M
3. Orientation Centers				M		M
4. Global Mindset Education	C/M	C/M	C/M			C/M
5. Global Business Training	C/M	C/M	M			M
6. Cross-Cultural Management Training	M	M	C/M	C/M	M	M
7. Culture & Language Training				C/M		M
8. Multi-cultural Team Building		M	C	C/M	M	M
9. Staff Exchanges & Network Development	M		C/M	M		M
10. Performance Management		C/M	C		C	C
11. Relocation Transfer, Mentoring, and Re-entry	C/M	C/M	C/M	C/M	C/M	C/M
12. Global Career Pathing	C/M	C/M	C		C/M	C/M
Mindset (M)	Broad	Balance	Process	Diversity	Change	Open

decades of routinely appointing managers from its domestic operations to key positions in overseas subsidiaries came to understand that this practice not only was insensitive to local cultural needs, but greatly underutilized its pool of non-American international managers who many times were more appropriate for expatriate assignments than their American managers.

Much of this philosophy, however, was developed in the 1960s and 1970s under pressure from the developing world, and later from the industrial world, for the development of local executive talents and skills. It eventually also became good financial policy for many corporations as they have seen their costs for expatriate relocation and maintenance skyrocket over the last two decades.

Unfortunately, the move from international or multinational to global must jar this cozy congruence of philosophy and finances. **Global corporations cannot afford to be geographically bounded in their human resource policies.** Global corporations must be able to recruit, train, and place their best experts and most effective managers in the geographic locations where the demands of the market, technology, and the environment require the best skills, regardless of nationality.

Assessment and Selection

A good global human resource strategy cannot begin too early *and must be strategically linked, especially for globalization.* Far too many companies have decided to globalize and then looked around for global managers. Developing global managers, like developing global corporate cultures is a minimum three to five year endeavor. If you or your company anticipate going global in any sense of the word in the next three to five years, you cannot lose a minute in putting a global HRD plan into place.

There is a great deal that needs to be done to develop assessment and selection methods for the competencies and characteristics (knowledge, conceptualization, flexibility, sensitivity, judgment, and reflection) we have outlined. There are also obviously different criteria used internationally for assessment and selection. At Matsushita, for example, managers are selected for international assignment on the basis of a set of personal characteristics described as SMILE.

- Speciality (the needed skill, capability, or knowledge).
- Management ability (particularly motivation).
- International flexibility (willingness to learn and adapt).
- Language facility.
- Endeavor (perseverance in the face of adversity).

These skills, however, are not always easy to assess. At this point, the best and easiest skills to assess are in the management of the competitive process-technical speciality, language, and perhaps endeavor. The former has well-developed courses and knowledge areas and the latter has some good instruments that have been developed over the last 20 years.

One new tool available from Moran, Stahl & Boyer's International Division in Boulder, Colorado, is an assessment instrument, the Overseas Assignment Inventory, which attempts to determine the cross-cultural sensitivity and adaptability of managers for assignment overseas. It is a research-based instrument, developed over 20 years of experience with a wide variety of clients.

This kind of assessment instrument, however, must be combined with on-the-job coaching and a career path that provides an opportunity for managers to correct areas of weakness and develop new skills and attitudes for effective global management. If it is seen only as a de-selection instrument, it will never pass the tests of organizational reality; line management does not really want to hear that the only bauxite engineer they have available for an important assignment in Peru cannot go, because he failed his test for cross-cultural sensitivity.

Global Orientation Centers

Assessment and selection is only the first part of preparing qualified global managers. When working in a disparate global organization, there is a constant need for orientation of people with many different backgrounds to the organization's corporate culture and the values and visions it has for itself.

In global corporate training, a large global corporation might select a major value or competence and periodically train its top 2,000 managers in internationally integrated groups of 20 to 40 people. This serves to compare and contrast different perspectives on the issue at hand and to develop wide-ranging global relationships that are important in managing the conflicting interests that inevitably arise in global operations.

Management training is not enough when it is done on a country-by-country basis or outside the global vision, values, and context of the corporation. Corporate global training programs must be utilized—just as corporate advertising campaigns are used with customers—to establish corporate identity and image with employees.

Arthur Anderson Consulting is one of the world's largest consulting firms. With 2,200 partners spread throughout the world, it needs to constantly share changes in it's corporate strategy, tactics, values, and culture with all its people worldwide to ensure continuity of practice and operations with its global clients.

To achieve this, Arthur Anderson has developed a Culture Training Center outside of Chicago in which multinational groups of managers are given the latest information about the corporation and have an opportunity to network with one another about the global trends and needs of the future.

To build a common commitment to the company at Matsushita, white-collar employees spend a great part of their first six months in what the company calls cultural and spiritual training. They study the credo of the company and the "Seven Spirits of Matsushita." Philips has a similar entry level training program (called organizational cohesion training) as does Unilever (Bartlett and Ghoshal, 1990, p. 143).

It should also be noted that global orientation centers can be excellent places for corporations to conduct research about their global markets and operations, as the managers who come through these centers can be polled on any number of current or future questions. Too few corporations use these centers for research, as well as education, and are missing a valuable input into their global planning process.

Global Mindset Education

Global mindset education is a new concept that I have developed in conjunction with the preparation of this book.

This has been tested most extensively at ARCO International and AT&T and involves a two to three day course that introduces managers to the basic themes of this book—the forces driving globalization, evolution of global organizations, and the six global management competencies involved in managing competitiveness, complexity, adaptability, multicultural teams, uncertainty, and learning.

This is an orientation, rather than a skill-building process, to provide an introduction to global management, which helps managers understand what they will be going through on a personal level.

After this introductory course, they are prepared and motivated to take a more formal global business curriculum in which they will learn the technical and business knowledge they need to utilize their new global mindsets and competencies.

Global Business Training

Executive education and development has become big business in the United States. In 1990 it was estimated that over 16,000 executives attended universities or other educational institutions of general management, while another 50,000 participated in internal programs, and over 3,000 were enrolled in one of the 100 executive MBA programs offered in the United States.

By the year 2000, estimates for executive education are as follows.

- University general management and functional programs: 22,000 at an estimated cost of $12,600 per attendee.

- Internal corporate programs: 60,000 at a cost of $5,800 per executive.

- Executive MBA programs: 4,000 at an average cost of $36,000 for two years.

- Hundreds of thousands of managers in two and three day programs at an estimated cost of $200–300 per/day (Moulton, 1991, p. 7).

Yet, at this point, the amount of money and space allocated to training global managers is infinitesimal. By the year 2000 it must be much larger than it is today.

The training challenge for global managers is considerable. There is the traditional need for knowledge in global strategies, structures, markets, products, and finances, as well as global and regional knowledge.

AT&T is a prime example of an American corporation caught in the wrenching throes of globalization, just after having struggled through a decade of deregulation. With over 300,000 employees, AT&T is working to provide basic global business education for its managers. AT&T has taken very seriously the need to go global.

Robert Allen, the AT&T chairman, has announced an objective of earning a much greater portion of profit outside the United States. For a company that was almost exclusively American until the 1980s, this presents a major human resource challenge.

The AT&T Global Business Curriculum includes business training, as well as global and area studies. At the most basic level, there are international systems and national area studies with which global managers must be conversant. This means some basic acquaintance with global economic, political, and social trends and some of the institutions affecting those trends like international trade and banking institutions, the Exim Bank (U.S. Export-Import Bank) and GATT (General Agreements on Trade and Tariffs).

AT&T managers must also have some basic understanding of foreign exchange, central banking, international transportation, telecommunications, and tax and legal considerations that may affect their industry. On a regional level, a global manager should know the major political and economic regional organizations like the EEC, European Investment Bank, LAFTA (Latin American Free Trade Association), Asian Development Bank, and other regional organizations affecting international trade and commerce.

Professional technical knowledge. It goes without saying, but I will say it anyway, that the successful global manager *has* to be competent in her or his professional/technical skills. This requires not just marginal competence, but more likely *superior* competence, as the world-class suppliers, customers, and competitors with whom one interacts are daily becoming better educated and more experienced.

In addition to competition, the increasing need for technology transfer means that foreign expatriate managers and representatives must not only know their product, but be able to transfer, adapt, adjust, and customize it to local needs. This ability to tailor products and teach local professionals how to work with the concepts and ideas behind the product, as well as the product itself, requires a much higher level of skills than those required to sell a product or service domestically.

The days are therefore gone when corporations can put people out to pasture by sending them on an international assignment. Today, global companies need to send their best and brightest abroad for seasoning and testing in preparation for executive leadership positions.

Managerial activities. As we have seen throughout this book, there are new managerial behaviors necessary for successfully managing global enterprises. In addition to these higher order management activities, global managers must also have basic skills in planning, budgeting, organizing, staffing, leading, and controlling just as they have always had since these terms were first outlined in the 1930s.

There is no substitute for basic managerial competence in performing well on a global basis.

Cross-Cultural Management Training

Another category of training that is needed in global organizations, but which up to the present has not been well developed, is comparative and cross-cultural management training for managers of global teams.

As we saw in Chapter Six, managing multicultural teams of different nationalities is not a simple matter. Different countries have completely different expectations concerning leadership, communications, coaching, appraising, and decision making, not to mention different patterns of thinking, which affect problem-solving preferences and many other more subtle aspects of organizational life.

In general, however, there have been few systematic attempts to acquaint global managers with ways of comparing different cultural approaches to management. This will take on increasing importance in the global corporations of tomorrow.

Cultural and Language Training

It goes without saying that some form of cultural and language training is necessary for people who are relocating abroad. Or at least it should. Interestingly, recent surveys of multinational corporations indicate that almost 50 percent of them do not have any predeparture language or cultural training for people being assigned abroad, although most provide in-country training.

While predeparture language and cultural training for an expatriate and his/her family should be routine practice in a global corporation, there are additional groups of people who also need cross-cultural sensitizing. These include managers who travel internationally, but hold positions in their home country, as well as managers in the home country who have to interact with foreign counterparts, customers, or suppliers. There are few companies that do an adequate job for these populations.

The recent wave of cross-border mergers and acquisitions have given rise to a need for greater cross-cultural training and awareness for many corporations. In Western Europe in particular, many companies are being rocked by their acquisition of companies with completely different corporate and national cultures.

Those who have believed that the Europeans are cross-culturally and globally more sophisticated than Americans because of their constant exposure to people of other nations in Europe are learning that exposure and understanding are two different things.

Country knowledge. On a national level, some understanding of social and economic development policies; the relationship between trade, export, industrial, and agricultural development policy; and currency, taxation, and banking is important in understanding the context in which your business is operating. Most countries are far more centralized in their economic and industrial policy than the United States and this affects governmental attitudes and regulations and regulatory agencies in their approach to foreign trade and investment.

Cross-cultural knowledge and skills. It is clear that becoming a global manager is ultimately a personal challenge—a challenge not only to learn about the world and the application of business principles, technology, and competitiveness to the international arena, but ultimately a challenge that becomes deeply personal in accepting and adjusting to other values, experiences, and lifestyles.

One key to being a successful manager in a global organization is to understand cultural differences. The second is approaching multicultural teams and foreign business opportunities with an open attitude and willingness to explore the synergy of these differences. And the third key is having the analytical and behavioral skills to operate globally with people of different values, beliefs, and expectations concerning business and international management. The first requires knowledge, the second, the right attitude and the third, the skills.

While it is helpful to have some **knowledge** of local customs and cultural conditions, a truly global manager must have a broader framework within which to analyze many different cultures on a functional basis.

We saw in Chapter Six one framework that has been used that examines six key variables.

• The way people of any society *perceive themselves* as individuals or part of a collective group.

• The way people in a society *perceive their relations with others* in terms of formality, obligations, and depth.

• The way people in a society *perceive the world* around them, both animate and inanimate, from relationship with nature and the environment to attitudes toward time and space.

• The *patterns of thinking,* including problem solving, linear versus holistic analytical patterns, high and low contextual needs, and inductive versus deductive reasoning patterns.

You will recall the six variables shown in Figure 6-10, the last two of which are language and nonverbal behavior. These two areas are greatly affected by cultural differences and, while the first has been well studied, the second still needs a great deal of research on a country-by-country basis.

• The influence of *language* on culture, from its ability to handle abstract thinking to its capacity to convey sense of time, urgency, and deadlines.

• The way in which *nonverbal behavior* will affect interpersonal and business relations, including the use of silence, hand gestures, postures, colors, smells, and sounds.

The left-brain cultural knowledge outlined above cannot be dismissed. This framework constitutes an important part of the education of any global manager. At the deepest (or highest) level, it is also important to be conversant with the human condition around the world and how this relates to major religious and philosophical traditions that reflect on the current state of humanity and the spirit and soul of the people of the world.

The extent to which global corporations actually use the training opportunities available for international managers, especially at the levels of global and area studies, cross-cultural and attitudinal levels, however, remains amazingly sparse. Nevertheless, the HRD field has developed the capacity to prepare people in these areas if corporations will take the time to allow their employees to attend these courses.

Multicultural Team Building

The most advanced area of global management and organization development is multicultural team building. Grace Cocoa, a specialty foods division of W. R. Grace, has been using multicultural team building in its plants and its global functional groups, as well as with its multinational global senior management team for the last several years. And it has recently created a multicultural organization development task force to examine priorities for corporate culture change and alignment on a global basis.

Hoffman-La Roche, the Swiss-based pharmaceutical company, also uses strong team management methods and stresses the multicultural components of managing its international research and development teams.

In spite of the fact that multicultural team building is growing in popularity in global organizations as an integrating mechanism, as well as a method of increasing work productivity and effectiveness, there has been remarkably little systematic work in defining the specific characteristics of a well functioning multicultural team. Our formula outlined in Chapter Six provides one approach.

Staff Exchanges and Network Development

It goes without saying that staff exchanges are an important part of building a global corporate culture. It also goes without saying that there are some guidelines for conducting useful and beneficial staff exchanges, which are little known in global corporations.

The biggest problem in arranging staff exchanges is to be clear about the purpose, length, and structure of proposed exchanges.

It is critically important to be clear about the purpose; the rest will follow. Personal biases such as, "you can't learn anything in two weeks" from people who have spent three months on a staff exchange should be ignored. The fact is, if you are interested in establishing acquaintances and testing chemistry between people at different ends of the globe in order to facilitate daily telephone contact, two-week staff exchanges are extremely useful.

If, however, you need to exchange staff to gain professional knowledge, skills, market information, or specialized orientation, then a period of four weeks is more likely appropriate.

Staff exchanges of three months to a year fall into another category and are generally used for more in-depth technical or professional training and development for persons who will be taking over responsibilities in another location.

Ericsson is built on networks and actively develops them. It has developed a policy of sending large numbers of people back and forth between headquarters and subsidiaries for a year or two. Where NEC may transfer a new technology through a few key managers, Ericsson will send a team of 50 or 100 engineers and managers from one unit to another. This flow is often two way as a means of strengthening the global corporate culture, as well as transferring technology.

International Mentoring and Re-entry Planning

It has become clear that re-entry is a major problem for many managers who accept an assignment abroad. **A global organization that does not adjust its corporate culture, policies, and procedures to deal with re-entry problems will never have a talented and adequate cadre of global managers.**

Too many managers have become disillusioned upon their return from an overseas assignment. There are several factors which lead to this.

• There is a definite drop in status when one returns from an expert position in an outpost to a normal line job at home.

• There usually are financial and status benefits associated with expatriate living that do not follow a manager and his or her family home.

• There is a period of cultural adjustment, many times to the different pace of life in one's home country.

• These problems are exacerbated if an expatriate has not been kept up to date with headquarter's thinking while abroad and does not have a real job when returning.

• Finally, this process may be further complicated when there are no opportunities to apply the knowledge and perspectives gained abroad and no appreciation of the way in which foreign experience could benefit operations in the new location.

To avoid these pitfalls, a carefully developed plan of information sharing, job planning, and appreciation of diverse job experience must be put into place. Mentors should be assigned to share information with managers when they are abroad. These same mentors should represent the career interests and job possibilities for managers as they return. And the corporation should work to develop a set of global corporate values that includes an appreciation for and incorporation of foreign experience into the local management practices, whether local is in the field or headquarters.

Global Career Pathing for Key Management Cadre

Charles Handy notes that 30 years ago when he started to work for a famous multinational company, he was given an outline of his future career. The outline ended with him as chief executive of a particular company in a particular far-off country. He left before his career had advanced very far, but notes that by now "not only did the job they had picked out no longer exist, neither did the company I would have directed nor even the country in which I was to have operated" (Handy, 1990, p. 6).

This can serve as a word to the wise for those who may think that global career pathing means establishing a predictable course for the future. A recent review conducted by the *Economist* of 15 global corporations from the United States, Europe, and Asia cites the following factors in planning for international careers.

- Top managers should have worked outside their own country.
- Local managers should have worked outside their own country and a corporate center.
- Corporate center staff should have worked abroad.
- International experience should be provided early in a career.
- International jobs are both jobs to be done and development opportunities.
- Organizations must stretch to meet their global human resource obligations and needs.
- The manager, spouse, and family must be treated as one unit.

Unilever, one of the best and oldest of the global human resource programs, believes that management development should be centrally controlled because only in that way can you develop the kind of managers needed for an international concern. Ericsson works with a worldwide management planning system. Rhone-Poulenc has an international human resource committee. Fiat internationalizes all management projects.

Accor notes that "becoming international involves achieving a fit between strategy, structure and people." They do this through five activities.

- Creating an international spirit (culture).
- Training a worldwide view of human resources.
- Confronting dilemmas of international management development.
- Planning international careers.
- Using management education to build the international organization and develop strategy.

It is not necessary for everyone, but it is definitely necessary for some well-identified management cadre to be on a global career path. This includes anyone who has the talent or aspirations to eventually be in the executive suite.

In many of the world's most sophisticated global corporations, the identification, monitoring, and transfer of the top cadre of senior executives is the responsibility of none other than the corporation's board of directors or management committee.

There are obvious contradictions in the development of this global sourcing philosophy at a time when dual career marriages are resulting in a greater desire on the part of many managers to stay put. There is no easy answer to this issue other than to develop HRD policies that are sufficiently attractive to the family as a whole so that they are seen as conducive to family life as well as corporate life.

With the influx of a new generation of managers who are increasingly demonstrating new and different values, the incentive packages for global service will need to be modified accordingly. Different companies have found different methods of dealing with this, but none have found it easy. This is especially true if you consider that the values and needs of people in different countries around the world are at different stages in their development and based on different cultural heritages.

One answer to this dilemma is to view the development of a global career path as a combination of achievement, financial, and cultural needs. Needs for achievement and upward mobility must be blended with financial incentives, but modified by cultural backgrounds and values that may alter what is perceived to be the most attractive package for success in global management. Perhaps we need social scientists, in addition to financial compensation and benefits specialists to think about what it means to have a global career path track in a global corporation.

Performance Management

As a manager, you know that the best way to encourage new behavior is to set goals around new directions and reward them, either financially or with other kinds of recognition.

An integrated approach to global management development, therefore, cannot be effective without building the desired behavior into the performance management system of your organization.

Very simply, this means that global managers must not only be offered orientation, training, and education opportunities, but must be coached and counseled into taking advantage of these opportunities and, in the end, must have their performance and rewards managed against the successful development of these competencies.

One of the ways this can be done is by installing within your organization a global career path that does not punish, but rewards and nurtures people through the predeparture, overseas assignment, and re-entry process, which has been such a dismal failure at so many international and multinational corporations.

A recent study in Europe has revealed some interesting differences in the way in which managers from different countries see the criteria for career promotion (Laurent, 1986, pp. 91–102).

In an international questionnaire distributed to managers of a major American multinational corporation with an excellent reputation for human resource management, American managers felt the single most important criterion for a successful career was ambition and drive.

French managers believed that being labeled as having high potential was the critical factor for success, while the British managers felt it was important to create the right image and be noticed for what they do. German managers believed that technical expertise and creativity were critical for a successful career.

The subject of successful criteria for international assignments is not new by any means. Nasmiji Itabashi, one of the early founders of international education in Japan, identified as early as 1934 that to be an international person, as he described it, one had to cultivate the following qualities.

1. Sincerity and dependability.
2. An understanding of one's own culture and institutions.
3. A global perspective and insight.
4. Proficiency in at least one foreign language.

This is still not a bad list today. In fact, it is very insightful in many ways, not the least of which is an emphasis on cultural *self*-awareness over the learning of other specific cultures. And there are many people from the third world who would tell you that if American managers learned more about sincerity and dependability they would gain many more contracts and have many more successful joint ventures abroad than has been the case over the last 50 years.

Successful global companies today, however, are clear about their promotion criteria for global managers. For Shell, the four qualities most associated with potential are:

• A sense of imagination.

- A sense of reality.

- The individual's power of analysis.

- The "helicopter quality," or capacity to envision facts and problems in a wider context.

Philips also uses four criteria that are known throughout the company as the basis for assessing executive potential. These are:

- Conceptual effectiveness (vision, synthesis, professional knowledge, business directedness).

- Operational effectiveness (individual effectiveness, decisiveness, and control).

- Interpersonal effectiveness (network directedness, negotiating power, personal influence, and verbal behavior).

- Achievement motivation (ambition, professional interest, and emotional control).

Bristol-Myers Squibb has recently created a Global Leadership Task Force comprised of all the vice-presidents of their business units to review the criteria used for assessing and developing their managers. They believe some modifications will be needed in their HRD system as a result of their company's new global strategic direction.

Developing a truly global career path system requires not only policies, but clear corporate values that are communicated throughout the organization. At firms like ICI, British Petroleum, and Philips, board level attention is devoted to international executive development (Evans, Doz, and Laurent, 1990, p. 122).

One of the best ways to create matrix minds is through mobility. In the 1970s over 90 percent of top management of American multinational corporations did not have passports. Today, many companies are using temporary assignments of up to one or two years to broaden executive thinking and facilitate corporate decision making.

It is also important not to become caught in the trap of the international corporate service corps comprised of roving managers who never come home again. IBM has a policy that 99 percent of its people on overseas assignment are temporary, with positions waiting for them back home. Only 1 percent of its expatriate managers are careerists in the international arena. In this way, the international perspectives gained through service abroad become integrated back into the home organization.

DIFFERENT DEGREES OF
GLOBAL MANAGEMENT

It is important to acknowledge that not *all* managers in a global organization need an equal amount of global mindsets, characteristics, and competencies. As Barnevik, the head of ABB has noted:

> A global company does not need thousands of global managers. We need maybe 500 or so out of 15,000 managers to make ABB work well—not more. I have no interest in making managers more 'global' than they have to be. We can't have people abdicating their nationalities, saying 'I am no longer German, I am international.' The world doesn't work like that. If you are selling products and services in Germany, you'd better be German! [Taylor, 1991, p. 94]

One useful way of looking at different managers in a global organization has been suggested by Enrico Auteri and Vittorio Tesio of Fiat (Auteri and Tesio, 1990, p. 10). They have developed four categories of positions operating at different levels in a global organization.

• *Transnational positions* operate over the whole geographic area pertaining to the business without segmentation or limitations.

• *Multinational positions* operate in the context of several countries defined by specific limitations.

• *Open local positions* operate within the context of a single nation, with significant links, reference points, and dependence on elements outside the country.

• *Local positions* operate within the context of a single nation on the basis of locally determined variables, without significant interaction with other countries.

Within this definition, Auteri and Tesio found that more than 40 percent of the managerial positions at Fiat worked with international interaction. The most exposed areas were commercial, administrative, planning, and personnel.

If one examines this four-level categorization, it is clear that the first two levels need global management education and career pathing. What has been less clear up to now, however, is that there is a great need for global management education and skills at level three, open local positions.

Open local positions involve national managers who report in a matrixed fashion to someone outside their country, regional or district managers who must coordinate functional policies with colleagues in other countries, or local managers who are sourcing or selling to suppliers or customers in other countries. If one considers the direction of business in the world's organizations today, this third category of managers could easily amount to 25–40 percent of the managers in most global corporations.

This group of local/global managers will need special attention, training, recognition, and career pathing in the years ahead. They are the largest and most important group to develop a global mindset—after a small group of transnational and multinational managers have been identified. This will be a major area for global human resource development and application in the 1990s.

Life Cycles and Organizational Learning

The idea of organization development through different life stages has become increasingly popular. You will remember that in Chapter Six we discussed the stages of group development—forming, storming, norming, and performing—which had been identified by Tuckman (1977).

You can see in Figure 8-2 that this concept of development stages has operated for many years among psychologists and organizational theorists.

As far back as 1950, Erik Erikson wrote about the eight ages of man. Erikson, a psychiatrist, was interested in the causes of abnormal behavior and discovered that much could be explained by individuals who became fixated or stuck at particular stages of their life development.

In such cases, they might become obsessed or blocked, For example, their inability to solve the autonomy issue in stage two could lead to problems with further development at later stages. Similarly, an inability to resolve the intimacy/isolation challenges of young adulthood could lead to difficulty in working in teams or groups at later stages of one's life.

The purpose here is not to make you a clinical psychologist, but merely to introduce to you the fact that human behavior, whether at the individual, group, or organizational level, has certain similar developmental patterns. In order to manage learning successfully, whether for the individual manager, the multicultural team, or the global organization as a whole, HRD managers must be aware of the effect of developmental stages on learning.

Ichak Adizes, in his book *Corporate Lifecycles,* has developed an excellent cycle of organizational development in which he demonstrates the different goals faced at different stages of development (see Figure 8-3).

In addition, Adizes has developed a system to manage each growth stage, which requires a different combination of emphasis on performance (P), administration (A), entrepreneurship (E), and integration (I). While his theory is too complex to adequately convey in the brief space available here, it is important to know that he believes that different stages of the corporate life cycle will require different combinations of managerial skill. For example, during the infant stage, there is a strong need for entrepreneurship (E), but less need for administration (A).

FIGURE 8-2
Stages of Development

Organization

Corporate lifestyles
(Adizes, 1988)

Group

Stages of development
(Tuckman, 1977)

Individual

Eight stages of man
(Erickson, 1950)

For each phase of development, corporations, like individuals, must learn lessons that become cumulative and create organizational learning. In other words, they must not only become trained in how to deal with each challenge, but they ultimately must become educated concerning how to respond to unexpected challenges in the future.

To achieve this, organizations build capacity—and that capacity most often resides in its people. While systems, policies, and procedures are certainly part of an organization's capacity, they, like training, are primarily built on experience of past failures and successes and as such are more backward than forward oriented.

To build more forward oriented capacity into an organization, one must educate its people. Herein lies the capacity to define visions for the future, to develop means for dealing with unexpected turns of events, and to dis-

FIGURE 8–3

Adizes's Corporate Life Cycle with Associated Goals

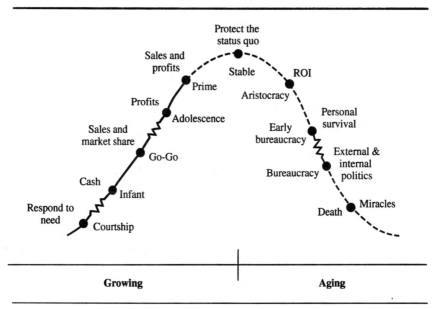

Source: Adizes, *Corporate Lifestyles*, Prentice Hall/A Division of Simon & Schuster, Englewood Cliffs, N.J., 1988, p. 103

cover new technologies to bring the organization through its next developmental impasse.

Ray Sata, chairman of Analog Devices, believes that the capacity and rate at which organizations and people learn may become the only sustainable competitive advantage of the future, especially in knowledge-intensive industries. He believes the management challenge is to accelerate organizational learning by building a change oriented corporate culture that welcomes change, learns from it, and incorporates it into future plans on a total systems basis (Stata, 1989, p. 64).

Jack Welch, the change-oriented master of GE, has invented three new methods to enhance organizational learning during his second decade as chairman. These are workouts, best practices, and process mapping (Stewart, 1991, p. 41).

Workouts are held in retreat settings. A group of 40 to 100 employees, selected by management from all ranks of an organizational unit, are taken to a hotel or conference site for a three-day session. The boss rolls out the agenda and then leaves people for small group brainstorming of as many ideas as they can for improving the quality and productivity of the organization.

On the third day, the boss re-enters the room and, with senior executives watching, must respond to employee suggestions with one of three answers: agree, disagree, or ask for more information. Many times the senior executives sit in the back of the room so there is no eye contact between the manager and his boss.

The workout saves money and brings the employee directly into the change process in a way that is controlled, but also out of control.

GE's second project called *best practices* that involves interviewing other companies to find out what is the secret of their success. It is interesting to note that almost all companies interviewed emphasized processes, not functions or structures. In other words, they did not focus on the operations of a single department, but on the processes that facilitated departments working together on a global basis.

Finally, GE, as a complex global organization, developed something called *process mapping* as a means of managing change on a global scale. Process mapping involves a flowchart showing every step, no matter how small, that goes into making or doing something. GE has discovered that when a process is mapped, the ability of managers to manage it is greatly enhanced.

Rodger Briknell, who leads one of GE's power systems plants in Schenectady, New York, has perhaps the best description of the new synergy that develops between a company and its employees when it has become a learning organization. He says, "If you teach a bear to dance, you'd better be prepared to keep dancing till the bear wants to stop" (p. 49). Is that managing change—or chaos?

National Culture and Personal and Organizational Learning

As Andre Laurent has pointed out, the approach to organization change cannot be the same in every culture. Therefore, the learning and development process itself, will be more complex in a global than in a national organization. Laurent notes:

> When a majority of German managers perceive their organization as a *coordinated network of individuals making rational decisions based on their professional knowledge and competence,* any process of planned organizational change in Germany will have to take this into consideration.
>
> When a majority of British managers view their organization primarily as a *network of interpersonal relationships* between individuals who get things done

by influencing and negotiating with each other, a different approach to organizational change is needed in England.

And when a majority of French managers look at their organizations as an *authority network* where the power to organize and control actors stems from their positioning in the hierarchy, another change model may be called for in France. [Evans, et. al., 1990, p. 92, emphasis added]

While stages of growth at the individual, group, and organizational level (which we reviewed in the last section) are posited as universal, their particular method of expressing themselves will be subject to cultural differences.

As we can see in Laurent's description above, German, British, and French managers have very different definitions of the nature of organizational life. In a multicultural team composed of German, British, and French managers, therefore, the stages of growth, while following Tuckman's thesis, will contain different concerns at each stage.

For example, in the forming stage of group development, a German may be concerned about developing clear roles and responsibilities and decision-making procedures. A Brit may want to get to know the other people in his or her group and understand how they can work together as a group of individuals. The Frenchman, on the other hand, may be concerned about power and authority, what the rights of the leader and the individual members of the group will be, and how much authority he will have over his own actions.

As an American manager of this group, how would you begin your team-building meeting to begin to form your group and create a common understanding of how you will work together? I'll give you a hint. First get everyone to acknowledge that there might be different agendas, relate that to cultural differences in general, state some of your own biases as an American, and see if you can get people to deal with one another and the group development within the context of cultural and personal expectations. That should give you enough to do in your first meeting.

Peter Senge, approaching this subject notes the delicate relationship between thinking patterns and organizational change. He states:

From a very early age, we are taught to break apart problems, to fragment the world. This apparently makes complex tasks and subjects more manageable, but we pay a hidden, enormous price. We can no longer see the consequences of our actions; we lose our intrinsic sense of connection to a larger whole. When we then try to 'see the big picture,' we try to reassemble fragments in our minds, to list and organize all the pieces. . . .

When we give up the illusion that we can do this—we can then build 'learning organizations'—in which people continuously expand their capacity to create the results they truly desire, where new and expansive patterns of thinking are nurtured, where collective aspiration is set free and where people are continually learning how to learn together. [Senge, 1990, p. 3]

You will remember that our first mindset for the global manager was driving for the bigger, broader picture. This is very much related to Senge's concept of seeing the big picture. Both contain the mandate to look beyond our own technical specialization and to see the world not as something to be analyzed, broken down, and controlled, but expanded, explored, and investigated.

Learning how to learn is a concept that was introduced 30 years ago in the early days of group dynamics. Now, in the 1990s, individuals and organizations are asking how they will establish methods and procedures to learn how to learn. We are developing good experiential and interactive training programs and are beginning to develop good reflective experiences for organizations to examine their mission, vision, values, and culture. Executive retreats and team building, organizational audits, corporate culture surveys, benchmarking best practices, peer and upward assessments, assessment centers, and more consciously coordinated alignment of corporate culture and people with corporate visions are producing ways for corporations and individuals to learn how to learn, not just from their experiences, but from an understanding of where they want to go and what will be required to get there.

Despite this progress, there remain a range of challenges for all human resource professionals and m line managers as we approach the 21st century. Managing global organizations is only one of them. Let's take a minute to briefly review some of the trends we will all need to work with during the years ahead.

GLOBAL HUMAN RESOURCE CHALLENGES FOR THE 21ST CENTURY

Reflecting on the point we have come to in our journey, it might be useful to take a moment and see what the implications of our observations might be for basic human resource challenges as we stand at the edge of the millennium.

Five basic themes emerge which comprise a human resource agenda that will keep us all stretched and challenged for the foreseeable future. These are:

1. Rethinking all boundaries.
2. Multinational, multicultural, and intercultural interaction and cooperation.
3. Decentralization, intrapreneurship, and entrepreneurship.
4. Retraining.
5. Personal and organizational adaptability and learning.

Let's take a moment to summarize each of these trends.

Rethinking All Boundaries

The first theme that emerges is that boundaries are not what they used to be, either physically, organizationally, or psychologically. Boundary redefinition will occur on the following three levels.

Global, national, regional, and local boundaries. The clearest boundaries being reorganized daily are geographic. With this comes a reconceptualization of who we are, who our neighbors are, and in some cases who are our enemies. This is certainly the case in Western, Eastern, and Central Europe.

Between EC 1992 and the reconfiguration of Eastern and Central Europe, the world has been turned upside down for a large portion of the world's population.

Structural and functional boundaries. Decentralization, de-layering, and cross-functional coordination are the themes of the customer-driven organization and total quality management (TQM). While this has been driven by global competition and more educated customers, it has been facilitated by advances in microchip technology and the vast computerization of global manufacturing, transportation, and marketing operations.

Teams, competitors, and allies. Strategic alliances are daily transforming lifelong competitors into tentative allies, requiring new kinds of risks and new forms of cooperative/competitive behavior. Teams are increasingly diverse and multicultural and the ability to work with constantly changing teams means stronger corporate cultures and common shared visions, values, and methods of operation.

Multinational, Multicultural, and Intercultural Interaction and Cooperation

Culture—in all its glory—has taken center stage. Increased diversity in the American work force, ethnic strife in Eastern and Central Europe, cultural differences in cross-border joint ventures, mergers, and acquisitions are trends that have demonstrated how little many of us know about cultural differences and how to manage them. This will be a growth area for the 21st century.

This new emphasis on culture will take three forms.

Cultural self-awareness. An area that has been only tentatively developed is cultural self-awareness training. In this field, people are taught what biases and beliefs they have based on their own background as a means of better understanding and relating to people from other cultural backgrounds. This area, which has great potential, would enable people to operate in many different countries, without specific country training for each world area.

Cultural adaptability. We must not only learn to be culturally self-aware in order to work with people from other cultures, but we must also become facile in our ability to adapt to a range of foreign environments which themselves may have a great variety.

Cross-cultural management. We will need to adapt our personal management styles for multicultural teams and have a much better understanding of comparative management practices as they exist in different countries around the world. Cultural managerial analysis and similar frameworks will need to be developed to provide analytical perspectives from which various management practices can be related to cultural values and merged together for global cultural synergy.

Decentralization, Intrapreneurship, and Entrepreneurship

Creativity, innovation, and spontaneity are the watchwords for success in a fast-moving world. Corporations around the world are shedding bureaucracy and finding ways to encourage experimentation among their employees. Continuous improvement, driving out waste, and skunk works are among the methods used to encourage more innovation in global organizations. Three factors push in this direction.

Think globally, act locally. Entrepreneurship and innovation require mindset changes, as well as structural adjustments to free the people to move more toward systems thinking. Thing globally, act locally, is one of the context building phrases of the 21st century.

Mass customization. Global efficiency and local responsiveness find their answer in mass customization, the method by which mass products like cabbage patch dolls are customized for individuals by special order. John Naisbitt and Patricia Aburdene's *Megatrends 2000,* was published simultaneously in 19 countries and in each case the local publisher included local examples of the trends the authors identified in the United States and around the world.

Quick, creative responsiveness.   Just-in-time inventories, long-term, limited supplier relations on the supply side, and Domino's pizza on the distribution side represent the move to relationship building through the use of time. Suppliers win contracts by delivering materials just in time and producers win customers by producing products just in time (in Domino's case it's 30 minutes). Speed, responsiveness, flexibility, innovation—these will be the competitive advantages of the future. It will be the responsibility of the human resource professionals to deliver the people with the mindsets and skills to make all this happen.

Retraining

We have not yet begun to deal with the challenge of retraining. There are three factors converging to make retraining a major human resource requirement during the next century.

Global work force dislocation due to political/economic changes. The scene in Eastern and Central Europe will be a scene of human trauma for many years to come. Millions of people will lose their jobs through privatization. This will include both government and party workers, former security and military personnel, as well as others who will be terminated in attempts to make newly privatized companies profitable. Estimates of the amount of redundancies in most of the formerly socialist countries run between 10 and 25 percent of the work force. We have never dealt with anything like this in modern history.

Management dislocations due to downsizing, acquisitions, and mergers.   In the United States and Western Europe, workers, technicians, professionals, and executives are faced with the need for retraining as acquisitions and mergers produce redundant positions and excess headcount. Downsizing to retain competitive advantage as a low-cost producer also places pressure on middle management, as well as blue-collar workers.

Industry shifts in the transition from the industrial to the information age and the industrial to the service economy.   Basic structural readjustments are occurring throughout the Western world as major portions of the world's economies emerge into transitions from one age to another. The result is displaced workers, outdated skills, and new skills such as computer literacy that will place great new demands on the human resource function.

Personal Flexibility and Adaptability to Change

A basic theme of this book has been the need to develop new managers who are more flexible and adaptable than those of the past. This drive also comes from three specific trends.

Increased base rate of change. People are familiar with a base rate of unemployment and base rates of inflation. I would suggest that we may be experiencing an escalation in the base rate of change. All societies exist within a certain rate of change that has become comfortable and manageable.

In the former Communist countries it was imperceptible, in Western Europe and the United States it has been perhaps 5 percent. Eastern and Central Europe are now experiencing a complete breakdown of their societies and a change rate probably exceeding 50 percent, while the United States and other parts of the world have probably doubled their rate to 10 percent. All this places great pressure on people to adjust to new circumstances in ways that are totally new.

New change professions. We have not yet begun to develop the helping professions necessary to assist people through these transitions. Indeed, in many instances we have not recognized the transition itself, let alone conceptualized it, analyzed it, and trained people to assist with it. I am involved in teaching students at Moscow State University to become organization development specialists. It is a formidable task, because the macro socioeconomic-political context is so unstable that most Western theories about micro-change on an individual, team, or organizational level are irrelevant.

NEW DIRECTIONS

These trends constitute major challenges and opportunities for human resource professionals for many years to come. We need everything from research to conceptualization to theory building. We also need to develop new intervention methods, from selection and assessment to training and performance management to enable people and corporations to meet the demands of the 21st century. It is an exciting time—and a complex time; but the time is great for human resource people who have the skills and motivation to rise to the occasion.

Organizations that follow the integrated agenda recommended here can make significant progress toward the human side of globalization work.

Given the accelerating needs of customers from Europe and Japan, it is necessary for organizations in the United States to develop new ways to align their people and cultures with their global strategies and structures.

In the end, what we may need is a Baldrige Award for Global Competitiveness. U.S. corporations may need to be challenged to adopt the best practices in global strategy, structure, culture, and skills in the same way they are being challenged to tackle quality.

If we can develop corporations that are consumer driven, quality focused, and globally effective, we will have gone a long way toward restoring America's competitiveness and ensuring our continued prosperity into the 21st century.

KEY PRACTICES AND TASKS FOR MANAGING LEARNING

You may want to examine the list of practices and tasks associated with managing personal and organizational learning to determine where you should begin to work in this area.

Competence VI: Managing Learning

Definition: Ability to manage personal and organizational learning and improvement on a continuous basis through the exploration of new fields of knowledge, new cultural perspectives, and through seeking feedback on a global basis.

Action and Mindset: Seeking openness

Personal Characteristic: Reflection

Key Practices and Tasks

1. Develop a *capacity for systems thinking* at every level of personal and organizational functioning, searching for contexts and broader influences on a global basis which may affect personal or organizational success.

    1.1 Analyze how your job and function are dependent on other jobs or functions within your organization and develop annual goals to anticipate how changes in these areas may affect your work.

1.2 Examine what global trends could affect your work over the next three years and begin now to develop methods for using these changes as new opportunities for personal and organizational growth.

2. Develop a *working knowledge of international relations, international economics, and cross-cultural differences* that will allow effective interaction of foreign suppliers, customers, and partners.

    2.1 Attend one internationally oriented seminar, workshop, or conference every other year to broaden your exposure to international thinking and perspectives.

    2.2 Read magazines and newspapers that reflect the national or regional perspective of your target audience.

3. Consider personal and organizational *learning as a lifelong process.*

    3.1 See yourself as one of the new knowledge workers and constantly gather, analyze, and reflect on information on a global basis, utilizing global resources for new concepts, perceptions, and opportunities for personal, professional, and organizational effectiveness.

4. Develop a *sense of meaning and purpose* in personal and organizational life that transcends the immediate job or annual objective and can be related to a higher or broader contribution to the human condition.

    4.1 Develop your own personal reason for staying in your job, profession, or organization which has a global implication that is meaningful to you and which motivates you to get up in the morning.

    4.2 Become aware of the impact or relationship of your work to people in other countries and try to make your work a net contribution to the human condition on a global basis.

This becomes translated into the final global competency learning cycle in Figure 8–4.

The commitment to lifelong learning is not a simple commitment to make. It requires the willingness to live with unfinished business; the faith that people can constantly grow and develop for the better; and the sense that there is some larger reason for existence than getting up in the morning to make a buck.

FIGURE 8–4
Global Competency Learning Cycle (Managing Learning)

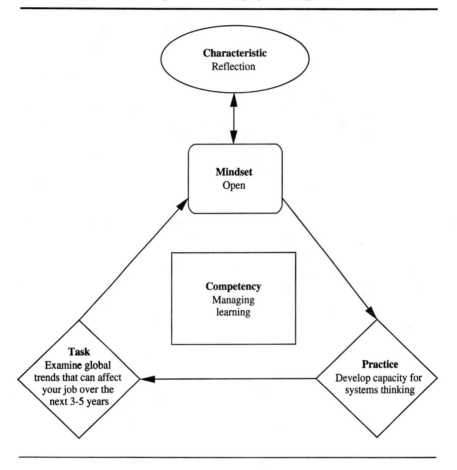

People and organizations who are committed to learning as the central aspect of their life not only survive better, but are often more attractive to others, more vibrant in their ideas, and more fulfilled in their pursuits.

Being a successful global manager or a socially responsible global organization requires an integrated approach to the world that develops the capacities needed to flourish, while knowing that these capacities will never be enough to replace a sense of purpose, mission, and the willingness to trust process and let go.

AFTERTHOUGHTS FOR GLOBAL MINDSETS

You might want to review the 21st century challenges in the last section to determine areas that you would like to explore further. There are enormous opportunities for leadership in the human resource field as people begin to address the issues outlined.

If you are a line manger, you will see areas where you also will need to develop new mindsets, behaviors, and skills to deal with the demands of the next century. You may want to think about how these trends will impact your business and how you and your HRD people can work together to ensure your competitiveness in the months and years ahead.

It is important that you determine where you and your organization are in the identification of needs for global mindsets, behaviors, and skills in your executives, managers, professionals, and workers throughout the world. You may want to convene a task force or find some other way to examine what are the critical success factors for your business, what target populations should be identified to be developed, and what combination of human resource strategies and tactics (selection, training, etc.) should be used against each population, mindset, behavior, and skill.

Chapter Nine

Integration

A finite game is played for the purpose of winning, an infinite game is played for the purpose of continuing the play.

Carse, p. 3

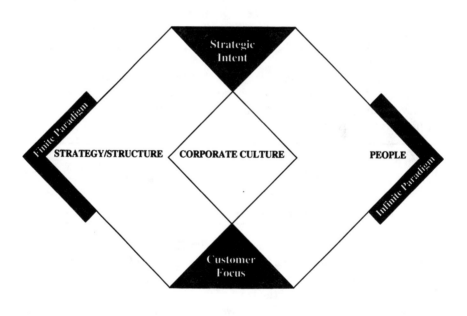

FORETHOUGHTS FROM A GLOBAL MIND

We are nearing the end of our journey—and the beginning. Hopefully you are feeling a little more global than when you began and you are beginning to feel comfortable with your new, more global mindset.

There are still many unclear areas and many uncharted waters, both personally, organizationally, and internationally. The transformation of Eastern and Central Europe from centrally planned and structurally driven political and economic systems is giving way to process-driven free markets and process-driven democracies. The role and relationship of the United States, Japan, and Germany in a post-cold war world remains to be developed. The speed and pace of technological change continue to challenge all organizational strategies and affect all individual lives.

It is apparent that globalization is something larger than a change in the strategy or structure of an organization. It is also probably greater than the global corporate cultures we have been discussing or people like you and I who are coping with these transformations.

There is something greater going on in the universe and only global minds may be able to discern the new dynamics of this evolving world.

Perhaps we should all take a lesson from the Tao and look for the flow of the pendulum from yang to yin. In this adventure that we have taken, we have tried to point out some of the beginning definitions and directions in the hope that you will be intrigued enough to begin the journey of developing your own global mindset and competencies to become an active player in this new world.

This is not the last chapter of the book, but the first. As Carse has noted, the purpose of the game for which we have been preparing you in this journey is not to win and go have a beer . . . but to continue the play and get high from constant motion.

THE NEW PARADIGM—FINITE TO INFINITE GAMES

Throughout this book you have followed Jim Carse as he painted a picture of the emergence of a new paradigm at the beginning of each chapter. The new paradigm is the infinite game.

In Figure 9–1 you can read the flow of the chapters and Carse's thoughts. In closing I would like to reflect on how I see Carse's observations related to the journey we have been on.

Going Global

No one can play the game alone.

No one can play a global game alone. We all need colleagues to cope with the complex and broad-based world that we face. And we will also find that

FIGURE 9-1
Outline of Book and Carse Quotes

Chapter	Subject	Quotation
One	Going Global	"No one can play the game alone."
Two	Global Mindsets and Competencies	"Finite games can be played within an infinite game, but infinite games cannot be played within finite games."
Three	Competitiveness	"The rules of a finite game are the contractual terms by which the players can agree who has won."
Four	Complexity	"Finite players play within boundaries; infinite players play with boundaries."
Five	Adaptability	"Culture . . . is an infinite game. Culture has no boundaries . . . for this reason it can be said that where society is defined by its boundaries, a culture is defined by its horizons."
Six	Teams	"No one can play the game alone. One cannot be human by oneself. There is no selfhood where there is no community. We do not relate to others as the person we are; we are who we are in relating to others."
Seven	Uncertainty	"The rules of the infinite game must change in the course of play."
Eight	Learning	"Because infinite players prepare themselves to be prepared for the future, they play in complete openness. To be prepared against surprise is to be trained . . . to be prepared for surprise is to be educated."
Nine	Integration	"A finite game is played for the purpose of winning, an infinite game is played for the purpose of continuing the play."

there are many other people who are willing and able to play the game with us.

Our key challenge is to try to develop as many infinite, rather than finite games as possible.

It is also impossible to gain a balanced picture of the world if you only look at your side of the elephant. Working as a successful manager in a global organization, therefore, requires you to constantly *drive for the bigger, broader picture.*

As Americans we are at a cultural disadvantage in looking for larger contexts. As we have noted earlier, the anthropologists who have studied such subjects, characterize Americans as low-context. In a low-context culture, people are happy to accept the situation as they see it if it meets their needs. In fact, they are inclined to believe that the world as they see it *is* reality. All they need to do is to reinforce those things they like, and over-come those things that stand in the way, and life will be very good. This is what sociologists call an instrumentalist view of the world—you do whatever gets you there.

Many people who teach cross-cultural relations have noted that one of the sources of difficulty between the French and Americans is that while Americans are constantly asking how, the French are asking why. *How* leads to pragmatic descriptions of how to get things done; *why* leads to philosophical considerations of the broader, historical context and framework for the current situation. This is the difference between high- and low-context.

The Japanese culture, as we have seen, also drives toward high-context, not from a philosophical viewpoint like the French, but from a group perspective. The Japanese need to know what groups you belong to, where you fit into social, economic, and educational hierarchies, and what your family background and history is before they can place you in the current situation and determine how to deal with you. One might say that if the American question is how and the French is why, the Japanese equivalent might be where.

In any case, you can see how both the French and the Japanese are more driven to the bigger, broader picture than Americans. We have already discussed the impact of different thinking patterns on French, Japanese, and American approaches to exploring systems versus rational, linear perspectives. It is clear, therefore, that if you are an American working in a global organization, you will need to practice systems thinking and systems analysis, forcing yourself into the bigger, broader picture to understand the forces affecting global organizational life. In the process, you will hopefully come to appreciate contradictions as part of the more complex arena of world operations, rather than as impediments to your current project.

Global Mindsets and Competencies

Finite games can be played within an infinite game; but infinite games cannot be played within finite games.

Finite games are, very simply win-lose. While we play many finite games in the world of global business in our competition for customers, suppliers, technology, and profits, to be successful we must be playing an infinite strategic game that is larger than any of the local tactical contests we may win.

Michael Macoby, in his best-selling book of the 1970s, *The Gamesman,* described the devastating end faced by managers who spent their entire lives winning battles, but losing the war. These people spent their lives winning games, but lost any sense of cumulative purpose or accomplishment.

It is best to remember in global gamesmanship that the purpose of the exercise is to keep the larger game going (better life for people of the planet) and to ensure that you have a broad enough mindset to encompass the needs of others in your global play.

Competitiveness

The rules of a finite game are the contractual terms by which the players can agree who has won.

As already mentioned, global management is filled with win-lose, competitive games. Make no mistake about it. In areas like managing the competitive process, it is extremely important to understand the rules that other players are playing by.

Cross-cultural negotiating styles, international marketing techniques, global entry, and development strategies are all aspects of the global win-lose finite game that confront you as a global manager every day. If you do not play these finite games well, your life as a global manager will be remarkably short.

At the same time, Carse has a message for you as an individual—and perhaps for your corporation. He stresses that you and perhaps your company, always have the option to focus on the larger picture, the infinite game, and walk away from finite games that threaten to destroy your larger purpose, mission, or value. These are the elements of the infinite game, which prevent you from becoming one of Macoby's victims of the finite play.

Complexity

Finite players play within boundaries; infinite players play with boundaries.

The complexity of global organizations can suffocate you. But it doesn't have to. Carse has a way out—play *with* boundaries rather than *within* them. To do this you need to focus on your conceptual skills and concentrate on reframing your current view of the world.

Developing a balanced perspective about the global world in which you work requires not getting bogged down in details. If you are driving for the bigger, broader picture, this should help, but in addition, you need to use your intuitive and analytical skills to continuously reframe the world you deal with.

Reframing has been a subject of great inquiry in recent years. A number of good books have been written about how to think creatively and intuitively to get out of boxes in your life (see Bolman and Deal, 1991 and

Barker, 1989 and 1991). Joel Barker calls this "paradigm shifting," Carse calls it "playing with boundaries." You can *call* it whatever you want, but the action you need to take is to look at problems from different angles, brainstorm new visions, and try to ensure that you do not get caught in old ways of thinking that bog you down.

We have discussed the need to live with the contradictions and paradoxes inherent in global organizational life. We have noted the need to incorporate these contradictions into larger systems of thinking and to understand that the most important ingredient in holding contradictory ideas is developing balance.

What we have not emphasized enough, however, is that you will probably not be motivated or able to do any of these things unless you appreciate contradictions for the energizing role that they can play in global organizations. Let's look at a few.

First of all, **contradictions are the essence of diversity.** Contradictory ideas, opinions, and perspectives are the engine of creativity. Brainstorming, a technique in which people are allowed to put up contradictory ideas without discussion, many times leads to new creative ideas that derive from contradictory viewpoints on a flip chart.

Second, **contradictions are the engine of opportunity.** Every situation is skewed toward a particular strength on one side of the picture. Usually the entrepreneurial initiative will flow from the opposite, or underutilized side —the side that no one else sees, because we are all preoccupied with managing the current state.

Looking for the contradictions in the current state of things will often lead the way to the next generation of product, structure, or process that will be the competitive edge of the future. The full exploration of contradictions, when they go against your current strength, is key to ensuring the success and relevance of your organization in the future.

And third, **contradictions are the natural state of the world.** Remember the Tao and yin and yang, symbolized by the flowing opposite halves of a circle. This has reminded people for generations that the world is *rich* in its contradictions, and that there is great opportunity and pleasure to be gained from understanding and appreciating the flow.

Adaptability

Culture . . . is an infinite game. Culture has no boundaries . . . for this reason it can be said that where society is defined by its boundaries, a culture is defined by its horizons.

If culture is an infinite game, then corporate culture becomes one of the keys to successful global management. If a culture is defined by its horizons, it means that a corporate culture that is outward looking, rather than inward focused toward its boundaries is one that will be healthy and successful.

In the last 25 years, I have seen many organizations fail because they became too focused on defining their structure, their boundaries, their authority relationships, and their allocation of internal resources. Corporate cultures that focus on the horizons of new opportunity, the possibilities of new world order, and the visions of emerging ideas and people will flourish in today's global world, while the old order changeth and many don't see it, because they are too internally oriented.

The 21st century may well be dominated by headlines of new technological breakthroughs. But the real breakthroughs will need to come in our ability to manage our corporate cultures and people in their response to these new technologies and the changes they rein down on our lives.

It doesn't matter what position you have, because your position in your organization can neither protect you from global change nor make you capable of dealing with it. What will make you a successful manager in a global organization is your relationship to *process*—a theme that we have often heard throughout this book.

Those of us who have developed skills in the process and human side of organizational life will be key to the future success of our global corporations.

Teams

No one can play the game alone. One cannot be human by oneself. There is no selfhood where there is no community. We do not relate to others as the person we are: we are who we are in relating to others.

The teamwork era has arrived. It is also an era of team play. This means that teams will need to learn to work *and* play together. White-water rafting, outward bound, and other learning-play experiences will be part of the team that works in an integrated interdependent self-managed way.

These teams will also be self-managed in that they will construct constant learning loops. They will be self-managing in process as well as content, interpersonally as well as workwise, and self-correcting while continuously upgrading their standards of excellence.

In the end, however, the real advantage of teamwork in a global organization may be best described by Carse. Through cultural diversity and the rich variety of perceptions, values, and beliefs available in global organizations we can become much more than we ever could in a monocultural situation. Under these conditions, we are truly enriched if we are who we are in relating to others.

Uncertainty

The rules of the infinite game must change in the course of play.

To stay relevant to the present and the future, and to enable one to continue play, "the rules of an infinite game, must change in the course of play." In such a situation, change must become the norm, rather than an exception.

There will be rough spots in this scenario. One of the most difficult will be to learn, personally and organizationally, to deal with continuous change and conflict. The secret to living with uncertainty appears to be threefold.

- First, we must look for new order in disorder, which comes from putting on different lenses and new paradigms.
- Second, we must become comfortable with white-water rafting and structured process in which we are not wholly in control or out of control.
- And third, we will need to recognize that managing change will mean managing periods of alternating chaos and control, rather than managing something that is always in control.

We will also have to become comfortable with conflict. We will need to focus on the opportunities that conflict provides for new innovations and look for learning and growth for ourselves and our organizations from diversity and conflicting views. We will need to concentrate less on defending our position and more on understanding the possibilities and opportunities inherent in the other person's view. Like a black-belt judo expert, we must learn to use our opponent's momentum to move us both in new directions.

This will mean some work on ourselves. Psychologists have long believed that we fear most in others those things we have not resolved in ourselves. Self-work and personal growth and development will be important for keeping pace with continuous change, as well as for dealing with the differences that are inevitable in a global organization.

Learning

Because infinite players prepare themselves to be prepared for the future, they play in complete openness. To be prepared against surprise is to be trained . . . to be prepared for surprise is to be educated.

Personal and organizational learning are paramount to global success. As we saw in the last chapter, global managers must be trained in basic knowledge about the world, but, more importantly, they must be educated to be open for change, surprise, and uncertainty.

To be educated is a state of being. To be trained is a state of preparedness. *Since global management requires dealing with the unpredictable, global managers need to be educated, as well as trained.*

We have offered many thoughts about how you can prepare yourself to be surprised by the future—new theories, new formulae, new suggested actions and arenas for personal and organizational development. To explore these and build them into an integrated whole that works for you is your life's work as a global manager.

Global managers never stop learning. It is logical that if you stop learning you cannot be open to the surprises a constantly changing world will present to you. But it is equally true that you will never *know* enough. In the end, *being open for surprises is not a rational act—it is an act of faith*—faith in your own ability to flow with the future, faith in others' willingness to support you, and faith in some fundamentally larger forces in the world that use you for higher and better purposes than you can rationally construct.

Integration

A finite game is played for the purpose of winning, an infinite game is played for the purpose of continuing the play.

In the end, perhaps the most important skill for a global manager is to be able to manage meaning. Meaning comes from continuous play—from the ability to work toward something larger than the next win.

Managing meaning involves understanding not only the functional utility of an event, technique, or operation, but also understanding its context within the broader aspects of life, within the needs of the current situation, and within the needs, hopes, and fears of the people with whom you are working.

You have to know how to manage meaning to put together a globally inspiring mission statement, an organizationally motivating vision, or a personally engaging work plan. Meaning is the translation of a stimulus not just into a response, but first into a concept—which in turn generates a response. The search for meaning—for ourselves—for others—and for the world, is one of the most profound lifelong activities that global managers can undertake.

But it is almost impossible to provide meaning for yourself and others if you are not managing change. I have struggled throughout this discussion with the desire to declare that management of change is an obsolete idea.

Organization development, a profession barely 30 years old, has declared that it has expertise in planned change. That somehow seems anachronistic and leads me to wonder whether the profession has not lost its battle to manage and control the future to the flow and chaos of the world.

On the other hand, this whole book has been a "how to" guide on managing change and the future. To be open for surprises, as we have seen, we need not only the right attitudes, but also skills. To manage change we must also have skills, but in addition, an attitude that says that not all change can be controlled in the traditional sense.

Change, therefore, presents us with one of the most fundamental contradictions of organizational life. The very nature of an organization, with boundaries, norms, and purpose, means that there is something that is subject to change. If it is subject to change, it must be able to deal with change in some way that is not random. At the same time, if an organization only prepares for those changes it can control, it will miss the larger issues that may be beyond its control in the traditional sense, but not beyond its capacity to survive—if it is open to surprises, stays in shape for navigating new waters, and is constantly scanning for rocks in the rapids. All of which brings us to learning.

The key to all that we have described in this journey is learning. Personal learning, team learning, and organizational learning. Learning, in turn, is dependent not only on training and education, but on an open attitude and some interest and curiosity about the world around us.

I cannot imagine an effective global leader who is not interested and curious about the world. To be an effective global manager, you have to do more than exist, you have to thrive; rather than cope, you must take the initiative and instead of managing, you need to create.

Global management at its best is a testimonial to many of the world's better attributes—openness, creativity, resiliency, adaptiveness, understanding, sensitivity, empathy, analysis, anticipation, challenge, and, yes, control.

To achieve such a state is a lifelong quest, and to be an effective manager is a lifelong quest. Learning from experience, learning from others, learning from history, learning from the present—global management requires constant attention to learning. It also requires the development of a worldview—a viewpoint and a personal philosophy about the world and your role in it.

In this journey I have shared some of my own beliefs, doubts, and convictions about the world and the world of global management. Some views you may have found interesting, some overdone, some boring. I would hope that you have had all those feelings, because this is part of the contradictions that are part of me and my world.

My challenge to you now is to develop your own viewpoint, philosophy, and worldview about your role and life as a global manager. You are at the center of a rapidly evolving world. It has great potential and if you grab onto it and go for the ride, you will have a wonderful and challenging life.

Sister Corita, a Catholic nun who painted many pictures in the 1960s that incorporated abstract color with poetry and prose created one of my favorite paintings on which she quoted an Italian writer, Ugo Betti, who wrote:

To believe in God is to know that the rules are fair and that the world is full of wonderful surprises.

Prepare yourself to be open for these surprises and to move in the world with a spirit that inspires yourself and others to live life to its fullest. Good luck.

A FINAL AFTERTHOUGHT FOR YOUR GLOBAL MINDSET

Well—that's it. You are now a chartered explorer in global mindset management—a CEGMB for those of you who like to put letters after your name.

You are an explorer, because you will never know where home is again, nor will you be satisfied with one area of the world. You are chartered, because you have gone through a course that has pointed directions, imparted some lessons, and raised awareness about the terrain.

Hopefully, you will apply the lessons and philosophies of this book to becoming a more effective global manager in your organization, and to encourage others to take the steps necessary to develop the behaviors and skills for successful global management.

Developing a global mindset, in the end, is not just a perceptual or attitudinal venture, but also a philosophical one. It requires a concern about the planet, a respect for distant people and their perspectives, and an interest in the human condition in its broadest sense, from the historical days of our forefathers to the future of our grandchildren.

Carse has said that "infinite players are not serious actors in any story, but the joyful poets of a story that continues to originate what they cannot finish." This is an intergenerational issue. One in which the work we do today is for the future.

This is quite a scope of time and space with which to become engaged. If you do, however, you will find your horizons broadened, your spirit invigorated, and your effectiveness blossom as you work with others to improve not only your organization's global efficiency and effectiveness, but also to enhance your participation as a contributing member of the world community.

APPENDIX

Appendix

Summary of Six Competencies, Mindsets, Characteristics, Practices, and Tasks

COMPETENCY #1: MANAGING THE COMPETITIVE PROCESS*

Definition

Ability to gather information on a global basis concerning the global sourcing of capital, technology, suppliers, facilities, market opportunities, and human resources, and the capacity to utilize the information to increase the competitive advantage and profitability of the organization.

Action and Mindset: Driving for the bigger, broader picture

Personal characteristic: Knowledge

Key Practices and Tasks

Practice #1: Set *critical success factors* (CSFs) for the organization's global competitiveness and use these as a framework to filter global information for key trends.

---

*Note: A *competency* is a specific capacity to execute action at a skill level sufficient to achieve the desired effect. Each competency requires *practices* that are distinctive and contribute to the competency. These practices, in turn, must translate into a series of *tasks* that global managers execute to be effective.

• Determine the most important tasks to be done in your job to ensure that your function is managed well on a cross-functional and international basis.

• Use CSFs as a framework to search for and filter information on a global basis which will affect your ability to be successful in the execution of your job responsibilities.

Practice #2: Establish *personal and organizational information systems* that scan globally for trends, best practices, and resources that provide new opportunities for increased competitive advantage and profit.

• Read professional and commercial publications that track your functional and industry trends and practices on an international, rather than national, basis.

• Join international professional associations and attend meetings and conferences that stress the global aspects of your job responsibilities.

• Search for best practices in your job on a global basis, both within your organization and within your industry or profession.

• Develop one new idea each year to increase your productivity or organization's competitiveness, the seeds of which you have obtained from outside your country.

Practice #3: Establish information processing systems that *deliver the right level of information to the right people at the right time* for the most effective and timely decision making on a worldwide basis.

• Share information you gain that is relevant to increasing your productivity or effectiveness with others in your organization on a global basis who could benefit from it.

• Ensure that people you manage or with whom you work abroad have the information they need to make as many decisions locally as possible to. increase the quality of their decisions and their speed of response to local customer needs.

Practice #4: Track *global merger and acquisition activity and foreign investment patterns* of competitors and potential competitors.

• Conduct and update your competitive analysis on an ongoing basis to ensure that you are aware of what your key competitors are doing on a worldwide basis, even if some activities may seem to be irrelevant to your current interests or priorities.

• Continually scan the global environment for potential competitors who could come from suppliers or customers who might want to vertically integrate, as well as for diversified multinational corporations who might look to expand through merger and acquisition in your industry.

Practice #5: Monitor *international trade, tariff, economic, social, and political changes* that may affect local, regional, or international competitiveness.

• Read broadly in your industry and professional press and in popular literature about international social, political, and economic megatrends.

Overview

Managing the competitive process requires a manager to be curious and to be constantly attentive to the world and its changing social, economic, and political conditions. It is an engagement with life that can be vibrant and exciting for those involved.

COMPETENCY #2: MANAGING COMPLEXITY

Definition

Ability to identify, analyze, and intuitively manage complex relationships on a global basis which affect personal and organizational effectiveness.

Action and Mindset: Balance of Contradictions

Personal characteristic: Conceptualization

Key Practices and Tasks

Practice #1: Manage *relationships which are simultaneously cooperative and competitive* such as strategic alliances, headquarters-field relations, and functional, geographic, and product matrices.
• Analyze which aspects of cooperative/competitive relationships should be cooperative and which need to remain competitive, and compartmentalize your information, decision making, and operations accordingly.
Practice #2: Look for *contradictions and paradoxes* in your work and, rather than trying to eliminate them, determine how they can be managed for richer decisions.
• In situations of generic conflict between functions or interests, use the conflicting positions as a check and balance system to ensure the best decisions.
• Learn to manage and feel comfortable with conflict in order to ensure that you do not prematurely close off decisions that could lead to better solutions, because of anxiety over differences.

Practice #3: Use *intuitive* as well as analytical skills to assess the feel for the information gathered and the direction of things.

- Be willing to make decisions without adequate information.
- Learn to trust your sense of things rather than waiting for all the facts to make a decision for you.
- If your intuitive skills are not strong, find people who are and bring them around you so they can influence your decision making.

Overview

Managing complexity requires thinking skills and conflict management skills, both mentally and interpersonally. *All* global organizations are more complex than domestic organizations and they experience much more conflict as a result of the diversity of views and perspectives that must be brought to bear in decision making.

This complexity and conflict in turn require managers who are simultaneously able to see the validity of conflicting viewpoints while making decisions that reflect the best interests of the organization.

COMPETENCY #3: MANAGING ORGANIZATIONAL ADAPTABILITY

Definition

Ability to appropriately centralize and decentralize decision making for various businesses, functions, and tasks to provide the quickest, best, and most coordinated decisions and actions on a global basis, and to develop and dissolve temporary teams and mechanisms to deal with environmental change.

Action and Mindset: Trust Process

Personal characteristic: Flexibility

Key Practices and Tasks

Practice #1: Determine *which decisions should be centralized* for coherency and efficiency and *which decisions should be decentralized* for local responsiveness by business, function, and task.

• Research practices in your industry and function concerning central-ization and decentralization of various policies, practices, and tasks.

• Analyze your managerial area to decentralize as many marketing, sales, and customer-oriented operational decisions as possible, while retaining central control over general policies and operational areas such as finance and research where technology or practices can provide policy coherence and/or cost efficiency.

Practice #2: Develop a *global strategy and structure that is fixed,* but a *global corporate culture that is process driven and flexible* to changing world conditions through the use of global task forces, temporary decision com-mittees, regional coordination groups, and global integrators.

• Look for opportunities to make your job and function as flexible as possible by establishing annual or semiannual cross-functional reviews and building in feedback loops on your performance from internal and external customers on a global basis.

• Look for extraordinary individuals who seem to have an ability to see many sides of an issue and use them for global troubleshooting and analysis, regardless of their full-time position and responsibilities.

• Ensure that your reward systems and criteria are re-enforcing the global cultural values and behavior that you want to see in your unit.

Overview

The management of global corporate culture could well be the most impor-tant task of a global manager. Herein lies the manager's and the organiza-tion's capacity to respond to the rapid changes in the environment on a global basis which affects the organization's survival and growth.

To be a successful manager of global corporate culture, one must be willing to occasionally break all rules, be committed to change, and be able to thrive on chaos.

COMPETENCY #4: MANAGING MULTICULTURAL TEAMS

Definition

Ability to manage teams that represent diversity in functional skills, experience levels, and cultural backgrounds with cultural sensitivity and self-awareness. Ability also to use differences for creative innovations, while managing con-flicts constructively.

Action and Mindset: Value Diversity

Personal characteristic: Sensitivity

Key Practices and Tasks

Practice #1: Learn and use an understanding of the basic *dimensions of cross-cultural behavior* and their impact on managerial style and organizational functioning.
• Read management literature that describes how managers in other cultures manage their work and their people.
• Apply management ideas from other societies to your own unit to improve its productivity and/or effectiveness.
Practice #2: Develop *cultural self-awareness* which allows one to contrast one's own culture with other cultures to allow flexible movement from one culture to another.
• Read books that describe the cultural perceptions, values, and behavior of people from your culture and become aware of the biases you bring to your job as a result of your national background.
• Ask a colleague from another culture to give you semiannual feedback on how your management actions are seen from his or her cultural perspective.

Overview

Along with flexibility, cross-cultural sensitivity is one of the most important characteristics of a global manager.
The truth is that a successful global organization must provide cross-cultural exposure and develop cross-cultural sensitivity in *all* its managers, whether domestic or international, so that they are able to work with other parts of the organization around the globe with whom they are interdependent, as well as global customers, suppliers, and competitors.

COMPETENCY #5: MANAGING UNCERTAINTY

Definition

Ability to manage continuous change and uncertainty on a personal and organizational level, ensuring that an adequate blend of flexibility and control are achieved, which enables the organization to be responsive to changes in the environment in a timely fashion.

Action and Mindset: Flow With the Change

Personal characteristic: Judgment

Key Practices and Tasks

Practice #1: Work with *continuous global change,* rather than stability as the norm and learn to navigate in perpetual white water.
• Analyze what aspects of your job are subject to outside change, which should be reviewed for change from the inside, and what the shelf life of your policies, practices, and procedures should be to remain relevant to changes in your industry and profession.

Practice #2: Create *new opportunities out of change and chaos,* rather than trying to re-establish the old order.
• Examine the changing conditions around you for new products, policies, practices or procedures that can increase your personal, professional or organizational efficiency and/or effectiveness.

Practice #3: Manage *change as a cyclical process* of taking charge and letting go, using right-brain as well as left-brain thinking skills.
• Determine which phases of change must be controlled and which phases must be left alone for their own development, thereby resisting the tendency to manage the change process through continual control.

Overview

Often the greatest barrier to the successful management of change is the fear that managers experience when they experience uncertainty. Most managers have been paid throughout their lives for being dependable and not making mistakes. Managing change, however, requires overcoming the sense of uncertainty that comes from knowing that some process may be out of control, but that one has the skills to bring it back or rebuild from where it leaves off.

Without a willingness to lose control on a temporary basis, it is almost impossible for a global manager to be successful. White-water rafting is here to stay as a management metaphor for success in the global arena (Vaill, 1989).

COMPETENCY #6: MANAGING PERSONAL AND ORGANIZATIONAL LEARNING

Definition

Ability to manage personal and organizational learning and improvement on a continuous basis through the exploration of new fields of knowledge, new cultural perspectives, and through seeking feedback on a global basis.

Action and Mindset: Seeking Openness

Personal characteristic: Reflection

Key Practices and Tasks

Practice #1: Develop a *capacity for systems thinking* at every level of personal and organizational functioning, searching for contexts and broader influences on a global basis that may affect personal or organizational success.

• Analyze how your job and function are dependent on other jobs or functions within your organization and develop annual goals to anticipate how changes in these areas may affect your work.

• Examine what global trends could affect your work over the next three years and begin now to develop methods for using these changes as new opportunities for personal and organizational growth.

Practice #2: Develop a *working knowledge of international relations, international economics, and cross-cultural differences* that will allow effective interaction with foreign suppliers, customers, and partners.

• Attend one internationally oriented seminar, workshop, or conference every other year to broaden your exposure to international thinking and perspectives.

• Read magazines and newspapers that reflect the national or regional perspective of your target audience.

Practice #3: Consider personal and organization *learning as a lifelong process.*

• See yourself as one of the new knowledge workers and constantly gather, analyze, and reflect on information on a global basis, utilizing global resources for new concepts, perceptions, and opportunities for personal, professional, and organizational effectiveness.

Practice #4: Develop a *sense of meaning and purpose* in personal and organizational life that transcends the immediate job or annual objective and can be related to a higher or broader contribution to the human condition.

• Develop your own personal reason for staying in your job, profession, or organization which has a global implication that is meaningful to you and which motivates you to get up in the morning.

• Become aware of the impact or relationship of your work to people in other countries and try to make your work a net contribution to the human condition on a global basis.

Overview

The commitment to lifelong learning is not a simple commitment to make. It requires the willingness to live with unfinished business; the faith that people can constantly grow and develop for the better; and the sense that there is some larger reason for existence than getting up in the morning to make a buck.

People and organizations who are committed to learning as the central aspect of their lives not only survive better, but are often more attractive to others, more vibrant in their ideas and more fulfilled in their pursuits.

Being a successful global manager or a socially responsible global organization requires an integrated approach to the world that develops the capacities needed to flourish, while knowing that these capacities will never be enough to replace a sense of purpose, mission, and the willingness to trust process and let go.

Selected Bibliography

Adizes, Ichak. *Corporate Lifecycles: How and Why Corporations Grow and Die and What to Do About It.* Englewood Cliffs, N.J.: Prentice Hall, 1990.

Adler, Nancy. *International Dimensions of Organizational Behavior.* Boston: Kent Publishing, 1986.

Adler, Nancy and Dafina N. Izraeli, eds. *Women in Management Worldwide.* Armonk, N.Y.: M.E. Sharpe, 1988.

Allen, Robert F. and Charlotte Kraft. *The Organizational Unconscious: How to Create the Corporate Culture You Want and Need.* Englewood Cliffs, N.J.: Prentice Hall, 1982.

Argyris, Chris. *Overcoming Organizational Defenses: Facilitating Organizational Learning.* Needham Heights, Mass.: Allen & Bacon, 1990.

"AT&T Global Service." *New York Times,* March 11, 1992, p. D4.

Atkinson, Philip E. *Creating Culture Change: The Key to Successful Total Quality Management.* Bedford, UK: IFS Publications, 1991.

Attali, Jacques. *Millennium: Winners and Losers in the Coming World Order.* New York: Times Books, 1991.

Austin, Clyde, ed. *Cross-cultural Re-entry.* Abilene, Tex.: Abilene Christian University Press, 1986.

Auteri, Enrico and Vittorio Tesio. "The Internationalisation of Management at Fiat." *Journal of Management Development,* February 1991, pp. 27–36.

Barham, Kevin and Clive Rassam. *Shaping the Corporate Future.* London: Unwin Hyman, 1989.

Barnum, Cynthia. "Effective Membership in the Global Business Community." In *New Traditions in Business.* ed. John Konesch. San Francisco: Sterling & Strong, 1991.

Barnum, Cynthia and Natasha Wolniansky. "Globalization: Moving a Step Beyond the International Firm." *Management Review,* September 1989, pp. 30–33.

Barker, Joel Arthur. *Discovering the Future: The Business of Paradigms.* St. Paul, Minn.: ILI Press, 1989.

Barnard, Chester. *The Functions of the Executive.* Cambridge, Mass.: Harvard University Press, 1936.

Barr, Lee and Norma Barr. *The Leadership Equation: Leadership, Management and the Myers-Briggs.* Austin, Tex.: Eakin Press, 1989.

Bartlett, Christopher and Sumantra Ghoshal. *Managing Across Borders: The Transnational Solution.* Cambridge, Mass.: Harvard Business School Press, 1989.

——. "Matrix Management: Not a Structure, a Frame of Mind." *Harvard Business Review.* July–August 1990, pp. 138–45.

——. "Organizing for Worldwide Effectiveness: The Transnational Solution." *California Management Review* 31, no. 1 (1988).

Barnum, Cynthia and David R. Gaster. "Global Leadership." *Executive Excellence,* June 1991, pp. 19–22.

"Being a Global Leader." *Directors & Boards Chairman's Agenda* 16, no. 1 (Fall 1991).

Bennis, Warren. "Leadership in the 21st Century." *Training,* May 1990, pp. 43–48.

Bleeke, Joel A. and Brain A. Johnson. "Signposts for a Global Strategy." *The McKinsey Quarterly,* Autumn 1989, pp. 60–71.

Bloom, Allan. *The Closing of the American Mind.* New York: Simon and Shuster, 1987.

Bolman, Lee and Terrence Deal. *Reframing Organizations.* San Francisco: Jossey-Bass, 1991.

Boulding, Kenneth E. *The World as a Total System.* Beverly Hills, Calif.: Sage Publications, 1985.

——. *Human Betterment.* Beverly Hills, Calif.: Sage Publications, 1985.

Boyatzis, Richard E. *The Competent Manager: A Model for Effective Performance.* New York: John Wiley, 1982.

Brake, Terence, Kimberley Sullivan, and Danielle Walker. *Doing Business Internationally—The Cross-Cultural Challenges.* Princeton: Princeton Training Press, 1992.

Brock, William and Robert Hormats, eds. *The Global Economy: America's Role in the Decade Ahead.* New York: W. W. Norton & Company, 1990.

Brown, Ina Corinne. *Understanding Other Cultures.* Englewood Cliffs, N.J.: Prentice Hall, 1963.

Burke, W. Warner. *Organization Development: A Normative View.* Reading, Mass.: Addison-Wesley OD Series, 1987.

Caiden, Gerald. *Administrative Reform Comes of Age.* New York: Walter de Gruyter, 1991.

Capra, Fritjof. *The Turning Point: Science, Society and the Rising Culture.* New York: Bantam Books, 1982.

Carnevale, Anthony Patrick. *America and the New Economy: How New Competitive Standards are Radically Changing the American Workplace.* San Francisco: Jossey-Bass, 1991.

Carr, Clay. "Managing Self-Managed Workers." *Training and Development Journal,* September 1991, pp. 36–42.

Carse, James. *Finite and Infinite Games.* New York: Ballantine Books, 1986.

Chang, Chung-yuan. *Tao: A New Way of Thinking.* New York: Harper & Row, 1975.

Chesanow, Neil. *The World-Class Executive.* New York: Rawson Associates, 1985.

Christopher, Robert C. *The Japanese Mind.* New York: Fawcett Columbine, 1983.

Clegg, S. R. and S. G. Redding, eds. *Capitalism in Contrasting Cultures.* New York: Walter de Gruyter, 1990.

Cleveland, Harlan. *The Future Executive.* New York: Harper & Row, 1972

Cohen, Roger. "For Coke, World its Oyster." *New York Times,* November 21, 1991, p. D1.

———. "The Very Model of Efficiency." *New York Times,* March 2, 1992, p. D1.

Conference Board. *Building Global Teamwork for Growth and Survival.* Research Bulletin No. 228. New York: The Conference Board, 1990.

Contractor, Farok and Peter Lorange. *Cooperative Strategies in International Business: Joint Ventures and Technology Partnerships between Firms.* Lexington, Mass.: Lexington Books, 1988.

Copeland, Lennie and Lewis Griggs. *Going International: How to Make Friends and Deal Effectively in the International Marketplace.* New York: Random House, 1985.

"Corporate Culture." *Business Week,* October 27, 1980, pp. 34–38.

Csikszentmihalyi, Mihaly. *Flow: The Psychology of Optimal Experience.* New York: Harper, 1990.

Davis, Stanley M. *Comparative Management: Organizational and Cultural Perspectives.* Englewood Cliffs, N.J.: Prentice Hall, 1971.

———. *Future Perfect.* Reading, Mass.: Addison-Wesley, 1987.

De Menthe, Boye. *Japanese Etiquette & Ethics in Business.* 5th ed. Lincolnwood, Ill.: NTC Business Books, 1988.

———. *Korean Etiquette & Ethics in Business.* Lincolnwood, Ill.: NTC Business Books, 1987.

Deal, Terrence E. and Allan A. Kennedy. *Corporate Cultures: The Rites and Rituals of Corporate Life.* Reading, Mass.: Addison-Wesley, 1982.

Desatnick, Robert L. and Margo L. Bennett. *Human Resource Management in the Multinational Company.* Westmead, England: Gower Press, 1977.

Dlugos, Gunter, Wolfgang Dorrow, and Klaus Weiermair, eds. *Management Under Differing Labour Market and Employment Systems.* New York: Walter de Gruyter, 1988.

Doz, Yves. *Strategic Management in International Companies.* New York: Pergamon Press, 1986.

Dredge, C. Paul. "Corporate Culture: The Challenge to Expatriate Managers and Multinational Corporations." In *Strategic Management of Multinational Corporations: The Essentials,* by Heidi and Lawrence Wortzel. New York: John Wiley & Sons, 1987, pp. 410–23.

Drucker, Peter F. *Managing in Turbulent Times.* New York: Harper & Row, 1980.

———. *The Changing World of the Executive.* New York: Times Books, 1985.

———. *The New Realities.* New York: Harper & Row, 1989.

————. "The New World According to Peter Drucker." *Business Month,* May 1989, pp. 48–59.

Eccles, Robert G. "Managing through Networks in Investment Banking." *California Management Review,* Fall 1987, pp. 176–95.

Erikson, Erik. *Childhood and Society.* Rev. ed. New York: W. W. Norton, 1963.

Ernst & Young. *Guide to Expanding in the Global Market.* New York: John Wiley & Sons, 1991.

————. *Resource Guide to Global Markets.* New York: John Wiley & Sons, 1991.

Evans, Paul, Yves Doz, and Andre Laurent, eds. *Human Resource Management in International Firms: Change, Globalization, Innovation.* New York: St. Martin's Press, 1990.

Faison, Seth. "Morgan Stanley Makes High-Level Changes." *New York Times,* March 11, 1992, p. D 4.

Ferguson, Henry. *Tomorrow's Global Executive.* Homewood, Ill.: Dow Jones-Irwin, 1988.

Fisher, Glen. *Mindsets: The Role of Culture and Perception in International Relations.* Yarmouth, Me.: Intercultural Press, 1988.

Fisher, Roger and William Ury. *Getting to Yes.* Cambridge: Harvard Negotiation Project, 1985.

Fombrun, Charles, Noel M. Tichy, and Marry Anne Devanna. *Strategic Human Resource Management.* New York: John Wiley & Sons, 1984.

Foster, Richard. *Innovation: The Attacker's Advantage.* New York: Summit Books, 1986.

Fulghum, Robert. *All I Really Need to Know I Learned in Kindergarten.* New York: Villard Books, 1989.

Garland, John and Richard Farmer. *International Dimensions of Business Policy and Strategy.* Boston: Kent Publishing, 1986.

Geneen, Harold. *Management.* New York: Basic Books, 1982.

Ghadar, Fariborz, Phillip D. Grub, Robert T. Moran, and Marshall Geer. *Global Business Management in the 1990s.* Washington, D.C.: Beacham Publishing, Inc., 1990.

Gibney, Frank. *Miracle by Design: The Real Reasons Behind Japan's Economic Success.* New York: Times Books, 1982.

Gleick, James. *Chaos: Making a New Science.* New York: Penguin Books, 1989.

Gross, Thomas, Ernie Turner, and Lars Cederholm. "Building Teams for Global Operations." *Management Review,* June 1987, pp. 32–36.

Grove, Andrew S. *High Output Management.* New York: Random House, 1983.

Grove, Cornelius and Constance Franklin. "Using the Right Fork Is Just the Beginning: Intercultural Training in the Global Era." *International Public Relations Review* 13, no. 1 (1990), pp. 13–21.

Grub, Phillip D., Fariborz Ghadar, and Dara Khambata, eds. *The Multinational Enterprise in Transition*. Princeton, N.J.: Darwin Press, 1986.

Hall, Edward T. *Beyond Culture*. Garden City, N.Y.: Anchor/Doubleday, 1976.

———. *The Hidden Dimension*. New York: Anchor Press, 1966.

———. *The Silent Language*. New York: Doubleday & Company, 1959.

Hall, Edward T. and Mildred Reed Hall. *Hidden Differences: Doing Business with the Japanese*. Garden City, N.J.: Anchor Press/Doubleday, 1987.

Handy, Charles. *The Age of Unreason*. Boston, Mass.: Harvard Business School Press, 1990.

Harper, Bob and Ann Harper. *Succeeding as a Self-Directed Work Team*. Croton-on-the-Hudson, N.J.: MW Corporation, 1990.

Harris, Philip, ed. *Global Strategies for Human Resource Development*. Washington, D.C.: American Society for Training and Development, 1983.

Harris, Philip and Robert Moran. *Managing Cultural Differences*. 2nd ed. Houston: Gulf Publishing Company, 1987.

Harrison, Phyllis A. *Behaving Brazilian*. Cambridge, Mass.: Newbury House Publishers, 1983.

Hayes, Michael. "Internationalising the Executive Education Curriculum at General Electric: A Case Study of Trends in the 1980s." *Journal of Management Development,* February 1991.

Heenan, David A. and Howard Perlmutter. *Multinational Organization Development*. Reading, Mass.: Addison-Wesley, 1979.

Hersey, Paul and Kenneth Blanchard. *The Management of Organizational Behavior.* 3rd ed. Englewood Cliffs, N.J.: Prentice Hall, 1976.

Hickman, Craig R. and Michael A. Silva. *Creating Excellence: Managing Corporate Culture, Strategy and Change in the New Age*. New York: New American Library, 1985.

Hofheinz, Roy, Jr. and Kent E. Calder. *The Eastasia Edge*. New York: Basic Books, 1982.

Hofstede, Gert. *Culture's Consequences: International Differences in Work-Related Values*. Beverly Hills, Calif.: Sage Publishing Co., 1980.

———. *Cultures and Organizations: Software of the Mind*. London: McGraw-Hill, 1991.

———. "Motivation, Leadership and Organization: Do American Management Theories Apply Abroad?" *Organizational Dynamics,* Summer 1980, pp. 42–63.

Huey, John. "Nothing is Impossible." *Fortune,* September 23, 1991, pp. 135–38.

Ibe, Masanobu and Noriko Sato. "Educating Japanese Leaders for a Global Age: The Role of the International Education Center." *Journal of Management Development,* February 1991.

Imai, Masaaki. *Kaizen: The Key to Japan's Competitive Success*. New York: Random House, 1986.

Info-Line. "Discovering and Developing Creativity." January 1989, Issue 901. Alexandria, Va.: American Society for Training and Development.

Info-Line. "Fifteen Activities to Discover and Develop Creativity." February 1989, Issue 902. Alexandria, Va.: American Society for Training and Development.

Ishihara, Shintaro. *The Japan that Can Say No.* New York: Simon and Shuster, 1989.

Jacques, Elliot and Stephen D. Clement, *Executive Leadership: A Practical Guide to Managing Complexity.* Cambridge, Mass: Basil Blackwell, 1991.

James, Muriel. *The Better Boss in Multicultural Organizations: A Guide to Success Using Transactional Analysis.* Walnut Creek, Calif.: Marshall Publishing, 1991.

Johnston, William B. "Global Workforce 2000: The New World Labor Market." *Harvard Business Review,* March–April 1991, pp. 115–27.

Joynt, Pat and Malcolm Warner, eds. *Managing in Different Cultures.* Oslo: Universitetsforlaget, 1985. (U.S. distributor: Columbia University Press.)

Kanter, Rosabeth Moss. *The Change Masters: Innovation for Productivity in the American Corporation.* New York: Simon and Shuster, 1983.

———. *When Giants Learn to Dance.* New York: Simon and Shuster, 1989.

Keirsey, David and Marilyn Bates. *Please Understand Me: Character and Temperament Types.* Del Mar, Calif.: Prometheus Nemesis Book Company, 1984.

Kennedy, Gavin. *Negotiate Anywhere!: How to Succeed in International Markets.* London: Arrow Books, 1987.

Kiezun, Witold. *Management in Socialist Countries: USSR and Central Europe.* New York: Walter de Gruyter, 1991.

Kinlaw, Dennis C. *Developing Superior Work Teams.* San Diego: University Associates, 1991.

Klineberg, Otto. *The Human Dimension in International Relations.* New York: Holt, Reinhart and Winston, 1964.

Kissler, Gary D. *The Change Riders: Managing the Power of Change.* Reading, Mass.: Addison-Wesley, 1991.

Kluckhohn, Florence and Frederick L. Strodtbeck. *Variations in Value Orientations.* Evanston, Ill.: Row, Peterson and Company, 1956.

Kolde, Endel-Jakob. *Environment of International Business.* 2nd ed. Boston: Kent Publishing, 1985.

Koopman, Albert. *Transcultural Management: How to Unlock Global Resources.* Oxford: Basil Blackwell, 1991.

Korn/Ferry International and Columbia School of Business. *21st Century Report: Reinventing the CEO,* New York: Korn/Ferry International, 1989.

Kotter, John P. *A Force for Change: How Leadership Differs from Management.* New York: Free Press, 1990.

Kras, Eva S. *Management in Two Cultures: Bridging the Gap between U.S. and Mexican Managers.* Yarmouth, Me.: Intercultural Press, 1989.

Kuhn, Theodore. *The Structure of Scientific Revolutions.* Chicago: University of Chicago Press, 1962.

Kupfer, Andrew. "How to be a Global Manager." *Fortune,* March 14, 1988, pp. 43–48.

Lamont, Douglas. *Winning Worldwide: Strategies for Dominating Global Markets.* Homewood, Ill.: Business One Irwin, 1991.

Lane, Henry W. and Joseph J. DiStefano. *International Management Behavior.* Scarborough, Ontario: Nelson Canada, 1988.

Laurent, Andre. "The Cross-cultural Puzzle of Human Resource Management." *Human Resource Management* 25, no. 1, (Spring 1986), pp. 91–102.

Lawrence, Paul R. and Charalambos A. Vlachoutsicos, eds. *Behind the Factory Walls: Decision Making in Soviet and U.S. Enterprises.* Boston: Harvard Business School Press, 1990.

Lessum, *Global Management Principles.* Englewood Cliffs, N.J.: Prentice Hall, 1989.

Levitt, Theodore. "The Globalization of Markets." *Harvard Business Review,* May–June 1983, pp. 92–102.

Little, Reg and Warren Reed. *The Confucian Renaissance.* Sydney: The Federation Press, 1989.

Lobel, Sharon A. "Global Leadership Competencies: Managing to a Different Drumbeat." *Human Resource Management* 29, No. 1 (Spring 1990), pp. 39–47.

Lorenz, Christopher. "The Birth of the 'Transnational.'" *The McKinsey Quarterly,* Autumn 1989, pp. 72–93.

Macoby, Michael. *The Gamesman: The New Corporate Leaders.* New York: Simon and Shuster, 1976.

Makridakis, Spyros G. *Forecasting, Planning and Strategy in the 21st Century.* New York: Free Press, 1990.

Marsick, Victoria J. and Lars Cederholm. "Developing Leadership in International Managers—An Urgent Challenge!" *The Columbia Journal of World Business* XXII, no. 4 (Winter 1988).

McClelland, David C. *The Achieving Society.* Princeton, N.J.: D. van Nostrand, 1961.

McGrath, Joseph P. *The Social Psychology of Time.* Newbury Park, Calif.: Sage Publications, 1988.

McGregor, Douglas. *The Human Side of Enterprise.* New York: McGraw Hill, 1961.

Meyer, Marshall W. and Lynne G. Zucker. *Permanently Failing Organizations.* Newbury Park, Calif.: Sage Publications, 1989.

Miller, Lawrence. *American Spirit: Visions of a New Corporate Culture.* New York: William Morrow and Company, Inc., 1984.

Mitroff, Ian. *Business Not as Usual.* San Francisco: Jossey-Bass, 1987.

Mole, John. *Mind Your Manners: Culture Clash in the Single European Market.* London: The Industrial Society, 1990.

Montville, Joseph V. *Conflict and Peacemaking in Multiethnic Societies.* Lexington, Mass.: Lexington Books, 1990.

Moran, Robert and Philip Harris. *Managing Cultural Synergy.* Houston: Gulf Publishing, 1982.

Morgan, Gareth. *Riding the Waves of Change: Developing Managerial Competencies for a Turbulent World.* San Francisco: Jossey-Bass, 1988.

Morgan, Patrick. "International HRM: Fact or Fiction?" *Personnel Administrator,* September 1986, pp. 43–47.

Morris, Desmond, Peter Collett, Peter Marsh, and Marie O'Shaughnessy. *Gestures.* New York: Stein and Day, 1980.

Moulton, Harper. "Executive Development and Education: An Evaluation." *Journal of Management Development* 9, no. 4 (1991), p. 8.

Muna, Farid A. *The Arab Executive.* London: Macmillan Press, 1980.

Myers, Isabella B. *Gifts Differing.* Palo Alto, Calif.: Consulting Psychologists Press, 1980.

Naisbitt, John. *Megatrends: Ten New Directions Transforming our Lives.* New York: Warner Communications, 1982.

Naisbitt, John and Patricia Aburdene. *Megatrends 2000: Ten New Directions for the 1990s.* New York: William Morrow and Company, 1990.

———. *Re-inventing the Corporation.* New York: Warner Books, 1985.

Nakamura, Hajime. *Ways of Thinking of Eastern Peoples.* Honolulu: East-West Center Press, 1964.

Nelson-Horchler, Joani. "Desperately Seeking Yankee Know-How." *Industry Week,* March 4, 1991, pp. 52–56.

Nydell, Margaret K. *Understanding Arabs: A Guide for Westerners.* Yarmouth, Me.: Intercultural Press, 1987.

Ohmae, Kenichi, *Beyond National Borders.* Homewood, Ill.: Dow Jones-Irwin, 1987.

———. *The Borderless World.* New York: Harper Business Press, 1990.

———. "The Logic of Strategic Alliances." *Harvard Business Review,* March–April 1989, pp. 143–54.

———. *The Mind of the Strategist.* New York: Penguin Books, 1983.

———. *Triad Power.*

Ouchi, William G. and Alfred M. Jaeger. "Type Z Organization: Stability in the Midst of Mobility." *Academy of Management Review,* April 1978.

Overman, Stephanie. "Shaping the Global Workplace." *Personnel Administrator,* October 1989, pp. 41–44 and 101.

Paradigm 2000 Newsletter 1, no. 1 (April/May 1990).

—— 1, no. 2 (June/July 1990).

Pascale, Richard Tanner. *The Art of Japanese Management: Applications for American Executives.* New York: Simon and Shuster, 1981.

Pascale, Richard T. *Managing on the Edge: How Successful Companies Use Conflict to Stay Ahead.* London: Viking Penguin, 1990.

Parsons, Talcott and Edward A. Shils, eds. *Toward a General Theory of Action.* New York: Harper, 1962.

Peak, Martha H. "Developing an International Management Style." *Management Review,* February 1991, pp. 32–35.

Pedersen, Paul. *A Handbook for Developing Multicultural Awareness.* Alexandria, Va.: American Association for Counseling and Development, 1988.

Perlmutter, Howard V. and David A. Heenan. "Cooperate to Compete Globally." *Harvard Business Review,* March–April 1986.

Peters, Thomas. *Thriving on Chaos: Handbook for a Management Revolution.* New York: Harper & Row, 1988.

—— and Robert H. Waterman. *In Search of Excellence: Lessons from America's Best-Run Companies.* New York: Harper & Row, 1982.

Phatak, Arvind. *International Dimensions of Management.* 2nd ed. Boston: Kent Publishing, 1989.

Popcorn, Faith. *The Popcorn Report.* New York: Doubleday, 1991.

Porter, Michael, ed. *Competition in Global Business.* Cambridge, Mass.: Harvard Business School Press, 1986.

Prahalad, C. K. and Yves Doz. *The Multinational Mission: Balancing Local Demands and Global Vision.* New York: Free Press, 1987.

Punnett, Betty Jane. *Experiencing International Management.* Boston: PWS-Kent Publishing, 1989.

Quelch, John A. and Edward J. Hoff. "Customizing Global Marketing." *Harvard Business Review,* May–June 1986, pp. 59–86.

Randlesome, Collin. *Business Cultures in Europe.* Oxford: Heinemann Professional Publishing, 1990.

Randolph, Benton. "When Going Global Isn't Enough." *Training,* August 1990, pp. 47–51.

Ray, C. "Organizational Learning—The Key to Management Innovation." *Sloan Management Review* 30, no. 3 (Spring 1989), pp. 63–74.

Reich, Robert B. *The Work of Nations: Preparing Ourselves for 21st Century Capitalism.* New York: Alfred A. Knopf, 1991.

——. "Who is Them?" *Harvard Business Review,* March–April 1991, pp. 77–88.

——. "Who is Us?" *Harvard Business Review,* January–February 1990, pp. 53–64.

Rhinesmith, Stephen H. "Americans in the Global Learning Process." *The Annals of the American Academy of Political and Social Science* 442, (March 1979), pp. 98–108.

——. "An Agenda for Globalization." *Training and Development Journal,* February 1991, pp. 22–29.

——. *Bring Home the World: A Management Guide for Community Leaders of International Exchange Programs.* New York: Walker and Company, 1985.

——. *Cultural-Organizational Analysis: The Interrelationship Between Value Orientations and Managerial Behavior.* Cambridge, Mass.: McBer and Company, 1971.

——. "Going Global from the Inside Out." *Training and Development Journal,* November 1991, pp. 42–47.

——, John N. Williamson, David M. Ehlen, and Denise S. Maxwell. "Developing Leaders for a Global Enterprise." *Training and Development Journal,* April 1989, pp. 24–34.

Ricks, David A. *Big Business Blunders: Mistakes in Multinational Marketing.* Homewood, Ill.: Dow Jones-Irwin, 1983.

Rogers, Carl. *On Becoming a Person.* Boston: Houghton-Mifflin, 1961.

Ronen, Simcha. *Comparative and Multinational Management.* New York: John Wiley, 1986.

Rossman, Marlene L. *The International Businesswoman: A Guide to Success in the Global Marketplace.* New York: Praeger, 1986.

SRI International Business Intelligence Program. "Strategic Partnering: Keys to Success in the 1990s." D88-1255, 1988.

——. "More About Strategic Alliances." D88-1256, 1988.

Salacuse, Jeswald W. *Making Global Deal: Negotiating in the International Marketplace.* Boston: Houghton-Mifflin, 1991.

Sathe, Vijay. *Culture and Related Corporate Realities.* Homewood, Ill.: Richard D. Irwin, 1985.

Schein, Edgar H. *Organizational Culture and Leadership.* San Francisco: Jossey-Bass, 1989.

Senge, Peter. *The Fifth Discipline: The Art & Practice of The Learning Organization.* New York: Doubleday, 1990.

Shaeffer, Ruth G. "Building Global Teamwork for Growth and Survival." *The Conference Board Research Bulletin.* No. 228.

Shames, Germaine W. and W. Gerald Glover. *World-Class Service.* Yarmouth, Me.: Intercultural Press, 1989.

Sheth, Jaqclish and Golpira Eshghi (eds). *Global Human Resource Perspectives.* Cincinnati: South-Western Publishing, 1989.

Singer, Marshall R. *Intercultural Communication: A Perceptual Approach.* Englewood Cliffs, N.J.: Prentice Hall (Simon & Shuster), 1987.

Siu, R. G. H. *The Portable Dragon: The Western Man's Guide to the I Ching.* Cambridge, Mass.: MIT Press, 1971.

————. "Management and the Art of Chinese Baseball." In *Readings in Managerial Psychology*. Harold J. Leavitt and Louis Pondy. Chicago: University of Chicago Press, 1980.

Skinner, B. F. *About Behaviorism*. New York: Random House, 1976.

Smith, Peter B. and Mark F. Peterson. *Leadership, Organizations and Culture*. Beverly Hills, Calif.: Sage Publications, 1988.

Soros, George. *Underwriting Democracy*. New York: The Free Press, 1991.

Stacey, Ralph D. *Managing Chaos: Dynamic Business Strategies in an Unpredictable World*. London: Kogan Page, Ltd., 1992.

Stacey, Ralph D. *The Chaos Frontier: Creative Strategic Control for Business*. Oxford: Butterworth-Heinemann, 1991.

Stata, Ray. "Organizational Learning—The Key to Management Innovation." *Sloan Management Review*, Spring 1989, pp. 64–74.

Steingraber, Fred G. "Managing in the 1990s." *Business Horizons*, January–February 1990, pp. 49–61.

Stevens, William K. "Balance of Nature? What Balance is That?" *New York Times*, October 22, 1991, p. C3.

Stewart, Edward C. and Milton J. Bennett. *American Cultural Patterns: A Cross-Cultural Perspective*. Rev. ed. Yarmouth, Me.: Intercultural Press, 1991.

Stewart, Thomas A. "How to Manage in the Global Era." *Fortune*, January 15, 1990, pp. 58–72.

————. "GE Keeps Those Ideas Coming." *Fortune*, August 12, 1991, pp. 41–49.

Stopford, J. M. and L. T. Wells, Jr. *Managing the Multinational Enterprise*. New York: Basic Books, 1972.

Tachiki, Dennis S. "Japanese Management Going Transnational." *Journal for Quality and Participation*, December 1991, pp. 96–107.

Tayeb, Monir. *Organizations and National Culture: A Comparative Analysis*. Beverly Hills, Calif.: Sage Publications, 1988.

Taylor, William. "The Logic of Global Business: An Interview with ABB's Percy Barnevik." *Harvard Business Review*, March–April 1991, pp. 91–105.

Terpstra, Vern and Kenneth David. *The Cultural Framework of International Business*. 2nd ed. Pelham Manor, N.Y.: South-Western Publishing, 1985.

The Forum Corporation. *Documentation of the 1991 Influence Research Project*. Boston: Mass.: The Forum Corporation, 1991.

————. *Leadership: Training Workbook*. Boston, Mass.: The Forum Corporation, 1990.

Thiederman, Sondra. *Bridging Cultural Barriers for Corporate Success: How to Manage a Multicultural Workforce*. New York: Lexington Books, 1991.

Thurow, Lester. *Head to Head: The Coming Economic Battle Among Japan, Europe and America*. New York: William Morrow and Company, 1992.

Tichy, Noel and Mary Anne Devanna. *The Transformational Leader.* New York: John Wiley & Sons, 1986.

Toffler, Alvin. *Powershift: Knowledge, Wealth and Violence at the Edge of the 21st Century.* New York: Bantam, 1990.

Tregoe, Benjamin. *Vision in Action.* New York: Simon and Shuster, 1989.

Tuckman, Bruce W. and M. A. C. Jensen. "Stages of Small Group Development Revisited." *Group and Organization Studies* II, no. 4 (December 1977), pp. 419–27.

Vaill, Peter B. *Managing as a Performing Art: New Ideas for a World of Chaotic Change.* San Francisco: Jossey-Bass, 1989.

Varney, Glenn H. *Building Productive Teams.* San Francisco: Jossey-Bass, 1989.

Walton, Mary. *The Deming Management Method.* New York: Putnam Publishing, 1986.

Webber, Ross A. *Culture and Management.* Homewood, Ill.: Richard D. Irwin, 1969.

Weinshall, Theodore, ed. *Culture and Management.* New York: Penguin Books, 1977.

"Wharton Rewrites the Book on B-Schools." *Business Week,* May 13, 1991, p. 43.

Williams, Robin M., Jr. *American Society: A Sociological Interpretation.* New York: Alfred A. Knopf, 1961.

Wing, R. L. *The I Ching Workbook.* New York: Doubleday, 1979.

Wolniansky, Natalia. "International Training for Global Leadership." *Management Review,* May 1990, pp. 27–28.

Wonder, Jacquelyn and Priscilla Donovan. *The Flexibility Factor.* New York: Doubleday, 1989.

Wycoff, Joyce. *Mindmapping: Your Personal Guide to Exploring Creativity and Problem-Solving.* New York: Berkley Books, 1991.

Yankelovich, Daniel. "Tomorrow's Global Businesses." *The Futurist,* July–August 1991, p. 60.

Young, Stephen, James Hamill, Colin Wheeler, and J. Richard Davies. *International Market Entry and Development,* Englewood Cliffs, N.J.: Prentice Hall, 1989.

Index

**FOR INFORMATION ABOUT COMPANION TRAINING PROGRAMS TO
THIS BOOK, PLEASE CALL:**

PRINCETON TRAINING PRESS
1-609-497-0645

OR WRITE:

PRINCETON TRAINING PRESS
247 Nassau Street
Princeton, NJ 08542

Fax: 1-609-497-1295